PAUL'S IDEA OF COMMUNITY

*The Early House Churches in their
Historical Setting*

PAUL'S IDEA
OF
COMMUNITY

*The Early House Churches in their
Historical Setting*

Robert Banks

WILLIAM B. EERDMANS PUBLISHING COMPANY
GRAND RAPIDS, MICHIGAN

Library of Congress Cataloging in Publication Data

Banks, Robert J.
    Paul's idea of community.
        Bibliography: p. 199
        1. Bible. N.T. Epistles of Paul — Theology.
    2. Bible. N.T. Pastoral epistles — Theology.
    3. Church — Biblical teaching. 4. Freedom
(Theology) — Biblical teaching. I. Title.
BS2655.C5B36   1980   262   80-20417
ISBN 0-8028-1830-7

Contents

Abbreviations

In addition to standard literary abbreviations, the usual ones are employed for the books of the Bible.

1. *Books of the Apocrypha*

Jud.	Judith	Ecclus.	Ecclesiasticus
Est.	Additions to Esther	1 Macc.	1 Maccabees
Wisd.	Wisdom of Solomon	2 Macc.	2 Maccabees

2. *Pseudepigrapha*

3 Macc.	3 Maccabbees	Test. Lev.	Testament of Levi
Jub.	Jubilees	Sib. Or.	Sibylline Oracles
Apoc. Mos.	Apocalypse of Moses	Arist.	Letter of Aristeas
1 En.	1 Enoch	2 Bar.	2 Baruch

3. *Dead Sea Scrolls*

IQS	The Community Rule	IQM	The War Scroll
CDC	The Damascus Rule	IQH	The Thanksgiving Hymns

4. *Mishnah*

Ber.	Berakoth	Yeb.	Yebamoth
Pea.	Peah	Ket.	Ketuboth
Dem.	Demai	Sot.	Sotah
M. Sh.	Maaser Sheni	Gitt.	Gittin
Shabb.	Shabbath	Kidd.	Kiddushin
Pes.	Pesahim	B.M.	Baba Metzia
Yom.	Yoma	Makk.	Makkoth
Sukk.	Sukkah	Eduy.	Eduyoth
R. Sh.	Rosh-ha-Shanah	Ab.	Aboth
Taan.	Taanith	Bekh.	Bekhoroth
Meg.	Megillah	Arak.	Arakhin
Hag.	Hagigah	Tam.	Tamid

5. *Tosephta*

T. Ber.	Berakoth

6. *Miscellaneous*

LXX	The Septuagint
RSV	Revised Standard Version

Preface

This is not a technical book, nor a popular one either. We already
have a number of stimulating technical works on Paul's view of
the church, and many popular books on church life build on
aspects of Paul's view in their presentation. But the former are too
linguistically daunting for most readers, while the latter are too
particular in their emphasis or psychological in their orientation
to be fully satisfactory as treatments of Paul. I have written this
for those who find themselves caught in the middle — seeking a
comprehensive account of what Paul said, yet in terms they can
understand. And I am not thinking of the Christianly-inclined
only. Paul's idea of community is too historically interesting and
significant to be closeted among the religious.

This has affected the form of the book. It seeks not only to interpret Paul, but to set him firmly in his context. Only by comparing
him with his contemporaries do the genuinely distinctive elements
in his approach come into focus. For while in many respects Paul
was very much a man of his times, in others he was astonishingly
ahead of them. Many people today are finding that he speaks
more relevantly about the meaning and practice of community
than representatives of the counter-culture groups and church
structures. Meanwhile the sociologists of religion are beginning to
discover that Paul is someone with whom they have not yet fully
come to terms. Initially this book contained additional material
for those who have such interests, but I did not have enough space
to carry this through properly. Still, those who wish to explore
further the sociological character of Paul's ideas will find here
much that is helpful. And those seeking a more precise identification of the culturally conditioned and permanently relevant

aspects of his thought will discover much to help them. At a later stage I hope to give more concentrated attention to these two areas.

Though this is not a technical work, it is based on a thorough investigation of the relevant primary and secondary sources, and suggests a number of new interpretations of the material involved. My first enquiries were made more than fifteen years ago and in varying degrees the subject has preoccupied me ever since. Almost five years have passed since a first draft of part of this book was completed and it has gone through many revisions before reaching its present form. For me, interest in Paul's view has been stimulated not only by reading and thinking about it at an academic level, but also by involvement in groups which feel what Paul said still has continuing relevance for their community life. We learn about the past not just by rational reflection upon it, but also by personal involvement in those aspects of our present which have common links with it. This is true not only for people in general but for those of us who are historians as well. It sharpens the questions we ask of the past and deepens our empathy with it. Since the book does contain several new lines of thought, sets Paul's ideas in a broader historical context than is customary and approaches him as a social thinker rather than a systematic theologian, I hope it will be read by some biblical scholars, ancient historians and historians of ideas, as well as those for whom it is chiefly designed.

In setting out the footnotes and bibliography I have borne in mind those who will mainly use them. References to secondary works have been excluded from footnotes to avoid unnecessarily weighting the presentation. Instead I have provided a carefully chosen bibliography, geared around the main themes of the book. This includes works supporting in more detail many lines of argument within it, broader treatments of various aspects of Paul's view and certain alternative views to those I have advocated. Certain references to primary sources will be found for convenience in the text but longer sets of references will generally be found in the footnotes. Citations are comprehensive as far as Paul's writings are concerned. Other contemporary documents are cited representatively, since here I am summarizing bodies of evidence rather than treating them exhaustively. In view of the relative inaccessibility of some sources, e.g. collections of Greek papyri and inscriptions and some rabbinic commentaries and codes, I have referred only to those which the general reader will find more readily available. Those specialists who wish to consult the more technical sources should not have any difficulty finding the re-

quired references. These are in the books mentioned in the
bibliography accompanying each chapter. However, where more
inaccessible items have been gathered into anthologies such as C.
K. Barrett's collection of background documents to the New
Testament, I have included reference to them. At the close of the
book there is also a glossary containing descriptions of the main
figures, works and movements cited in the text and footnotes for
those who may be unfamiliar with them.

I have appreciated the encouragement of various people in the
writing of this book, too many unfortunately to name. But I must
thank Donald Robinson, now Bishop of Parramatta in the
Diocese of Sydney, who in his lectures some years ago first opened
my eyes to some of the distinctive features of Paul's view of
church; and my good friend Geoffrey Moon who, in countless
discussions, has stimulated and sharpened my thinking on many
issues involved. Thanks are also due to John Waterhouse, at the
time Manager of Anzea Publishers, for convincing me of the need
for a more general work on the subject rather than yet another
technical monograph, and also for carefully editing the original
manuscript. I have also valued the way in which Mr. B. Howard
Mudditt, until lately the Managing Director of Paternoster Press,
maintained constant interest in the project. The editors of *Interchange* and the *Journal of Christian Education* freely agreed to my
using some paragraphs from articles on 'Paul and Women's
Liberation' (*Interchange,* Number 18, 1975, pages 81-105) and
'Freedom and Authority in Education — I: Paul's View of
Freedom; II: Paul's View of Authority' (*Journal of Christian Education,* Number 55, 1976, pages 40-48 and Number 56, 1976, pages
17-24). Edwin A. Judge, Professor of Ancient History at Mac-
quarie University, and James D. G. Dunn, Lecturer in New
Testament at Nottingham University, kindly read the final draft
and made a number of helpful suggestions.

I am also grateful to Stephen Barton and Peter Marshall, two of
my postgraduate students, for correcting the initial typescript,
and to Dr. Robert Withycombe, Warden of St. Mark's Institute,
Canberra and to the Rev. David Durie, Principal of the College
of Ministry, Canberra, for helping me check the final proofs. Encouragement and help of a more personal kind was given by
Audrey Duncan throughout the years it took to write. My wife
Julie helped me clarify many basic ideas in our frequent discussions of the book's contents and also assisted me in checking the
manuscript. Our children Mark and Simon patiently bore with it
all and will, I hope, one day understand more fully how Paul
could so grip one's imagination — as for me he does.

Introduction

The Christian writings of the first century reflect a variety of attitudes towards the meaning and practice of community. But it is the earliest amongst them, Paul's letters, that contain the most detailed information. The remainder deal with the matter only intermittently or in an indirect way, or are too brief to yield any rounded portrait. Though virtually all of them were composed later than Paul's writings, they sometimes preserve traces of an approach to community that precedes these. Paul was not the first to formulate a Christian idea of community. But there can be no doubt that he gave more attention to this than anyone else during that period. In every one of his writings aspects of community life come in for discussion and, in a few, it emerges as the main issue for consideration.

It is not merely the extent of Paul's contribution that sets it apart from others in the first century, but its quality. We find here the most clearly developed and profound understanding of community in all the early Christian writings. Not that he provides any systematic treatment of the idea. For the most part he worked out his views in response to the problems of particular communities. Only a few of his writings were designed for a wider audience and deal with the subject in more general terms. Even these do not display a strictly systematic mind at work. But they do reveal an energetic and creative thinker who has the ability to engage in both theoretical reflection and the subtleties of argument. Also his writings reveal one unfailingly concerned with the practical consequences of his viewpoint and personally involved in the actual outcome of his recommendations.

Until the last century, and in some conservative circles up to the present time, the dogmatic approach to the New Testament tended to result in a monochrome treatment of its contents. This meant that the views of even highly individual authors like Paul were too often interpreted by statements contained in the writings of other early Christian figures. It also meant that the possibility of development in his views over a period of time was rarely given serious consideration. The emergence of a more historical approach to the New Testament rightly queried both of these procedures. But the first reassessments of Paul produced by it severed him too drastically from his first-century Christian contemporaries, and reduced too arbitrarily the number of writings alleged to come from his hand. These initial experiments in the revaluation of Paul have been generally rejected as unsound, both in their methodology and their conclusions. More moderate assessments have come to prevail, recognizing the links between Paul's interpretation of Christianity and others in the New Testament and extending the number of letters felt to come from his pen.

Yet the distinctiveness of Paul's contribution remains — nowhere more so, I would argue, that in his idea of community. In the detailed exploration of his writings that follows, we will look in turn at key aspects of his approach, taking care to note how he arrives at and argues from the basic principles which underlie his understanding. Two comments should be made here. First, it is the internal dynamics of Paul's communities that we are chiefly concerned to investigate, not the external responsibilities of their members to the world around them. The latter would require a full-scale treatment of its own. In any case, for Paul it is not as a community but as individuals, families and small groups that Christians undertake and fulfill these responsibilities. Secondly, since the different aspects of his approach all have their basis in what for him is the fundamental reality around which everything, his own life included, revolves — the gospel — certain themes are bound to reappear at regular intervals throughout this study. It could not be otherwise. Paul's thinking about community cannot be compared to an argument which proceeds logically from one point to another, each stage containing the seeds of the next and unfolding naturally into it. It is more like a composition built up on a single underlying motif, each section providing a variation of this basic theme, with the motif itself resurfacing at various points in the work. We shall encounter this pattern many times in the following pages.

This investigation is primarily based on Paul's letters. Although some uncertainty surrounds the genuineness of 'Ephesians' — actually a general letter addressed to a broad group of Christians rather than a communication to a specific church — I have decided to include it in the discussion that follows and treat it as if originally coming from the apostle. But I have generally indicated when I am using it to make a point not found in the other letters, so that the reader can judge for himself whether or not it is consistent with them. The Pastoral letters (1 and 2 Timothy, Titus) present a more difficult problem, since the question of their authenticity continues to be decided more uniformly in a negative direction, even by some conservative scholars. No one doubts that they emanated from circles deeply influenced by Paul's thought. But there are also a number of uncharacteristic features in them and perhaps they are later compositions which, like Luke's reconstructions of Paul's speeches in Acts, were compiled to preserve some of his instructions for the next generation. Since for me too their place is uncertain, and yet it is unwise to be too dogmatic on the issue, I have discussed them separately at the close of the book where their compatibility or incompatibility with what is drawn from the other writings is left for the reader to gauge. Material from Acts, relating to Paul's activities in founding communities, is included in the main text. Luke's work contains valuable historical information on such matters, though this must always be checked against his tendency to idealize the earlier situation and also his occasional anachronisms. The probable order of composition of Paul's letters I take to be 1 and 2 Thessalonians, Galatians, 1 and 2 Corinthians, Romans, Philippians, Colossians, Philemon, followed by 'Ephesians' — all of them written in the space of a comparatively short period of time, *c.* AD 50/51 to 61/62.

CHAPTER ONE

The Social and Religious Setting

PAUL: A MAN OF HIS TIMES

PAUL: A MAN OF HIS TIMES

It is not possible to understand a man or his activities apart from
the times in which he lived. This is especially the case with Paul.
In responding to the call of Jesus he did not withdraw from the
world about him. Rather he found himself thrown more violently
into it. As a consequence he criss-crossed vast tracts of the
Mediterranean region several times over in the course of the next
thirty years. In doing so he met people from a variety of racial and
national backgrounds, among them Jews from the Dispersion;
homeland and immigrant Greeks; Romans at the heart of the
Empire and in some of its distant outposts; Cypriots, Macedo-
nians and the inhabitants of local districts in different parts of
Asia Minor — even small groups from Egypt, Crete, Malta and,
apparently, Scythia. On these travels he encountered competing
philosophical schools, in particular Stoicism and Epicureanism,
and alternative religious movements, especially traditional Greek
city-state cults and imported Oriental mystery religions. At different points in his journeyings he also came into conflict with a
wide range of civil and political authorities and experienced at
first hand the ramifications of a variety of legal processes and decisions. So Paul was extensively involved in, and affected by, many
of the significant tendencies and tensions of his day and cannot be
studied in isolation from them.

There is a further reason for insisting that Paul be approached in this way. For he not only encountered the ideas and institutions of the people amongst whom he moved but adopted a deliberate policy of accommodation to them. This comes out most clearly in his first letter to the Christians at Corinth: 'I have become all things to all men', he says, 'that I might by all means save some' (1 Cor. 9:22). This does not mean that Paul compromises his beliefs and practices by simply conforming them to those he happens to be addressing at any particular time. It means that he is always taking such beliefs and practices into account and making them the starting point for his own message and behaviour. Wherever he can do so, he acknowledges the validity of other approaches and incorporates them into his own (Acts 17: 22-39). Where he cannot, he asserts the superiority of his approach over others and argues that it fulfils the aspirations that have been misguidedly invested in them (Col. 2: 8-23). Either way the things he is saying and doing cannot be properly appreciated without reference to the context in which he is speaking and acting.

Another aspect of this is Paul's frequently expressed concern with the social attitudes and structures of his day. While, on occasions, he calls these into question and contradicts them by his own statements or behaviour (1 Cor. 6: 1-6), on others he insists they be carefully noted and followed (11: 14-15). Where accepted conventions come into conflict with a basic implication of the gospel message, there is no doubt in his mind as to which has to give way (10: 14-22). Where less central implications of the gospel are concerned, and where there is the likelihood of causing offence among those outside the Christian group, there should be a willing avoidance of practices which, all things being equal, are quite legitimate in themselves (8: 7-13; 10: 23-30). This means that in some measure the activities of Christians in his communities were conditioned by the values and patterns of the society around them, and cannot be rightly understood unless considered in relation to them.

Many treatments of Paul's view of community are inadequate in this respect. Instead of seeing Paul's views in their historical setting they discuss them independently of the wider context in which they emerged. This results in a primarily doctrinal study of Paul's outlook, unrelated to many of the circumstances that played a part in its development. Yet it was through interaction with the society about him, as well as involvement with his communities, that Paul came to hold the views expressed in his letters, not through theological contemplation removed from the cut and thrust of daily life. This is why they have the stamp of reality about them and are so full of life and creativity. He was constantly being forced to justify conclusions he had already reached and demonstrate their relevance to situations that had arisen. He was also frequently under pressure to deepen his convictions in order to deal with new difficulties that had appeared. Paul's understanding of community is never static or frozen into a theological system. It is a living thing, always open to development and in touch with the practicalities of the moment.

THE GRAECO-ROMAN WORLD: CHANGING CONCEPTIONS OF COMMUNITY

The Graeco-Roman world in the middle of the first century was characterized by great variety and vitality. Although Rome now dominated the whole of the Mediterranean region and Greek culture had penetrated to the furthest reaches of the Empire, not only did local patterns of rule and ways of life continue to survive, but relatively new trends in social organization began to flourish and attract an increasing number of people. Traditionally there had been two main types of community with which people might associate themselves: *politeia*, the public life of the city or nation state to which people belonged; and *oikonomia*, the household order into which they were born or to which they were attached. For some, involvement in communities of both types could be a very full and satisfying affair. The Greek citizen in fifth-century Athens played a vocal part in the *polis*, the city-state in which he lived, as well as a leading role in the *oikos*, the family unit of which he was the head. His Jewish counterpart in eighth-century Israel, as an elder in his local town or village, made a real contribution to civic affairs and had important obligations to fulfil within the extended family for which he was responsible. But there were always others who were unable to participate in the life of either of these two kinds of communities in a freely-chosen or meaningful way. Among them were slaves, dependants of various kinds, adults who remained unmarried and outcasts of society.

By the first century, even those who had previously played an influential part in their respective civil and household communities found their freedom to do so dwindling in the face of changes that were overtaking both institutions in society. Well before the rise of Rome, but accelerated by the growth of the Empire, political power tended to become concentrated in fewer and fewer hands and to remain in those hands for longer and longer periods. This was so even in Rome itself. Though in the wake of the victorious legions the traditional republics were still often created elsewhere, independence was never fully granted to them and authority was generally vested in an aristocratic, often self-advancing, minority. Disenchantment with the *polis* not only took place among the politically disadvantaged sections of society but also increased among those who, in earlier days, had found their identity partly within it. To some extent the household community was the beneficiary of this exclusion from the real bodies in which civil power resided. What men could not find in the wider community to which they belonged they sought in the smaller community in which they lived. Its breadth of membership and intimacy of relationship lent themselves well to this. Yet the desires of many could not be satisfied for long within so narrow a sphere, while the hopes of others were forever being frustrated by the subordinate position they occupied within the household framework. For these reasons men's aspirations and allegiances tended to drift away from the *oikos* in another direction.

Some of the more thoughtful, and devout, members of society began to look beyond the public life of the *polis* in which they lived towards a cosmopolitan order which would encompass all men. They wrote or dreamt of a universal commonwealth, an international brotherhood, in which the basic divisions that presently separate men had been, or were to be, resolved. Whether this was viewed as a Stoic commonwealth in which reason reigned, or as an international theocracy ruled from Jerusalem by the Messiah, this idea maintained a powerful grip on the minds of many Greeks, Romans and Jews.

However for others these expectations proved too abstract and elitist on the one hand, or too violent and utopian on the other. In increasingly greater numbers such people began to find their desires fulfilled in a variety of voluntary associations that multiplied in cities all over the ancient world, especially in Greek centres. Though these associations had their precursors in groups formed for various purposes among the social elite in earlier centuries, it was in the late Hellenistic period that they came into their own and attracted a wide following — in part from the socially disadvantaged members of society. The novel feature of these groups was their basis in something other than the principles of *politeia* or *oikonomia*. They bound together people from different backgrounds on a different ground to that of geography and race, or natural and legal ties. Their principle was *koinōnia*, i.e. a voluntary sharing or partnership.

This does not mean that every such association was open to all who wished to join it. Many restricted entry to a certain nationality, family, class or sex in society and excluded all others. Only a few appear to have opened their doors, in some respects at least, to all. I say 'in some respects', for the majority were in any case established around a particular interest, vocation or commitment. These were extremely varied: political, military and sporting concerns; professional and commercial guilds; artisans and members of crafts; philosophical schools and religious brotherhoods. Although only some were purely religious in character (a religious dimension was present in nearly all such organizations, generally through the patronage of a deity and attachment to a shrine), the bulk were primarily designed to meet the social, charitable and funerary needs of their members. It was in such voluntary fraternities, which could number anything between ten and one hundred members but mostly averaged around thirty to thirty-five, that many people in the Hellenistic world began to find their personal point of reference and to experience a level of community that was denied to them elsewhere. In this proliferation of small clubs or associations, and in the significance they possessed for those who belonged to them, there is an interesting link between the first century and our own.

DISENCHANTMENT WITH TRADITIONAL RELIGION

(a) The Jews

Bearing in mind the wide range of associations that existed during this period, we need to look more closely at those which were predominantly religious in nature. A word first, however, about the religious scene in general during this time. Among the Jews, there was widespread dissatisfaction with the priestly hierarchy in Jerusalem, particularly in view of its collaboration with the Roman authorities and its absorption of Greek culture. In reaction against this, brotherhoods were formed to preserve the purity of the traditional faith, maintain the vigour of their messianic hope and promote adherence to the ethical code enshrined in their sacred books. To ensure this they developed an extensive network of regulations to protect their members against the encroachment of foreign influences or the relaxation of their religious obligations. For some, so apostate were the religious leaders and their cultic practices, and so impure the society around them, that they withdrew into monastic communities on the fringes of civilization or as conclaves within urban life. This was the course of action adopted by the Qumran community on the shores of the Dead Sea, and by the associated 'Essene' communities scattered throughout Jewish cities and colonies. Others formed fraternities within the flux of everyday affairs, to educate and encourage their members in ways of living a holy life in the midst of the world about them. Such, among others, was the practice of the 'Pharisees', a term which probably embraces a number of like-minded, though not identical, puritan groups in Jewish society. These formed themselves into *haburoth* in order to maintain rigid standards of purity and celebrate religious meals together.

Apart from the brotherhoods, there was another institution within Judaism which became a centre of religious and communal life, namely the synagogue. Its origin lay several centuries in the past and is partly clouded in obscurity. With the dissolution of the Israelite monarchies in the late-seventh and early-fifth centuries BC, and the consequent exile of the people from the land and Temple, the need for a new framework for preserving and nurturing the Jewish faith became necessary. It was probably at this time that local gatherings of Jews began to take place where the Law could be read and expounded, and prayer made. It is not clear which of these two elements, the educational or liturgical, was primary or whether both were inseparable from the beginning. After the return of the exiles from Babylon these gatherings seem to have continued, at least outside Jerusalem. In the capital, except for foreign residents, the rebuilt Temple provided a focus for worship and instruction.[1] Elsewhere, in northern districts like Galilee,[2] strong Hellenistic centres like Caesarea[3] and in cities throughout the Diaspora, synagogues (or 'prayer-houses' as they were often called outside Judea) multiplied, particularly during the second and first centuries BC.[4] The term *sunagōgē* at first referred to the gathering itself (Acts 13: 43), then by association to the community who assembled together,[5] and finally, as mostly in the New Testament, to the buildings which were provided especially for this purpose.[6] There is evidence to suggest that near the synagogue other buildings were sometimes constructed e.g. a guest house, baths, rooms etc., which could be used in association with it, especially by travellers.[7] While Pharisees were warmly welcomed by such groups because of their pious, thoughtful and practical approach to religion, they were not chiefly responsible

1. Josephus, *The Antiquities of the Jews*, XV, 380-425
2. Mt. 4: 23 and 9: 35; Lk. 4: 15
3. Josephus, *The Jewish War*, II, 285 and 289; compare *Antiquities*, XIX, 300
4. Philo, *Embassy to Gaius*, 156 and 311; *Vita Mosis*, II, 215; *In Flaccum, 45*
5. *Corpus Inscriptionum Graecarum*, 9909 (Barrett, p.50); Acts 6: 9 and 9: 2; Rev. 2: 9 and 3: 9
6. Philo, *Quod Omnis Probus Liber sit*, 81; Josephus, *Antiquities*, XIX, 305; and Acts 13-19 passim.
7. Theodotus Inscription (Barrett, pp. 51-52)

for the proliferation of synagogues — although they frequently made use of the synagogues to disseminate their teachings.

(b) The Greeks and Romans

Disenchantment with traditional religions also existed among Greeks and Romans. The reality or relevance of the official gods had been queried by the philosophers, and the ritual associated with their worship failed to satisfy the needs of those who were being awakened to greater individuality. Into the vacuum that was created stepped two main claimants for men's allegiance. First were the various philosophies of the day, which provided both an all-embracing world view and practical advice on the well-ordered life. These appealed to more thoughtful Greeks and Romans, their religious overtones strengthening their capacity to satisfy other aspects of the personality. Far and away the most influential of these in Paul's time, and the one that most seriously grappled with the communal tendencies within man, was Stoicism. This had its origins in the late fourth century. However it was Posidonius in the first century BC who did much to revitalize Stoic thought, giving it a more transcendental thrust and deeper religious character than it had previously possessed. This so-called 'Middle Stoicism' can be found in the writings of Paul's contemporary, the Roman philosopher-statesman Seneca, though representatives of a more traditional approach were also active, for example, Musonius Rufus and later, Epictetus. There were other philosophical outlooks but, unlike Stoicism, these had either failed to grip popular imagination — the fate of Epicureanism — or had not yet filtered down to the general educated consciousness — as with the revival of Platonism. Mention should also be made of the Cynics, those nonconformist itinerants who often shocked their contemporaries by their message and manner of life, and in part influenced Stoic ideas and practice. So much did these share in common in the first century AD that Cynicism may be aptly described as a kind of 'radical Stoicism'.

For others these philosophies were too cerebral a solution. Their individual quest for an assurance of immortality and place in the scheme of things led them to investigate the promises made by the various 'mystery' or secretive religions that poured into the Western Mediterranean world from the Eastern provinces. These had a long history, some originating in Greek folk-religions that persisted alongside the setting up of the official cults. At an early stage Eleusinian mysteries were integrated into the city cult at Athens, but for the most part mysteries continued alongside the official worship and did not demand withdrawal from it as a prerequisite for membership. One thinks here of the Dionysiac festivals or, a very different phenomenon, of the Orphic brotherhoods. Particularly from the third century BC a variety of Near Eastern local religions — Egyptian,[8] Phrygian,[9] Persian[10] and others — spread throughout the Hellenistic world. They were brought by emigrants, merchants, soldiers, even slaves, but by the second century AD were being promoted by some intellectuals and rulers as well. They established themselves as *thiasoi*, private cultic associations, though again participation in the official worship, or for that matter other mystery-cults, was not forbidden. So it was that the rites associated with such foreign deities as Cybele, Attis, Isis and Osiris, Adonis and, at a later date, the figure of Mithras, spread throughout the Empire. These catered for the psychological needs of people in a much more substantial way than the philosophical schools, chiefly through various dramatic rituals in which adherents participated and vivid mystical experiences to which they aspired.[11] Since such religions possessed a certain democratic tendency — they opened their doors to men of all nationalities, and to women and slaves as well — and maintained firm secrecy about their activities, they held a powerful attraction and fascination for many.

PAUL'S CONTACT WITH THE NEW RELIGIONS

How much contact did Paul have with these different groups? It is unlikely that he had been himself a member of anything but a *haburah*, a Pharisaic fellowship, and an attender of anything but the synagogue and Temple. He came to Jerusalem from Tarsus (the capital of Cilicia) at a young age, probably undergoing all his formal education there (Acts 22: 3 and 26: 4). His Pharisaic training in Jerusalem would not have permitted him to belong to any other association. His Diaspora origin also brought him into contact with synagogue life in Jerusalem, certainly with the synagogue of those from Cilicia and Asia, mentioned by Luke (7: 9; compare 24: 2). He was converted journeying to Damascus with an official commisson to seek out Christians in the synagogues there, but he proceeded to preach the gospel in these instead (9: 2 and 20), as he later did to the Hellenistic Jews in Jerusalem, probably in their synagogues (v. 29). When he subse-

---

8. Plutarch, *Isis and Osiris,* passim
9. Eusebius, *Praeparatio Evangelica,* II, ii. 22ff.
10. Mithras Liturgy (Barrett, pp. 102-104)
11. Apuleius, *Metamorphoses,* XI, passim

quently returned to Tarsus, and perhaps also initially at Antioch,[12] he presumably moved in synagogue circles. Once his wider missionary work had begun in earnest, synagogues consistently provided the contact-point with potential converts (Acts 17: 2), e.g. at Salamis (13: 5), Pisidian Antioch (v. 14), Iconium (14: 1), Philippi (where no building existed but simply a place of prayer) (16: 13), Thessalonica (17: 1), Beroea (v. 10), Athens (v. 17), Corinth (18:4) and Ephesus (18: 19 and 19: 8). There can be no doubt about Paul's wide acquaintance with synagogue practice.

It is more difficult to judge how much he knew about other voluntary associations in these areas, including the mystery-cults. He certainly came into conflict with them on occasions — directly with the guild of silversmiths at Ephesus (19: 24-27), and indirectly through his injunctions to the Corinthians about banquets in idols' temples and other references to the ecstatic and sensual character of cultic worship.[13] The widespread existence of such associations and the increasing penetration of the cults throughout the whole Mediterranean region suggests that Paul had other opportunities to learn about them, even if the secrecy imposed upon members of the mysteries made their affairs less public. The polemical use of their terminology at various points in his letters suggests this e.g. mystery,[14] knowledge,[15] visions (2 Cor. 12: 1; Col. 2: 18), though it is just possible that such language was in more general use. His encounters with members of the philosophical schools were probably less frequent, if for no other reason than their minority following. Alongside his well-known meeting with the Stoics and Epicureans at Athens (Acts 17: 18), contacts with such people can probably be deduced from his use of their venues, e.g. the hall of Tyrannus in Ephesus (Acts 19: 9), reference to their activities (1 Cor. 1: 20 and 2: 45) and echoes of their teaching (e.g. Acts 17: 28; 1 Cor. 15: 33). While we should not overlook the possibility that some acquaintance with the teachings of these groups formed part of Paul's education in Jerusalem, it seems likely that most of his information would have been gathered on his travels in a rather *ad hoc* fashion, supplemented by occasional debates with their representatives and discussions with converts from their way of life.

12. Acts 9: 30, 11: 25 and 26; compare Josephus, *War*, VII, 44
13. 1 Cor. 8: 7-13, 10: 14-22 and also 1 Cor. 12: 1-3, 13: 1
14. Rom. 16: 25; Col. 1: 26-27; Eph. 3: 3-4 and 9, 5: 32
15. See p. 74.

THE CHRISTIAN COMMUNITIES

The presence of different voluntary religious associations in the ancient world during this period means that, from one point of view, there was nothing particularly novel about the appearance of Christian communities alongside them. Judaism had its parties and, in the early days at least, the Nazarenes were regarded as an additional sect within Israel, not as a heretical departure from it. Hellenism had its cults and, in the initial stage of their development, Christians had their private gatherings. Because it centred around an Eastern divinity, Christianity may well have been regarded by some in terms of the mysteries, though the absence of normal cult-practices within it might have led others to view it as primarily a social rather than religious phenomenon, or perhaps as a new philosophical school. Quite apart from the way in which they were perceived at the time, Paul's communities must be seen in retrospect as part of a wider movement towards the spontaneous association of individuals in society, and as a parallel development to the religious fellowships that were growing in popularity within Judaism and Hellenism during that period. While, in view of Paul's pre-conversion background and missionary environment, it is the synagogue and mystery-cult that must be brought into closest comparison with his idea of community, the monastic fraternities and philosophical schools form part of the wider background to his approach. How far was it removed from the monastic order established at Qumran and how much does it have in common with the Stoic expectation of a universal commonwealth? How largely did it draw upon patterns of authority, worship and organization characteristic of the synagogue, and how extensively did it accommodate itself to the practices and structures of the mystery cults? In other words, how genuinely distinctive was it? These are questions which we must now examine.

CHAPTER TWO

The Arrival of Radical Freedom

THE THEOLOGICAL BASIS: FREEDOM THROUGH CHRIST

Along with a description of its historical setting, a proper introduction to Paul's idea of community must include consideration of the theological basis upon which it rests. This will involve drawing together relevant statements of Paul from all over his writings rather than following the development of his thoughts in successive letters. Here we are still dealing with preliminaries — a more sequential treatment would take too long to complete. Although the grounds on which Paul's view of community rests are generally investigated in terms of his understanding of 'salvation', I prefer here to group his various statements on the subject around the notion of 'freedom'. Paul uses the term *eleutheria*, freedom, or one of its cognates frequently throughout his writings, some twenty-nine times in all — only a little less often than *sōtéria*, salvation, or one of its allied terms. What is more, the notion of *eleutheria* carries over into his approach to community. Our examination of it here will provide the background for references to it later in this study. In fact most of the different aspects of Paul's idea of community are related in some way or other to his understanding of freedom.

We turn first to those passages where he is talking about the common predicament of individuals in this life. Though they are made for a relationship with God and are intended to be integrated persons, they are in reality divided beings who have

generally lost sight of their way.[1] Drawing upon terms with a
long history in Greek legal and political thought, and alluding to
observable patterns of behaviour as empirical support, Paul
asserts that people are so 'enslaved' by their baser inclinations
that they are no longer 'free' to properly know or pursue their real
potential and destiny. This takes place in three main ways:

1. They find themselves under an inner compulsion to 'sin',[2] and
to put their confidence in 'works' and the 'flesh'.[3] That is to say,
they are generally preoccupied with themselves, with their own
concerns and aspirations, and regard their own heritage or
accomplishments as the ground of their future expectations.

2. They are hampered, if Jews, from responding rightly to the
moral regulations in the Mosaic law (Rom. 2: 23 and 7: 7-12) or,
if Gentiles, to those moral demands of God inscribed upon their
wills (1: 32). This can take two forms. If they rebel against the
revealed or implanted 'law' of God, they drift into an amoral and
unnatural way of life (Rom. 1: 24ff.). If they focus all their
energies on the Law, it deceives them and becomes merely
another channel for their self-centred natures (Rom. 10: 1-3).

3. They are in bondage to certain realities outside themselves,
whether supernatural 'powers' which they allow to influence and
affect their lives,[4] the 'god of this world' — Satan himself — by
whom they are misled and manipulated (2 Cor. 4: 4; Eph. 2: 2),
or 'death' which, experienced spiritually now and physically
later, ultimately brings all their aspirations, relationships and
achievements to an end.[5] Thus people are not as 'free' as they
would like to think, but are 'in bondage to' baser inclinations,
moral obligations and alien forces. These largely shape their
characters and dominate their lives.

Although all are constrained in these various ways, this does
not mean that they are completely unfree. Paul allows that, up to
a point, people are able to know the truth about God and do what
is right,[6] just as those in authority over them are able to govern
society in a morally responsible fashion (Rom. 13: 1ff.). But their
capacity to do these things is limited.[7] So it is that every person —
beginning with 'the first man' through whose failure sin began to
exert its power in human affairs, law became necessary to contain

1. Acts 17: 27-30; Rom. 3: 9-18 and 7: 15-24
2. Rom. 6: 17 and 20; 7: 14 and 25
3. Rom. 2: 17ff. and 3: 20; Phil. 3: 3ff.; Gal. 3: 10
4. Gal. 4: 3; Col. 2: 8; Eph. 6: 12
5. Rom. 1: 32, 6: 13, 16, 21 and 23, 7: 5; Eph. 2: 2
6. Acts 17: 28; Rom. 1: 19-21; 2: 14-15; compare Phil. 4: 8
7. Rom. 1: 21-23; 1 Cor. 11: 32-33

it and death gained its abnormal significance — experiences a
solidarity with his fellows in 'Adam'. However, a second community has now come into existence through the achievement of
that other person whom Paul terms 'the second Man'. Through
his obedience the trend initiated by the first member of the human
race has been reversed (Rom. 5: 12ff.). Although the full impact
of sin fell upon him, it gained no control over him and was
defeated (2 Cor. 5: 21; Rom. 8: 3). Although he experienced the
condemnation meted out to the lawless, his behaviour trans-
cended the law and terminated it (Gal. 3: 13; Rom. 10: 4).
Although death unjustly made its claim upon him, he triumphed
over it and the alien powers as well (Rom. 1: 4; Col. 2: 15). Since
he did this not for his own sake but for the sake of all men as their
representative,[8] he is the foundation of a new community,
humanity or creation.[9]

Already we see how closely Paul's understanding of freedom,
or salvation, is bound up with his idea of community. He does not
view salvation as simply a transaction between the individual and
God. A person prior to his encounter with Christ belongs to a
community, however much his actions incline him to pursue his
own (or his immediate circle's) self-interest. And it is into a *new*
community that his reconciliation with God in Christ brings him,
however much he experiences that event as an individual affair.
Correlatively, the salvation effected by Christ follows from his
being not just an individual but a corporate personality, the
'second' and 'last' Adam (or, as it has been so strikingly expressed, 'Adam — at last!'). This means not only that Christ's actions
impinge upon the lives of others and are decisive for them but, as
we shall now go on to see, that his very life enters into them enabl-
ing theirs to enter into his.

THE FREEDOM OF CHRIST: THE ROLE OF THE SPIRIT

Those who acknowledge Jesus as having gained this victory on
their behalf, and who receive his Spirit into their lives, are
liberated from those things by which they were inexorably grip-
ped beforehand. They are free from the compulsion to sin and
from the tendency to rely on their own moral and religious
achievements.[10] They are free from the obligation to regulate their

---

8. Rom. 6: 3ff.; 2 Cor. 5: 14ff.; Col. 3: 3
9. 1 Cor. 15: 20ff.; 2 Cor. 4: 6 and 5: 17; Col. 3: 10; Eph. 2: 14-15
10. Rom. 6: 7 and 22, 8: 10-11; Eph. 2: 1-7

lives by reference to an instinctive or external moral code.[11] They are free from the bonds which death irrevocably puts around them (Rom. 6: 23 and 8: 21), and from those supernatural agencies which blinded their former judgement and influenced their former choices (Rom. 8: 38-39; Gal. 4: 8-11). Experience of the Spirit has the reverse effect. Instead of blinding and tyrannizing them, it has, since its gift is truth and its power love, released them and for the first time granted them freedom to choose a way of life for themselves (Rom. 5: 5; 1 Cor. 2: 10-11). This does not mean that they are altogether released from the pull of the old way of life. Far from it. In a frankly autobiographical passage Paul acknowledges: 'I am a divided being. In my innermost self, the thinking and reasoning part of me, I wholeheartedly endorse God's principles. But I am also aware of a different principle within me. This is in continual conflict with both my conscious mind and conscience, and makes me an unwilling prisoner to the power of sin which has such a grip on my personality. It is an agonizing situation to be in — to be torn by a conflict from which there is (as yet) no solution' (Rom. 7: 21ff.). According to Paul it is only in the resurrection at the Last Day that the final resolution of the conflict between the mind and the conscience will take place.[12] In the meantime one must live in the tension between them, conscious of the fact that in Christ the issue has already been decided and that through the Spirit this can now in part be experienced (Rom. 7: 25b - 8: 11).

This fundamental freedom is not merely an independence *from* certain things, but also an independence *for* others. As Paul says to the Galatians, 'It is *for* freedom that Christ has set us free', to which he adds, the corollary, 'Stand fast therefore and do not fall back into slavery again' (Gal. 5: 1). He goes on to explain that the positive expression of this independence leads, paradoxically, into a new form of 'service' (on a few occasions he even uses the term 'slavery'), though service of a qualitatively different kind to that experienced before. Instead of the compulsory service of sin, there is now the voluntary service of what Paul broadly terms 'righteousness' (Rom. 7: 17-18). Instead of conformity to a moral code of life, there is now conformity to what he calls the 'law' of Christ, that is the compassionate character and sacrificial behaviour of Jesus (1 Cor. 9: 21; Gal. 6: 2). Instead of the experience of spiritual and ultimately physical death, there is now the experience of 'life', a life which, even in suffering, will

---

11. Rom. 7: 4-6 and 8: 1-4; Gal. 2: 19-20; Col. 2: 16-23
12. Rom. 7: 24-25a; compare 1 Cor. 15: 53-57

eventually liberate believers and the cosmos itself from the bondage to decay.[13]

Quite apart from all these things, there is a new liberty towards *God*, which dispels fear and leads to freedom in his presence of a most intimate kind (Rom. 8: 15-18; Gal. 4: 1-7). (At this point Paul tends to drop the language of service and slavery in favour of that descriptive of family relationships.) This results in service to God which is quite free in character (Rom. 1: 9). It also leads to a new freedom towards *others*. This includes freedom from the fear of others' judgements as well as from one's own attempts to manipulate them.[14] It also includes freedom in the communication of one's thoughts, expression of one's emotions, the opening up of one's life and the sharing of one's possessions.[15] Indeed the free service of others, the voluntary giving of oneself in love to them, is at the very heart of this conception of freedom (1 Cor. 9: 19; 1 Thess. 2: 8). It also entails a more liberated attitude to the created things of *this world*. Since there is nothing in existence which is in principle out of bounds — 'All things are yours,' Paul insists, and 'To the pure all things are pure' — this opens up a freer, non-idolatrous use of possessions.[16]

So this freedom granted by God not only transfers men and women out of a broken relationship with God, and a defective solidarity with men, into a new community with both, but also inclines them to live the kind of life that will extend and deepen that new community itself. The integral connection between freedom and community in Paul's thinking once again becomes transparently clear.

ALTERNATIVE FIRST CENTURY VIEWS OF FREEDOM

In the Pharisaic and Qumran writings, as in Jewish literature generally, there are no formal discussions of the subject of freedom. This has led some commentators to suggest that it is a purely Greek conception. But this is highly questionable.

(a) The Pharisaic and the Qumran communities

The Old Testament, under such terms as 'redemption' and 'salvation', speaks frequently enough of the national freedom

13. Rom. 8: 18-23; 2 Cor. 4: 11-18
14. 1 Cor. 4: 3 and 9: 19; 2 Cor. 11: 20-21
15. 2 Cor. 3: 12, 6: 11, 7: 4, 8: 2 and 9: 13
16. Rom. 14: 14; 1 Cor. 3: 21-22

granted to Israel at the Exodus,[17] and occasionally of personal deliverances (e.g. Ps. 66: 2 and 89: 26) and the liberty experienced by obeying the Law (Ps. 119: 45). It also looks forward to the time when a greater spiritual and moral freedom will be granted to the individual by God (e.g. Is. 61: 1; Jer. 31: 33-34). In the rabbinic writings there is a reiteration of the Old Testament ideas concerning political freedom.[18] More personal freedom is also occasionally talked about,[19] though here a multitude of ritual and moral regulations encroach upon it[20] and its achievement is sometimes more grounded in human effort.[21]

At Qumran the emphasis is more upon the fulfilment of the Exodus events in the present deliverance of the community from association with false worshippers.[22] and its longed-for future deliverance from its enemies,[23] than on the deliverance of Israel as a past event. At the individual level, an even more rigid adherence to legal traditions[24] is combined with a stronger insistence upon the necessity of divine grace for their observance.[25] Paul shares with Pharisaism the recognition of an historical event as the foundation of freedom, but this is located for him in the history of a person rather than in certain national events, and is based more decisively on God's free will than on what is sometimes represented as a semi-contractual relationship between himself and his people. He shares with Qumran the celebration of God's grace as the source of freedom, but for him this is active through the presence of the Spirit in a way that the Qumran community could not envisage until the arrival of the Messianic Age.

In all three, service of God and others is a central concern, but in Paul it is not undertaken through the observance of a moral code regulating the greater part of life, so much as through the application of certain basic attitudes and principles to the varying circumstances of life. All three lead to the formation of communities in which the members possess a strong sense of responsibility for one another, though varying in the intensity of their common existence. Pharisaism, which tended to be an association of a religious elite, centred around the fulfilment of particular obligations of an occasional character; the Qumran sect estab-

17. E.g. Ps. 77: 15 and 111: 9
18. Pes. 10: 5-6
19. Ab. 2: 7 and 3: 15-16; Pea. 1: 1
20. Ab. 1: 1; Shabb. 7: 1f.
21. Makk. 3: 16
22. CDC 3: 5-21
23. 1QM 11: 9-10
24. E.g. 1QS 5-7; CDC 10-11
25. 1QS 9: 14-15, 11: 2-22

lished an isolated monastic order, with a self-contained life; while
the Pauline communities possessed a more open and 'everyday'
character than either of these approaches.

(b) The Stoic philosophers

So strong and pervasive is Paul's emphasis upon liberty in comparison with preceding and contemporary writings that many
have regarded him as indebted directly to Hellenistic, principally
Stoic, thought. The Stoics were certainly interested in freedom.
Epictetus, the freeman philosopher, talks about the subject in his
surviving writings proportionately about four times as frequently
as Paul. There is in both Paul and the Stoics, unlike earlier Greek
thought, a preoccupation with the question at the personal rather
than legal or political level. Both agree that freedom does not
come through subservience to an external law, but by conformity
to certain norms that are internal in character. They share the
belief that it can only be attained through freeing oneself from the
many false beliefs which bind man's thoughts and actions. The
two stress the necessity for liberation from certain passions, in
particular the fear of death. There is, too, a submission to the
divine as part of this whole process and the quest for unity with
other persons.

Closer inspection reveals that, despite these apparent conver-
gences, resemblances between the two are of a formal kind only.
While the quest for freedom is no longer to be pursued through
adherence to an external law, for the Stoic it is discovered through
self-understanding[26] while for Paul it is by possessing, through the
Spirit, the 'mind of Christ' (2 Cor. 6: 16). Although both require
an awareness of the illusory value of many received beliefs and external objects, for Paul it is precisely the ascetic response that
Stoicism endorsed[27] that is to be left behind (Col. 2: 16-23). True,
both the Stoics[28] and Paul required the renunciation of certain
passions, but for the latter it is only baser desires which are to be
sublimated, not the emotions as a whole. (This is why Paul can
call his readers to show an increase in such things as affection,
grief, earnestness, eagerness, indignation, zeal and so on (2 Cor.
6: 11-12, 7: 2 and 9: 11) and also speak constructively of his own
anguish, fear, sorrow, restlessness and longing — quite apart
from emotions of a more 'positive' character.[29]). For him freedom
also involves liberty for man's body and environment, i.e. resur-

26. Epictetus, *Dissertationes*, IV, 1: 52 and 63
27. Epictetus, *Encheiridion*, 15
28. Epictetus, *Ench.*, 12, 16 and 20; *Diss.*, III, 26 and 39
29. 2 Cor. 1: 8-9, 2: 3-4 and 12-13, 5: 3-5, 7: 5, 11: 28-29

rection of the body and the creation of a new universe, and it is not restricted to the intellectual and spiritual faculties.[30]

Whereas commitment to the divine is by no means absent from the Stoic approach, for all its new transcendental emphasis there is a strong pantheist element in the notion of divinity that is involved: since the inner self is also basically divine, the individual's self is more firmly anchored.[31] For Paul a genuine surrender of the ego itself to a personal God is involved, not for it to become a divine automaton but precisely in order that it might find and become its true self.[32] In addition, although the Stoics recognized a common bond between men and sought to develop it, this had its basis in the rational harmony of all things. The sympathetic integration to which this led frequently possessed an elitist character. Paul's view of community, with its foundation in an historical event and its emphasis upon sacrificial service, reconciliation and special regard given to the least qualified members, is a very different affair.

(c) The Mystery Cults

Another view of freedom with which Paul may have had to deal was that carried over into some of his communities from the mystery cults. Freedom was regarded in these circles as primarily freedom from fate[33] and, ultimately, freedom from the body.[34] There was also freedom from uncleanness, but this was mainly considered to be a ritual affair.[35] The positive freedom that was enjoyed was limited through adherence to various ritual and ascetic practices.[36] This tended to become an end in itself, only minimally subject to external law or inner self-control.

How did Paul's view of freedom differ from that of the mystery cults? The concept of fate was foreign to Paul. For him freedom was ultimately 'for' and not 'from' the body, and was explicitly other-directed rather than designed essentially for the individual's enjoyment. Also the freedom which the cults promised came through a secret and mystical experience, overwhelming the individual and, temporarily at least, fusing him with the divine

30. Epictetus, *Diss.*, IV, 1: 97ff., *Ench.*, 1
31. Epictetus, *Diss.*, I, 12: 26-35
32. Phil. 2: 15-16; Col. 3: 10; Eph. 4: 23-24
33. Apuleius, *Metamorphoses*, XI, 6, 12, 15 and 25
34. *Mithras Liturgy*, 3-7 (Barrett, pp. 102-104); compare Plutarch, *Isis and Osiris*, 78-79
35. Apuleius, *Met.*, XI, 23
36. Tibullus, *Elegy*, I, 23-32; Apuleius, *Met.*, XI, 27ff.; Plutarch, *Is. and Os.*, 6-8

power.[37] According to Paul however, God comes to a person through the Spirit and not merely as a power: since the individual is addressed by Christ rather than absorbed into him, the real identity of each is retained. Both approaches certainly possessed a corporate dimension, but the cults were fundamentally based on a community of interest rather than responsibility, and were characterized by shared ritual rather than mutual service. (The mysteries clearly differed from one another in emphasis here and some, such as the Isis cult in its late forms, attained a more personal conception of deity and moral understanding of obligation.)

THE DISTINCTIVENESS OF PAUL'S VIEW

Despite his Greek terminology then, and the presence of certain formal parallels with Stoicism, Paul's view of freedom is built on essentially Hebrew foundations, but differs from the freedom characteristic of the Pharisaic and Essene groups in his day. The centrality of love, rather than of a moral or legal code, self-control or self-abandonment, particularly marks off his concept of freedom from that of Judaism and Hellenism. To clarify this relationship between love and freedom would lead us into a full-scale study of Paul's ethical views. We are not able to undertake that here. But the centrality of love does mean that freedom is experienced not only as the content of the Christian life, but also as the process by which its texture is determined. For when Paul elaborates upon the nature and implications of love, he does not draw up an ethical code in which all its practical consequences are explored and established in advance. He draws attention instead to certain *general* attitudes with which love is associated or through which it is exhibited (Gal. 5: 13-23; Cor. 13: 2-11). Since discernment is required to know which of these is appropriate in any particular situation, freedom is very much involved in deciding what is or is not fitting 'in the Lord' in a certain set of circumstances.[38] Although in his writings Paul goes on to formulate broad principles of conduct to which these attitudes give rise (Col. 3: 8-4: 5; Eph. 5: 21-6: 9), as well as giving on occasion very specific injunctions to particular individuals or churches, these principles often require fresh application 'in the Spirit' to the changing contexts in which people are involved. The specific injunctions are not always able to be generalized into universal rules (though they may rest on principles which have a more general application). All this in-

37. Plutarch, *Is. and Os.,* 35, 68 and 77-78; Apuleius, *Met.,* XI, 24
38. Compare 2 Cor. 1: 23-2: 8 and 13: 2-11

dicates the flexibility in Paul's approach to decision-making and
the extent to which freedom permeates his understanding of it.
He gives clearest expresson to this in his assertion: 'Though I am
free from all men, I have made myself a slave to all . . . I have
become all things to all men, that I might by all means save some.
I do it all for the sake of the gospel that I may share in its blessings.' (1 Cor. 9: 19, 22 and 23).

To summarize, freedom for Paul consists of three main components:

Independence

* from certain things, e.g. sin, the Law, death and alien
  powers
* for certain things, e.g. righteousness, conformity to Jesus and
  suffering
* resulting in a personal and life-giving experience of liberty.

Dependence

* upon Christ, who terminated mankind's enslavement
  through his death and resurrection
* upon the Spirit, who communicates Christ's life and purpose
* received as a divine gift rather than innate possibility.

Interdependence

* with others, since liberty leads to service and can only be
  practically defined in relation to their needs
* with the world, since the universe itself will experience the
  liberty of transformation — along with those who are Christ's
* giving liberty a social and cosmic, as well as a personal and
  theocentric dimension.

In the light of all this, one can understand Paul's confidence that
'where the Spirit of the Lord is, there is freedom' (2 Cor. 3: 17).
The richness of his understanding of freedom is readily apparent.
As we have seen, much of his view of community is already
implicit in it.

CHAPTER THREE

Church as household gathering

THE GOSPEL AND COMMUNITY

In the wake of Paul's travels throughout the Mediterranean, Christian communities sprang up, consolidated and began to multiply. This was the outcome of a deliberate policy on his part. He not only proclaimed the message about Christ and brought people into an intimate relationship with God, but drew the consequences of that message for the life of his converts and led them into a personal relationship with one another. As we have seen, for Paul the gospel bound men and women to one another as well as to God. Acceptance by Christ necessitated acceptance of those whom he had already welcomed (Rom. 15: 7); reconciliation with God entailed reconciliation with others that exhibited the character of the gospel preaching (Phil. 4: 2-3); union in the Spirit involved union with one another, for the Spirit was primarily a shared, not individual experience.[1] The gospel is not a purely personal matter. It has a social dimension. It is a communal affair.

To embrace the gospel, then, is to enter into community. One cannot have the one without the other. But what *sort* of a community? Where does it exist? How is it expressed? Any discussion of these questions must begin with Paul's use of the term *ekklēsia*, church, or very soon come to grips with it. This word occurs some sixty times in his letters, more often than all the other occurrences

1. 2 Cor. 13: 14; Phil. 2: 1; Eph. 4: 3

of the word in the New Testament combined. It is his favourite way of referring to the communities to whom he is writing. The term itself may be found in Greek sources, including the Greek translation of the Jewish Bible, several centuries prior to its use by Paul. It is also present in Acts, where it comes early into prominence, and occasionally in Matthew, Hebrews and James — as well as the letter and apocalypse of John. We must now consider its pre-Christian meaning in some detail.

THE MEANING OF *EKKLĒSIA*

(a) Pre-Christian: 'any gathering of a group of people'

In Greek *ekklēsia* was a familiar word. From the fifth century BC onwards it referred to the regular 'assembly' of citizens in a city to decide matters affecting their welfare.[2] We have an example in the New Testament itself where *ekklēsia* is used to describe just such a meeting. This occurred during Paul's stay in Ephesus during his third missionary journey (Acts 19: 21-41). The silversmiths of that city, fearing for their trade in view of his preaching against idolatry, provoked a demonstration of the populace against Paul and his associates. The town clerk of Ephesus, probably the chief civil officer in the city, urged the crowd to restrain themselves, advising the silversmiths to make their complaint formally before the courts or proconsuls. If the people wished to take matters further they should do so in the lawful and regular *ekklēsia* where such matters were decided (v. 39), not in the unconstitutional and near-riotous *ekklēsia* now in session (v. 41). Here we have two typical instances of the Greek use of the word in reference to an assembly of the people. The term has also been found three times in inscriptions in relation to cultic societies, but in these as well the sense of 'meeting' or 'assembly' predominates. The term does not possess an inherently religious (let alone cultic) meaning.

In Jewish circles, as the Greek translation of the Old Testament (the Septuagint or LXX) shows, *ekklēsia* is generally used to translate the Hebrew word for the 'assembly' of the people of Israel before God,[3] though sometimes this is rendered by *sunagōgē*. It also describes other assemblies of a less specifically religious or non-religious kind, for example the 'gathering' of an army in preparation for war (1 Sam. 17: 47; 1 Chron. 28: 14) or the 'com-

2. Compare Thucydides, *Histories*, 1: 87 and 139, 6: 8 and 8: 69; Philo, *De Specialibus Legibus*, II, 44; *Quod Omnis Probus Liber sit*, 138 et al.
3. Dt. 4: 10 and 9: 10; Chron. 6: 3 and 12; Ps. 106: 32

ing together' of an unruly and potentially dangerous crowd (Ps. 25: 5; Eccl. 26: 6). All in all it occurs about one hundred times in the Septuagint, though predominantly to refer to Israel's meeting before God. Sometimes the whole nation appears to be involved, as on those occasions when Moses is addressing the people prior to their entry into the promised land. At other times it is only the chief representatives that seem to be present, as with the congregation of tribal heads, or patriarchal chiefs, at Solomon's dedication of the Temple in Jerusalem. (Josephus also uses the word frequently — eighteen times in LXX quotations and forty-eight times in all, always of a gathering. These vary in character, e.g. religious, political and spontaneous assemblies are mentioned.[4] Of Philo's thirty uses, all but five occur in quotations from the LXX, and these five in the classical Greek sense.) Despite the context in which the word generally appears in these writings, it is clear that it has no intrinsically religious meaning. It simply means an assembly or gathering of people in a quite ordinary sense so that, as in Greek usage, it can refer to meetings that are quite secular in character.

(b) Paul's use: 'a regular, local gathering before God'

How are we to discover what Paul himself meant by *ekklēsia?* Since the other occurrences of the term 'church' in the New Testament all postdate Paul's use of the word, we cannot draw conclusions from them as to the meaning he attached to it. Rather we must approach his writings as they stand (in the order in which they were written) and see whether Paul follows, develops or alters the sense which the term has in the Jewish and Greek sources.

Most probably the word 'church' was already in Christian use before he commenced his work, at least in Hellenistic-Jewish Christian circles. This means that from the earliest times such communities distinguished their gatherings from Jewish assemblies on the one hand and Hellenistic cults on the other. With one exception the Greek term for a Jewish community, *sunagōgē*, is never used of a Christian gathering in the New Testament. It is found in James, though even there alongside the term *ekklēsia*. The three usual terms by which the Hellenistic cults were described (*sunodos, thiasos* and *koinon*) do not occur at all. The reason for the absence of these terms is probably as follows: the synagogue was so centred around the Law and the mysteries so

4. Josephus, *The Antiquities of the Jews*, IV, 309; *Life*, 268; *The Jewish War*, I, 654 and 666

focused on a cult, that use of either word would have resulted in a misunderstanding of what *ekklēsia* was all about. (But more of this later, except to mention that Paul can still use the verbal form *sunagomai* alongside *ekklēsia*. Also later pagan writers and church fathers could refer to the Hellenistic churches as *thiasoi*.[5])

What is Paul's early usage of the term *ekklēsia*, church? He first uses the term in his greeting to the Christians in Thessalonica (1 Thess. 1: 1). Here he is using it in the same way as in Greek and Jewish circles, and yet consciously distinguishing the 'assembly' to which he is writing from others in the city. It is clear from the closing remarks of the letter that Paul has in mind either an actual gathering of the Thessalonian Christians or the Thessalonian Christians as a regularly-gathering community. He earnestly requests that his letter 'be read to all the brethren' and that they 'greet all the brethren with a holy kiss' (5: 26-27). Though, like other assemblies in the city, it is described as a 'gathering of the Thessalonians', it is marked off from the regular political councils by the addition of the words 'in God the Father', and from the weekly synagogue meetings by both the use of the term *ekklēsia* and the addition of the phrase 'in the Lord Jesus Christ'. The same ascription reappears in Paul's second letter to the same community (2 Thess. 1: 1). Elsewhere in these letters we have reference to other Christian gatherings only in the plural, viz to 'the churches of God' generally and to 'the churches of God' in Judaea (1: 4 and 2: 14). This suggests that the term could only be applied to *an actual gathering of people*, or to the group that gathers viewed as *a regularly constituted meeting* and not, as in today's usage, to a number of local assemblies conceived as part of a larger unit.

Now this does not appear to be always obvious from a casual reading of the New Testament writings. Indeed some statements seem to contradict it. There is for instance Paul's reminder early in Galatians of his original persecution of 'the church of God'.[6] This could be a reference to the church at Jerusalem *before* it distributed itself into a number of smaller assemblies in various parts of Judaea. It was that community which bore the brunt of Paul's vendetta against Jesus' followers. However most probably he refers to those he persecuted as a 'church' rather than as 'saints' (or some similar term) because, as Acts suggests, it was as they met that arrests were made — the fact of their gathering providing evidence of their Christian associations (Acts 8: 3; compare 2: 46). Something like this must be in mind, since a few lines

5. Compare Lucian, *The Death of Peregrinus*, 11; Origen, *Contra Celsum*, III, 2 and 3; Eusebius, *Ecclesiastical History*, X, 1
6. Gal. 1: 13 and later 1 Cor. 15: 9; Phil. 3: 6

further down Paul speaks distinctively of 'the churches of Judaea' in the plural (Gal. 1: 22).

This is supported by other literary evidence. In the greeting at the beginning of Galatians (Gal. 1: 2), throughout the following two letters to the Corinthians[7] and in Romans (Rom. 16: 4 and 16), we always find the plural form when more than one church is in view. The only exceptions to this are once where the distributive expression 'every church' (1 Cor. 4: 17) occurs, and twice where 'the church of God' (1 Cor. 10: 32) is mentioned in a generic or, just possibly, localized sense. Reference to 'the *churches* in Galatia' (Gal. 1: 2; 1 Cor. 16: 1), 'the *churches* of Asia' (1 Cor. 16: 19), 'the *churches* in Macedonia' (2 Cor. 8: 1), and 'the *churches* of Judaea' (Gal. 1: 22) demonstrates that the idea of a unified provincial or national church is as foreign to Paul's thinking as the notion of a universal church. Only if there were a provincial meeting of all Christians from time to time could he have spoken of them in this way. The names of the provinces, or inhabitants, simply provide him with a convenient way of grouping them in his thinking, though sometimes he can speak more generally just of 'the churches of the saints' and 'the churches of the Gentiles' (1 Cor. 14: 33 and Rom. 16: 4). The primary sense of 'gathering' is particularly clear in 1 Corinthians 11-14, especially in such expression as, 'when you assemble as a church' (1 Cor. 11: 18) and, 'It is shameful for a woman to speak in church.'[8] In the beginning of both letters, the church is described as belonging not to the people by whom it is constituted (as with the Thessalonians), nor to the district to which they belonged (as with the Galatians), but rather to the one who has brought it into existence (that is God) or the one through whom this has taken place (that is Christ).[9]

This means that the *ekklēsia* is not merely a human association, a gathering of like-minded individuals for a religious purpose, but a divinely-created affair.

THE CHRISTIAN GATHERINGS

(a) Their Location

So far as the location of these gatherings is concerned, we possess some hints in 1 Corinthians and further details in Paul's letter to the Romans. Towards the close of 1 Corinthians, probably written from Ephesus, Paul passes on greetings to his readers from

7. 1 Cor. 7: 17, 11: 16, 14: 33 and 34; 2 Cor. 8: 19 and 23-24, 11: 8 and 28, 12: 13

8. 1 Cor. 14: 35; compare 14: 4, 5, 12, 19 and 28

9. 1 Cor. 1: 1; 2 Cor. 1: 1 (cf. 1 Cor. 10: 32 and 11: 22) and Rom. 16: 16.

Aquila and Prisca, 'together with the church in their house'.[10]
This is the first time in Paul's writings that we come across this
expression. It could mean one of two things: the term *oikos,* house,
could refer to the *quarters* which Aquila and Priscilla occupied (or
possibly to a particular room within it, though this seems unlikely
here), or to the *household* which was in their charge. If it is to the
former, then the home of Aquila and Priscilla was the meeting-
place for some or all Christians in Ephesus. If the latter, which is
less likely, it was their whole household which comprised the
gathering. The incidence of household baptisms in Acts[11] and the
use of *oikos* to refer to the extended family, probably slaves, in the
Pastorals,[5] could point in this direction. However it is nowhere
stated in Acts, and their Jewish convictions make it unlikely, that
Aquila and Priscilla had a household of this kind. While *oikos* does
sometimes refer to slaves, it does not necessarily have that meaning. It is to their home then that the term *oikos* refers. We cannot
tell from it whether all the Christians in Ephesus met there or only
a number of them. Incidental remarks elsewhere in 1 Corinthians
and in Romans throw further light on the types of Christian
groups in a particular city, as well as on the places in which they
met.

In 1 Corinthians, Paul alludes to an occasion on which 'the
whole church' came together (1 Cor. 14: 23). This implies that at
other times the Christians in Corinth came together in small
groups, quite possibly as 'church'. The reference to various
groups in Corinth who owed their existence to the work of different apostles, viz Peter, Apollos and Paul, may be relevant here
(1: 12-13). In the concluding section of Romans, most probably
written in Corinth, Paul includes a greeting from one Gaius
whom he describes as 'host to me and to the whole church' (Rom.
16: 23). In the Greek Old Testament this expression consistently
refers to an assembly of all Israel; thus it must be the totality of
Christians in Corinth which is in view here (e.g. Exod. 12: 6;
Num. 8: 9). Gaius, like Erastus following, was probably one of
the more eminent men in the city. It is not surprising that his
home should be used for a gathering of the whole Christian community. Ample space would be required for such a meeting and it
is precisely this that a man of Gaius' status could provide. Once
again the qualification 'whole', unnecessary if the Christians of
Corinth only met as a single group, implies that smaller groups
also existed in the city.

10. 1 Cor. 16: 19; compare Acts 18: 18-19
11. Acts 10: 48 (compare 11: 14), 16: 15 and 33, 18: 8
12. 1 Tim. 3: 12; compare 3: 5 and 5: 14

This probability is confirmed by Paul's comments in Romans 16 about various Christian groups in the capital. There is no suggestion, presumably due to the size of the city, that Christians ever met as a whole in one place. Indeed, as much as a century later, Justin remarks that this still did not take place.[13] Mention is made only of smaller groups of believers. First to be named is that associated with Priscilla and Aquila, now back in Rome. Here again we have reference to 'the church in their house' (Rom. 16: 5). (Does this refer to the same group that was at Ephesus — in which case we have here a 'mobile church' — or did this couple maintain households in different centres as part of their commercial network?) The other four groups listed are not specifically described as churches, viz 'those who belong to the household of Aristobulus'; 'those . . . who belong to the household of Narcissus'; 'Asyncritus, Phlegon, Hermes, Patrobas, Hermas, and the brethren who are with them'; 'Philologus, Julia, Nereus and his sister, and Olympas, and all the saints who are with them' (Rom. 16: 11 and 14-16).

(b) Their Variety

What sorts of groups are in view here? There are three possibilities. They could be gatherings of the same kind as the church that met in the home of Priscilla and Aquila. Yet it is puzzling that Paul should not explicitly describe them as such. He shows no hesitation elsewhere in this matter. This suggests that his omission of the word here is deliberate and that something other than house-churches is in view.

Alternatively, do we simply have here mention of groups consisting of slaves who are in the service of several distinguished, non-Christian patrons (e.g. Aristobulus and Narcissus), or members of the same guild who work together — neither of whom meet with other Christians in any organized way? The others mentioned in Romans 16 do not seem to have formed part of the group around Aquila and Priscilla, otherwise Paul's greeting to the church in Aquila and Priscilla's house would be superfluous (16: 5). Yet Paul's injunction to 'greet one another with a holy kiss' (v. 16) suggests that some kind of group encounter took place. The answer may lie in the following.

The groups of people addressed, belonging as they did to households and guilds and living and working in close proximity with one another, probably fellowshipped together as they had opportunity, as part of their normal activities. Since they were

---

13. See Justin, *First Apology,* 67 and also *Acta Just. et Soc.,* 1

already in constant social contact inside and outside of working hours, they cannot strictly be said to gather, even if some lived semi-independently of the household. In any case they would not have been in a position to invite others to attend because of their pagan environment or work situation. For both these reasons, to describe such a group as an *ekklēsia* was inappropriate. It could well be that in Rome, where guild life was particularly strong and frequently concentrated in certain districts, two kinds of smaller Christian groups existed — the domestic or work group, and the house-church. Corinth was unique in that, while there were similar groups (e.g. 'Chloe's people, 1 Cor. 1: 11), the meeting of the whole church probably included people from all these sub-communities.

This helps to explain an unexpected feature in the opening lines of the Letter to Rome. Unlike the greetings in all five previous letters, Paul does not address himself here to 'the church' or 'the churches' but rather 'to all God's beloved in Rome, who are called to be saints' (Rom. 1: 7). Since for him *ekklēsia* cannot refer to a group of people scattered throughout a locality unless they all do in fact actually gather together, it is not possible for him to describe all the Christians in Rome as a 'church'. He could have done so only by giving the word a new meaning. By way of contrast the Christians in Corinth are an *ekklēsia*. Although they, like the Romans, meet together in smaller groups in different parts of the city, they also come together as a unit from time to time (as did earlier the believers in Jerusalem). This the Romans did not do. The 'whole church' never assembled in one place as it did in Corinth.

(c) Their Frequency and Size

Concerning the time and frequency of these early Christian meetings, Paul has little to say. He does request that contributions for the Jerusalem collection be set aside 'on the first day of every week' (1 Cor. 16: 2). But this refers to an individual rather than communal action, as the words 'and store it up' indicate, so may not allude to a weekly gathering. This expression, 'on the first day of every week', recurs in Luke's account of Paul's final meeting with the Christians in Troas (when all 'were gathered together to break bread' (Acts 20: 7)). But we cannot tell for certain whether the church regularly met on that day, or had chosen it because of Paul's departure the following morning. If it is the former, as is more likely, we are still not clear whether all the Christians assembled weekly or whether they did so generally in smaller groups. Paul's rather vague way of referring to meetings of the whole church suggests that its meetings were less frequent.[14] Since voluntary and cult associations met on a monthly basis, these larger Christian gatherings may well have followed suit. The Lucan passage describes a night meeting — understandable enough in view of the obligation upon most people to work during the day. Which evening is in view then, the Saturday or the Sunday? It is generally assumed that Luke had in mind the latter. But it is just possible that it was on the Saturday night that the Christians in Troas gathered together, the 'first day of the week' having begun at sunset. Though in Pliny's time and area a Sunday night meeting took place,[15] the evidence for the time at which early Christians met is so slender that it would be unwise to make any confident generalizations from the small hints that we possess. We are much more in the dark about the question than is commonly recognized.

In these early letters of Paul, the term *ekklēsia* consistantly refers to actual gatherings of Christians as such, or to Christians in a local area conceived or defined as a regularly-assembling community. This means that 'church' has a distinctly dynamic rather than static character. It is a regular occurrence rather than an ongoing reality. The word does not describe all the Christians who live in a particular locality if they do not in fact gather or when they are not in fact gathering. Nor does it refer to the sum total of Christians in a region or scattered throughout the world at any particular point of time. And never during this period is the term applied to the building in which Christians meet. Whether we are considering the smaller gatherings of only some Christians in a city or the larger meetings involving the whole Christian population, it is in the home of one of the members that *ekklēsia* is held[16] — for example in the 'upper room'.[17] Not until the third century do we have evidence of special buildings being constructed for Christian gatherings and, even then, they were modelled on the room into which guests were received in the typical Roman and Greek household.

This puts a limit on the numbers involved. The entertaining room in a moderately well-to-do household could hold around thirty people comfortably — perhaps half as many again in an emergency. The meeting in Troas, for example, was large enough for Eutychus to use the window-sill for a seat (Acts 20: 9). But it is

14. 1 Cor. 14: 23; compare 1 Cor. 11: 33
15. Pliny, *Epistulae*, X, 96-97
16. Compare also Acts 18: 7-8 and 20: 8
17. Acts 20: 8; compare Lk. 22: 12; Acts 1: 13

unlikely that a meeting of the 'whole church' could have exceeded forty to forty-five people, and many may well have been smaller. This would compare with the number of people who belonged to a voluntary association. Though there could be as few as ten (also the smallest number of men required to found a synagogue) and as many as one hundred, the average membership was around thirty people. The 'house-churches' and the domestic groups as well, would have been much smaller. In any event we must not think of these various types of community as particularly large. Certainly there is no suggestion that, as in the synagogue, ten adults had to be available before they could commence their gatherings. Even the meetings of the 'whole church' were small enough for a relatively intimate relationship to develop between the members. So long as they preserved their household setting, this was bound to be the case.

CHAPTER FOUR

Church as Heavenly Reality

PAUL'S LATER USAGE OF *EKKLĒSIA*

(a) Continuation of the earlier meaning

We now turn to the meaning of *ekklēsia* in the later writings of Paul. To begin with, we find Paul using it in the same way as in his earlier correspondence. In his letter to the Philippians he reminds them that 'in the beginning of the gospel, when I left Macedonia, no church entered into partnership with me in giving and receiving except you only' (Phil. 4: 15). Although in the letter he does not refer to the place where the church met, we can surmise from Acts that it was initially in the home of Lydia. It was in her home — as later in that of Prisca and Aquila in Corinth — that he stayed during his time in Philippi, and it was to it that he and Silas returned after their imprisonment to see 'the brethren' and exhort them before departing for Thessalonica (Acts 16: 15 and 40). We cannot tell whether there was only one Christian gathering in the city or several. If there were a number, presumably they must have also met as a whole, since the term *ekklēsia* can be used of them. How then do we account for the absence of the term *ekklēsia* in the opening greeting of the letter? There is no need to look very far for this, for the reason is contained in the wording itself: 'to all the saints in Christ Jesus who are at Philippi, with the *episkopoi* (bishops) and *diakonoi* (deacons)' (Phil. 1: 1). It is because Paul wishes to specify those people who have a special contribution to make to it, that he does not simply address the letter to the gathering as a whole.

The same appears to be the case in his letter to the Colossians where it is 'to the saints', the ordinary membership, and 'the faithful brethren', those who have a particular ministry to perform, that the letter is written (Col. 1: 2). Since Philemon was almost certainly a resident of Colossae, 'the church in his house', mentioned in the brief letter sent to him by Paul, must be either the church of the Colossians or one of the smaller Christian gatherings in the city (Philem. 2). Elsewhere in the letter to the Colossians itself there is a greeting to 'Nympha and the church in her house' in nearby Laodicaea, and a suggestion that the Colossians forward their letter to 'the church of the Laodicaeans' so that it may be read there as well (Col. 4: 15). It is again unclear whether the gathering in the home of Nympha and the church of the Laodicaeans are one and the same entity, or whether smaller and larger assemblies in the one city are in view. Since the letter to the Ephesians is not addressed to a particular locality, it is not surprising that the word *ekklēsia* is absent from its opening lines.

(b) A heavenly reality to which all Christians belong

In these later writings, however, an extension of Paul's understanding of *ekklēsia* also takes place. This is not an altogether new development, since the foundation for it had already been laid in his earlier letters. Compare the words *en Christō*, which in a number of places accompany Paul's use of the term *ekklēsia*. The 'in Christ' formula is the most frequently recurring phrase in Paul's writings. It occurs 164 times, though generally in contexts in which the individual Christian, rather than the Christian community, is in view. In these it refers primarily to the believer's dependence upon the work of the historical Jesus, and fellowship with the risen and heavenly Lord. Since individuals are in relationship with Christ not only when they are 'in church', and since even the dead can be so described (1 Thess. 4: 16), the possibility arises that a wider concept of *ekklēsia* than that associated with the local gathering is here hinted at by Paul.

How are we to envisage this? Does he think of this relationship as a spiritual fact which is then realized in practice when Christians do in fact meet together? This could provide the basis for a conception of a 'universal church' which is distributed throughout various local gatherings, and of an additional 'eschatological church' gathered around Christ into which one passes after death. Yet the idea of a 'universal church' is never developed in Paul's writings. Also the notion of the dead being included along with the living suggests that a broader conception of the church is present here than just that of an earthly community, however broadly understood. While he does speak elsewhere of an 'eschatological gathering', this is not primarily what Paul has in view when he uses *ekklēsia* in this extended sense, and entry into the former takes place not after death but on the Last Day (1 Thess. 4: 15-17). Alternatively, Paul could visualize an 'invisible church' consisting of all those who are in Christ, whether living or not, to which the genuine members of 'visible churches' also belong. This notion, though it has held a long and respected position in Christian thought, has no basis in Paul's teachings. The drift of his thought in the later writings is in a different, though not altogether unrelated, direction.

The first stratum of evidence comes in Galatians, where Paul contrasts the children of the 'present Jerusalem' with those who belong to the 'Jerusalem above' (Gal. 4: 25-27). The idea is developed further in his letter to the Philippians. In this Paul affirms that Christians alive on earth are at the same time members of a heavenly community. In a highly significant passage he contrasts those who have their 'minds set on earthly things' with those whose 'commonwealth is in heaven', his language probably echoing the privilege of citizenship conferred upon the whole Roman colony of Philippi (Phil. 3: 19-20). Membership in this heavenly community, together with all the benefits that accompany it, was as continuing an affair as membership in the Roman commonwealth. While each came to expression from time to time in an assembly, participation in their respective religious and political communities — the one with its focus around Christ in heaven, the other with its centre in Rome on earth — went on day after day as a permanent reality. (Incidentally we have in this passage a unique example of the way in which Paul's thinking on a particular subject was influenced by the circumstances he encountered on his mission. Though the basis for this view was already present in his earlier writings, it appears that the practical situation at Philippi has helped him arrive at a more definite conception.) The idea reappears in Ephesians (Eph. 2: 19).

In the Colossian and Ephesian letters, however, the term *politeuma* (place of citizenship) is left behind and in its place the term *ekklēsia* occurs. So in Colossians we are introduced to the idea of a non-local church of whom Christ is the head (Col. 1: 18 and 24). This notion is generally interpreted as a reference to the 'universal church' that is scattered throughout the world. However it is not an earthly phenomenon that is being talked about here, but a supernatural one. The whole passage in which the expression occurs focuses on the victorious Christ and his kingdom of light which believers have now entered (1: 9 - 2: 7). Though the prospect of the End is also in view, this is contingent upon what is viewed as a present reality (1: 11, 16, 22 and 28). While the members of this *ekklēsia* will be presented 'holy and irreproachable and blameless' before God in the future, elsewhere they are described as presently existing in a heavenly dimension as well as an earthly one. He reminds his readers that 'you have died and that your life is hid with Christ in God' (3: 3). Since 'you have been raised with Christ, seek the things that are above, where Christ is seated at the right hand of God' (v. 1). It is because they live with Christ in this heavenly realm that he promises them that 'when Christ who is our life appears then you also will appear with him in glory' (v. 4). The picture Paul draws here is of a *heavenly assembly* within which the Colossian Christians are *already* participating, and whose culmination will take place on the Last Day.

If any hesitation remains about the possibility of understanding *ekklēsia* this way in Colossians, it is dispelled by the language used in Ephesians. There it is explicitly said that God has 'made us alive together with Christ and raised us up with him, and made us sit with him in the heavenly places in Christ Jesus' (Eph. 2: 5-6). Compare the prayer with which the letter opens, where he acknowledges 'the God and Father of our Lord Jesus Christ, who has blessed us in Christ with every spiritual blessing in the heavenly places' (1: 3). Between these two passages, at the end of a celebration of Christ's heavenly authority, reference is again made to his headship over the *ekklēsia* (vv. 22, 23). Here again we see church taking place in heaven and Christians participating in it, even as they go about the ordinary tasks of their daily life. Metaphorically speaking they are gathered around Christ, that is, they are enjoying fellowship with him. Mention of the eschatological consummation is also present here (1: 14 and 2: 7), but the emphasis falls upon the completed action of Christ and its immediate heavenly implications. The heavenly church idea reappears in chapter 3 where Paul says that 'through the church the manifest wisdom of God might now be made known' — not to the world but 'to the principalities and powers in the heavenly places' (3: 10). It is probably present at the end of the chapter, especially in view of the phrases accompanying *ekklēsia* (viz 'to all generations', 'for ever and ever' (v. 21); lies behind the reference to the community in chapter 4 (v. 12), with its talk of gifts from him who has 'ascended far above all the heavens' (vv. 8-10), and is involved in the references to *ekklēsia* in chapter 5, which emphasize particularly the present character of Christ's relationship with it.[1]

According to Paul therefore, Christians belong both to a heavenly church which is permanently in session and to a local church which, though it meets regularly, is intermittent in character. This means that Christians are in a common relationship with Christ not only when they meet together — nor, for that matter, when they individually relate to him in thought and prayer — but at all times, wherever they are and whatever they do. Here we have an exalted conception, not easy to grasp. But it is certainly one of the most profound in the whole of Paul's writings.

THE RELATIONSHIP BETWEEN THE HEAVENLY AND THE LOCAL CHURCH

What is the relationship between these two churches — the permanent heavenly church and the local intermittent one? Paul does not spell this out in detail, but there are sufficient clues for us to move towards an answer. The language he uses indicates that the local gatherings are not *part* of the heavenly one any more than they are part of any alleged universal church. Paul uniformly speaks of them as *the* church which assembles in a particular place. Even when we have a number of gatherings in a single city, the individual assemblies are not regarded as *part* of the church in that place, but as *one* of 'the churches' that meet there. This suggests that each of the various local churches are tangible expressions of the heavenly church, manifestations in time and space of that which is essentially eternal and infinite in character.

We find no suggestion here of a visible, universal church to which local gatherings are related as the part to the whole. Nor does Paul speak of any organizational framework by which the local communities are bound together. He nowhere prescribes an ecclesiastical polity of this kind and nowhere suggests that the commmon life which communities share should be made visible in this way. As we have seen, he does occasionally group churches together in his letters by reference to the province in which they exist, e.g. 'the churches in Galatia'. But, as his consistent reference to such in the plural suggests, there is not even a hint of any idea of provincial government. As a background to such usage, we should probably see the language employed to describe the informal alliances of adjacent territories in parts of the ancient

1. Eph. 5: 23, 25, 27, 29 and 32

world around this time. These were matters of convenience only, had only a temporary existence and lacked any unified organisational framework.

This does not mean that links between local churches were absent. On the contrary, Paul both initiated and encouraged fellowship between them in a variety of ways. But he sought to build up enduring relationships of a personal, rather than institutional, character. This took place through the exchange of letters from their apostle (2 Col. 4: 16), the visits of individuals from one group to another (e.g. Rom. 16: 1), the sending of financial aid during time of need (e.g. 2 Cor. 8: 11-13), the burden of prayer on each other's behalf (e.g. 2 Cor. 8: 14), and the passing on of greetings and news through intermediaries.[2] These scattered Christian groups did not express their unity by fashioning a corporate organization through which they could be federated with one another, but rather through a network of personal contacts between people who regarded themselves as members of the same Christian family. This is so even with respect to the foundation church in Jerusalem. Paul is eager to gain its recognition of his missionary endeavours so as to avoid any division in the Christian movement between its Jewish and Gentile wings (Gal. 2: 1-10), for a denominationalism of this kind would be totally abhorrent to him. He is also concerned to gain the involvement of his Gentile churches in the collection for the poor in the church at Jerusalem (Rom 15: 25-27), so as to mark their acknowledgement that the gospel stemmed from them. Yet there is no sense in which his churches are subservient to the original Christian community or organizationally controlled by it. In saying this, I am anticipating the conclusions that emerge from later sections of this book where Paul's authority and the Jerusalem collection come in for closer consideration. It would be inappropriate to discuss these in detail here since they raise issues of a wider kind as well.

THE SIGNIFICANCE OF PAUL'S CONCEPT OF *EKKLĒSIA*

(a) In the context of his age

Comparison of Paul's understanding of *ekklēsia* with the intellectual and social climate of his day emphasizes both the comprehensiveness of his idea and its appropriateness for his times. Attention has already been drawn to three aspects in the contem-

2. 1 Cor. 16: 19; 2 Cor. 13: 13; Phil. 4: 22

porary scene that were particularly significant: those aspirations
for a universal fraternity which captivated the minds of educated
Greeks and Romans and devout Jewish leaders; the significance
of the household as a place in which personal identity and
intimacy could be found; the quest for community and immortality pursued through membership in various voluntary and
religious associations. In a quite remarkable way, Paul's idea of
ekklēsia managed to encompass all three:

1. It is a voluntary association, with regular gatherings of a
relatively small group of like-minded people. This it shares with
the synagogue and cults and, although it was a more exclusive
society, the Qumran community as well.

2. It has its roots in, and takes some of the character of, the
household unit. Neither the pagan *thiasoi*, nor the Pharisaic and
Essene *haburoth*, were consciously built up on this basis, and there
is little concern in Stoicism with the family group as such.

3. These small local churches were invested with a supra-
national and supra-temporal significance. They were taught to
regard themselves as the visible manifestation of a universal and
eternal commonwealth in which men could become citizens. This
has some overlap with the Stoic view, but differs from it in its
communal emphasis,[3] something that is even more apparent
when a comparison is made with the more individualistic Cynic
version.[4] Among contemporary religious groups, Qumran certainly did combine a clear view of this kind with its concrete sense
of assembly, but its vision had a much more limited horizon and,
in addition, retained a strong nationalistic emphasis (1QS 8: 4-7,
11: 3 and 6-9). The mystery-cults, for all their cosmopolitan
character, do not appear to have thought in terms of a 'com-
munion of souls' so to speak, chiefly because their anti-temporal
tendencies and individualistic emphasis did not provide them
with the framework for such a conception.

Only Paul's understanding of *ekklēsia* embraces all three ideas
of community to which people gave their commitment in the
ancient world at the time. This means that, psychologically speaking, Paul's approach had a decided advantage over its first century competitors, since it offered so much more than any of them
and offered things which elsewhere could only be found by adher-
ing to more than one religious group. Sociologically, the distinctive element in Paul's conception was its combination of all three
models of community. I am not suggesting that Paul systematic-

3. Contrast Cicero, *De Officiis*, I, 20-51; *De Natura Deorum*, II, 154-165; *De
Finibus Bonorum et Malorum*, V, 65; *De Legibus*, 22-39
4. See Diogenes Laertius, vi. 63 and 72

ally related each of these models, or even consciously viewed his idea as the fulfilment of contemporary strivings, merely that his view was conceptually richer and more socially relevant than others advanced in his day. In all this, by his use of the quite ordinary term for assembling in the ancient world *(ekklēsia)* and by his setting such gatherings in ordinary homes rather than cultic places, Paul shows that he does not wish to mark off his gatherings from the ordinary meetings in which others, including church members, were engaged. The novelty did not stem from the action of gathering itself, nor from its specifically religious intention. Parallels exist to both of these and, as we shall see later, Paul did not see such gatherings as more religious in character than any other activity in which Christians were involved. Even the household location of the meeting is not in itself distinctive, since occasionally private Hellenistic cults met in homes rather than in buildings constructed especially for the purpose. But this happened relatively rarely and, in any case, the homes concerned were turned into shrines and became the centre of cultic activities of various kinds. The synagogue as well, though originating probably in open air meetings, became in time a home-based institution. Yet by the first century special buildings were customarily reserved for its activities,[5] often in their design still reflecting their household antecedents. Even so, it was not so much the household basis of Paul's communities as the character of their gatherings and the source of their dynamic that distinguished them from their first-century counterparts.

(b) *For contemporary usage and practice*

We begin to see this by directing our attention away from the term *ekklēsia* to certain other terms and metaphors that Paul applies to his communities. But before doing this, I would like to make some final comments about his use of the word *ekklēsia* itself. Does it matter if Paul's understanding of it as 'gathering' in a dynamic local sense on the one hand, and a metaphorical heavenly sense on the other, later fell away in favour of a 'universal church'/'invisible church' conception? If this shift of meaning has nothing more than a semantic significance, then distinguishing Paul's view from subsequent usage has only linguistic interest and no important consequences flow from it.

Yet this is not the case. To begin with, the later extension of the term 'church' to cover not only the wider organization which binds local communities together, but also the various activities

5. See chapter 1, footnote 6

which it sponsors within the surrounding society, has created certain problems. These problems are compounded by applying those terms which only truly characterize the household gatherings and heavenly fellowship to such activities, or by requiring Christian communities to undertake responsibilities in the world that strictly belong to voluntary groups of Christians specifically called to the task. (More will be said about this later when Paul's 'work' comes in for detailed inspection.) All this leads to a confusion of descriptions and functions that has serious intellectual and practical repercussions. So more than a purely semantic or linguistic question is at issue.

That being said, Paul's predominant usage of *ekklēsia* to refer to the actual gatherings of Christians, and nothing more, means that the word is far less theologically significant than people generally assume. Its chief importance lies in the way it stresses the centrality of meeting for community life: it is through gathering that the community comes into being and is continually re-created. Although in his later writings Paul adds a new dimension to this activity — by seeing it as the expression of ongoing heavenly encounter with Christ — it is to other terms that we must turn if we are to penetrate the heart of his idea of community. The word *ekklēsia* brings us to the threshold of his understanding; it does not carry us over it.

CHAPTER FIVE

The community as a family

SOME METAPHORS FOR COMMUNITY

Paul frequently resorts to metaphors in his discussions on community. He thinks not just in terms of the logical development of arguments, but also of the illuminative significance of images. This was a characteristically Jewish way of proceeding — one which leaves its imprint everywhere in the biblical and intertestamental writings. Among the many metaphors applied to the Christian community by Paul, that of a 'building' comes before us several times in his letters. Sometimes an ordinary building is in view, sometimes the Temple — the latter being the building *par excellence* to a Jew. The more general use of the metaphor refers either to the work of the apostles in founding local communities — Paul describing himself as the 'master builder' in charge of operations[1] — or to the interdependence of the members of the community and their growth to maturity.[2] When Paul describes the community as a Temple, he is emphasizing its relationship with God through the Spirit and, as a consequence of this, its holiness and the wholehearted service it should render to God.[3]

Once again there appears to be a difference between the earlier and later writings. In the former the whole building represents the

1. Gal. 2: 18; 1 Cor. 3: 10-14; 2 Cor. 10: 8, 12: 19 and 13: 10; Rom. 15: 20; compare Eph. 2: 20 and 4: 12
2. 1 Cor. 14: 5, 12 and 26; Rom. 14: 19; Col. 2: 7; Eph. 4: 16
3. 1 Cor. 3: 16-17; 2 Cor. 6: 16; Eph. 2: 21-22

community and it is the local community which is in view. In the latter the corner-stone of the building is said to be Christ himself and the heavenly church is under discussion. (Christ is described as the 'foundation' of the building in the earlier writings, but that is not quite the same thing. In Ephesians it is the apostles and prophets who occupy that position rather than simply laying a foundation.) The metaphor can be applied to individual Christians as well as the community to which they belong. In a quite striking way they are described not merely as 'stones' in God's building, but individually as 'the Temple of the Holy Spirit' (1 Cor. 6: 19) himself.

A further set of metaphors comes from the world of agricultural labour rather than material construction, the community being described as a 'field', a 'grafting' (on an olive tree) and a 'planting'.[4] Other metaphors, such as the comparison of the church with 'dough' and of the offending member within it with 'leaven', are drawn from the domestic sphere.[5] But analogies with the world of nature (like the agricultural metaphors) or inanimate objects (such as the building metaphors), despite the presence of human participants, lack the dynamic element characteristic of human and divine-human relationships. This leads Paul on several occasions to follow traditional practice and link or mix his metaphors, so that the deficiencies of one may be remedied by the advantages of another.[6] Paul also shows a distinct preference for the 'body' metaphor, drawn as it is from the sphere of human existence, though even then (as we shall see) he has to portray and employ the metaphor in different ways to express his views. In the long term however, the inadequacy of the organic unity of the 'body' metaphor leads Paul to utilize the language of human, and especially family, relationships.

Although in recent years Paul's metaphors for community have been subjected to quite intense study, especially his description of it as a 'body', his application to it of 'household or 'family' terminology has all too often been overlooked or only mentioned in passing. This presumably stems from the fact that terms like *oikeioi,* 'household', occur so rarely in the Pauline writings. But, alongside this term, a number of related expressions are present which must be taken into account. So numerous are these, and so frequently do they appear, that the comparison of the Christian community with a 'family' must be regarded as the most significant metaphorical usage of all. For that reason it has pride of

4. 1 Cor. 3:9; Rom. 11: 17-24; Col. 2: 7; Eph. 3: 17
5. 1 Cor. 5: 6-7; compare Gal. 5: 9
6. E.g. 2 Cor. 9: 10; Col. 2: 7 and 19; Eph. 2: 19-22, 3: 17 and 4: 12-16

place in this discussion. More than any of the other images utilized by Paul, it reveals the essence of his thinking about
community.

A KEY IMAGE: FAMILY

(a) Description of membership

All Paul's 'family' terminology has its basis in the relationship
that exists between Christ, and as a corollary the Christian, and
God. Christians are to see themselves as members of a divine
family; already in his earliest letters Paul regards the head of the
family as being God the Father.[7] In a unique sense Jesus is his
Son, and it is only through his identification with men, and
actions on their behalf, that they are able to 'receive adoption as
sons' (1 Thess. 1: 10; Gal. 4: 4-5). As a result, says Paul in
Galatians, 'God has sent the Spirit of his Son into our hearts' so
that, along with Jesus, we are able to address him in the most
intimate terms as 'Abba! Father!' (Gal. 4: 6). This privilege, he
adds in Romans, confirms to our own spirit the fact that we are
indeed 'children of God, and if children, then heirs, heirs of God
and fellow heirs with Christ' (Rom. 8: 14-17). This fellowship of
Christians with God the Father and Jesus his Son is not at all like
the calling of a royal court in which the king holds audience with
his citizen subjects. Nor should we think of it in terms of the
assembling of a household in which the master is surrounded by
his loyal slaves. It is not even like the gathering of an ordinary
family in which the head enters into relationship with his infant
children. The meeting of Christians with their God is more
analogous to the encounter between *adult* children and their
father, where they are able to relate to him not only in the most
intimate, but increasingly in the most mature, fashion.[8]

Paul sees implications from this for the life of the local communities. Those who belong to them should see one another
primarily as members of a common family. So in Galatians Paul
encourages both himself and his readers, as they have opportunity, 'to do good to all men, and especially to those who are of the
household of faith' (Gal. 6: 10). According to the letter to the
Ephesians, the fellowship of Christians between Jews who were
members of the covenant race and Gentiles who were previously
aliens to the divine promises, experienced in the heavenly *ekklēsia*,

7. 1 Thess. 1: 1 and 3, 3: 11 and 13; 2 Thess. 1: 1-2 and 2: 16
8. Gal. 4: 1ff. and compare later Eph. 4: 13ff.

is to be viewed precisely in these terms. Referring to Christ, the author points out that 'through him we have access in one Spirit to the Father. So then you are no longer strangers or sojourners, but you are fellow citizens with the saints and members of the household of God' (Eph. 2: 19). Both the local gathering and heavenly 'assembly' are to be regarded as nothing less than God's family.

As well as *oikeioi*, a whole cluster of terms applied to the Christian community are drawn from family life. Some of these are among the most frequently used terms in Paul's vocabulary and, as much as anything, it is their very familiarity that has led to their unfortunate neglect. For example, the term *oikonomos*, 'steward',[9] which Paul uses of himself and other apostles, is drawn from the circle of 'household' personnel. It describes the responsible and accountable task which he has been given *vis-à-vis* his communities. But this word, used only twice, is drawn from the business side of family affairs, not from its more intimate side, whereas most of the terms Paul employs come from this latter sphere. True, we also have an occasional use of the term *doulos*, 'slave',[10] or *hupērētes*, 'servant' (1 Cor. 4: 1), underlining the kind of behaviour that should govern relationships between Christians in the community, just as it does his own behaviour towards them. But again this is not his most characteristic way of speaking. The term *adelphoi*, 'brethren', in paragraph after paragraph of his letters is far and away Paul's favourite way of referring to the members of the communities to whom he is writing. In spite of its frequency and its occasional use in a more technical sense, with respect to those who are colleagues in Paul's mission,[11] the term 'brethren' has not yet lost its basic meaning and become a mere formal description. There are many passages in Paul's writings where it is clearly expressive of the real relationship that exists between Christians,[12] not least when they come together as church. While some of the following examples are drawn from the sphere of relationships outside the actual gathering itself, they are no less pointers to the quality of relationship that should characterize it, as other passages more directly testify.

Paul for instance speaks movingly in 1 Corinthians of the concern that the stronger Christian should have for his weaker neighbour. The latter is described by him not only as 'the brother for whom Christ died' but quite personally as 'my brother' for whom

9. 1 Cor. 4: 1-2 and 9: 17; Col. 1: 25; Eph. 3: 2
10. 2 Cor. 4: 5; Rom. 1: 1; Phil. 1: 1; Col. 1: 7, 4: 7 and 12; Eph. 6: 6
11. Gal. 1: 2; 1 Cor. 16: 20; 2 Cor. 9: 3 and 5; Col. 1: 2 and 4: 15
12. Especially 1 Cor. 15: 58; Rom. 15: 14; Phil. 3: 1 and 4: 1; Eph. 6: 10

he has a direct responsibility (1 Cor. 8: 11 and 13). This kind of personal commitment to others is further illustrated by the way in which Paul talks in the warmest terms about certain fellow Christians, co-workers in his mission as well as members of local churches, with whom he had a close relationship. Tychicus, for example, is spoken of not only as a 'faithful minister and fellow servant in the Lord' but as 'a beloved brother' (Col. 4: 7; Eph. 6: 21). Paul refers to others, such as Sosthenes, Apollos and Quartus,[13] as 'our brother' in a similar fashion. 'I have derived much joy and comfort from your love, my brother', he says to Philemon and also writes of Epaphroditus in a personal, brotherly way (Philem. 7: Phil. 2: 25).

Terms descriptive of other family-type relationships are also used by Paul in his writings. Onesimus he regards as 'my child whose father I have become in my imprisonment', though he is also spoken of as 'the faithful and beloved brother' (Philem. 10; Col. 4: 9). 'I have no one like him', he says of Timothy, reminding the Philippians 'how as a son with his father he has served with me in the gospel' (Phil. 2: 22; Col. 1: 1) — though elsewhere he also designates him 'our brother' (1 Thess. 3: 22; 2 Cor. 1: 1). Then there are 'Apphia our sister' (Philem. 2), and 'our sister Phoebe', the latter being described as one who has been 'a helper of many and of myself as well'.[14] There is also that unnamed woman for whom Paul reserves one of his tenderest messages: 'greet Rufus, eminent in the Lord,' he begins, 'also his mother and mine' (Rom. 16: 13). Here we are given a glimpse, all the more significant for its incidental nature, into the quality of relationship that could exist between the apostle and his acquaintances. Indeed the whole of Romans 16, from which this reference comes, as well as the closing sections of many other Pauline letters, witness to the strong 'family' character of the relationships built up by Paul and various members of the churches amongst whom he moved. Here we also need to remember the way in which Paul speaks of his relationship to various communities as a whole by means of analogies drawn from family life, e.g. 'father', 'mother', 'nurse' and so on.[15] All these are quite clearly not merely relationships in name only, in some purely theological or superficially pious sense, but relationships of a very genuine and personal kind.

13. 1 Cor. 1: 1 and 16: 12; Rom. 16: 23
14. Rom. 16: 2, compare also 1 Cor. 7: 15 and 9: 5
15. 1 Cor. 4: 14-15 and 10: 14; Phil. 2: 12

(b) Quality of relationship

An inspection of other terms that spring from, or are most naturally located in, a family context confirms this conclusion. There are those, for example, whom Paul refers to as 'beloved' — among them Epaenetus, Ampliatus, Stachys, Persis, Tychicus, Onesimus and Luke.[16] Even whole churches — the Philippians for instance and, surprisingly, the Corinthians — are sometimes addressed by him in this way. 'How I yearn for you all with the affection of Christ', he exclaims to the Philippians (Phil. 1: 8; compare 2: 12), while his closing wish to the Corinthians, that most recalcitrant of communities, is that 'my love be with you all'.[17] He clearly expected Christians in their various local churches to enter into the same kinds of loving relationships with one another. He prays that the Thessalonians will 'increase and abound in love to one another as we do to you' (1 Thess. 3: 12). The Christians at Rome are reminded that in a very genuine way they should 'love one another with brotherly affection' *(philadelphia* here possessing a more intensive meaning than in earlier usage).[18] What such love involves is spelled out in the well-known passage from his first letter to the Corinthians:

> *Love is patient and kind;*
> *love is not jealous or boastful; it is not arrogant or rude.*
> *Love does not insist on its own way; it is not irritable*
>   *or resentful;*
> *it does not rejoice at wrong, but rejoices in the right.*
> *Love bears all things, believes all things,*
> *hopes all things, endures all things.*
> *Love never ends . . .* (1 Cor. 13: 4-8a)

It has to do with fundamental attitudes: patience, humility, tolerance, kindness, resilience, generosity, confidence, perseverance, optimism — attitudes that both here and elsewhere are discussed not so much in the context of the individual's relationship with God, as his interaction with his Christian brothers and sisters. These attitudes should not only accompany their communication with one another, but lead them into a real depth of relationship with one another.

So the Galatians, having been informed that 'love' is the chief 'fruit of the Spirit', are encouraged not merely 'to do good . . . to those who are of the household of faith' but also to 'bear one

16. Rom. 16:5, 8-9 and 12; Col. 4:7
17. 1 Cor. 16:24; compare 1 Cor. 4: 21 and 10: 14
18. Rom. 12: 9-10 and see 2 Macc. 15: 14 (LXX)

another's burdens and so fulfil the law of Christ' (Gal. 5: 22 and
6: 2). In 1 Corinthians Paul speaks of the need for the members to
'have the same care for one another' as well as suffer and rejoice
with one another in their humiliations and triumphs (1 Cor. 12:
25-26). In Romans he urges his readers not to please themselves
but for each to 'please his neighbour for his good, to edify him'
and 'to live in such harmony with one another, in accord with
Christ Jesus' that God might be unitedly acknowledged (Rom.
15: 1-2 and 5-6). In Philippians, there is to be mutual affection,
sympathy, love and harmony, with each unselfishly looking 'not
only to his own interests but to the interests of others' (Phil. 2:
1-4). In Colossians, they are to 'put on then, as God's chosen
ones, holy and beloved, compassion, kindness, lowliness, meekness, and patience, forbearing one another and, if one has a complaint against another, forgiving each other . . . And above all
these put on love, which binds everything together in perfect harmony' (Col. 3: 12-14). In Ephesians all this is summed up in the
injunction to the brethren to 'be kind to one another, tender-
hearted, forgiving one another'; thus 'walk(ing) in love, as Christ
loved us and gave himself up for us', and being 'imitators of God
as beloved children' (Eph. 4: 32-5: 2).

The centrality of *agapē* explains why Paul can sum up his
understanding of Christian responsibility as 'faith working
through love' (Gal. 5: 6b) and how he can conclude that members
of the community are to 'owe no man anything except to love one
another' (Rom. 13: 8). So basic is love that even the sacrifice of
one's life is worthless unless motivated and informed by it (1 Cor.
13: 3). Indeed love itself is the sacrifice God really requires (Eph.
5: 2). Although it should govern all social relationships, it has
pride of place within the community's internal life: it is the
'crown' of its endeavours, for it is above all love which 'binds' its
members together into a true unity.[19] Far from being a human
possibility however, it has its origin in God. Only through the
Spirit has it poured out into Christians' lives (Rom. 5: 5 and 15:
30). Far from being merely an attitude towards others, it
involves a purposive act of will. It is, as Paul says in one passage,
'a labour'[20] and it expresses itself not in mere feeling or inclination
but in concrete acts of service. While it delights in reciprocation,
love gives itself to others irrespective of the reaction it receives.[21]

It is precisely at this point that *agapē*, love, shows its difference
from the Greek ideal of *philia*, friendship, in which reciprocity

19. 1 Cor. 16: 14; Col. 2: 8 and 3: 14; Eph. 4: 1-3
20. 1 Thess. 1: 3; compare 2 Cor. 8: 24
21. Rom. 13: 10 and 20: 21

played such a central part. The concrete actions which characterize this community of love may be described as acts of identification on the one hand, or substitution on the other. Identification, the solidarity of the members with one another, goes beyond mere sociality, for each is inextricably involved in the life of the other. Prayer made by one member of the community for another, and especially suffering undergone by one member on behalf of another, are just two examples of what is here in view.[22]

EARLIER USES OF FAMILY TERMINOLOGY

What, then, of family terminology in general prior to Paul's use of it? It is not as common as might be imagined. Reference to Israel as a 'household' (Amos 5: 25; Jer. 38: 33), and to its members as 'brothers',[23] occurs earlier in Jewish literature, but nowhere in the Old Testament is Israel called *God's* family as such. The Greeks sporadically referred to members of the same political unit, or friends, as 'brothers'.[24] At Qumran both terms are more consciously used of the community created out of the broader society, but play only a minor role in comparison with other ascriptions. The Qumran community is depicted as a 'household', but of 'truth', 'holiness' and 'perfection' and members are described as 'sons', though of 'light', 'truth', 'righteousness' and 'heaven'.[25] 'Love of the members for one another is demanded, though only within the framework of a highly regulated life.[26] In one passage the overseer of the members is said to act as a 'father' to his 'children'[27] — echoing the intertestamental wisdom literature and its Old Testament antecedents.[28] The Pharisees too have their 'sons' and a rabbi is occasionally described as a 'father'.[29] But fraternal language does not seem to be particularly prominent and, among the Pharisees, references to love are again obscured by their preoccupation with the Law.[30] It is precisely the prominence of such language in Paul, along with

22. Compare Gal. 4: 19; 2 Cor. 4: 10-11; Rom. 9: 3; Col. 1: 24; Eph. 3: 13
23. E.g. Lev. 10: 4 and 19: 17; Dt. 15: 3; Philo, *De Specialibus Legibus,* II, 79f. and compare Mt. 5: 22-24 and 10: 6; Acts 2: 29 and 36, 13: 26
24. Plato, *Meno,* 239a; Xenophon, *Anabasis,* 7, 2: 25
25. IQS 1: 9, 3: 13, 20, 22 and 25, 4: 5-6 and 22, 5: 6, 8: 5 and 9, 9:6; CDC 3: 19 and Josephus, *The Jewish War,* II, 122
26. IQS 1: 9, 2: 24, 4: 4-5 and 5: 25
27. CDC 13: 9
28. Prov. 3: 12; Ecclus. 3: 1 and 6: 23-29
29. Makk. 23: 9; Eduy. 1: 4 and B.M. 2: 11
30. Ab. 1: 2; Sot. 5: 5

personalization by means of other words such as 'my', 'beloved' and so on, that distinguishes his understanding of community from these others. He also breaks convention by talking, in a virtually novel way, about 'sisters' as well as 'brothers'.[31] He can speak as intimately of them as of his 'brothers' and 'sons'.

In the mysteries, initiates do not seem to have been described as 'children' of the deities with whom they were joined, though there is talk of a father-son relationship between the initiate and his priestly guardian. The Cynic philosopher is also sometimes portrayed as a 'father' or 'nurse' to his hearers.[32] The Stoics often talk in terms of 'friendship' with the gods and one another. On the other hand their belief that all men were the 'offspring' of the gods and 'brothers' of one another, also frequently comes to expression.[33] Since this encompassed all men, and did not lead to the formation of communities even among one's Stoic neighbours, this does not have the same concrete ring about it as the Pauline conception. There are, in the papyri and inscriptions, occasional references in brotherly terms to members of the same religious society or guild. Here again though, family terminology and the language of love do not occupy the central position or possess the intensive meaning that they do in Paul's writings. Yet Paul was not the first to talk in this manner. It is Jesus who stands behind Paul's usage here — the one who looked at those sitting around him and said, 'Here are my mother and my brother! Whoever does the will of God is my brother, my sister and my mother'; the one who placed 'love' at the heart of his whole teaching about personal behaviour (Mk. 3: 34-35 and 12: 30-31).

THE RELATION BETWEEN 'FAMILY' AND 'FELLOWSHIP'

The metaphor of the family was a vital one to Paul. Paralleling the household *context* of community gatherings we have the use of household *language* to describe the relations between members. The correlation of the two may be accidental in Paul. Christians may not have had anywhere else to meet, especially since the synagogues soon became closed to them, and the rooms attached to local temples would have possessed unsavoury connotations. But

31. But see Num. 25: 8 and Cant. 4: 9
32. Apuleius, *Metamorphoses,* XI, 26; Dio Chrysostom, *Orationes,* IV, 73ff. and 77-78
33. Epictetus, *Dissertationes,* 1, 13: 4; Dio Chrysostom, *Orat.,* III, 100ff. but also Cleanthes, *Fragment* 537 (Barrett, p. 63) and Epictetus, *Diss.,* III, 22: 77ff.

just possibly the practical necessity for their use blended with a further, theologically-based consideration. For given the family character of the Christian community, the homes of its members provided the most conducive atmosphere in which they could give expression to the bond they had in common.

Before moving away from these various terms, all of which in one way or another stress the close relationship existing between Christians, we need to look at another term commonly believed to point in the same direction. Though not a family term, *koinōnia*, frequently translated 'fellowship', occupies a large place in many popular discussions of Paul's understanding of community. Paul uses the related adjectival noun *koinōnos* a few times in the sense of 'partner' in a joint activity[34] and the verb *koinōnein* five times, meaning either 'having a share' in some external activity[35] or 'making a contribution' of a financial or other kind (Rom. 12: 13; Gal. 6: 6). *Koinōnia* itself occurs some thirteen times but, as with these related terms, the sense of participation in some common object or activity is uppermost, e.g. participation in the Spirit, in someone's faith, in Christ and his sufferings, in the work of the gospel, in a financial contribution,[36] but not in the sharing of the people concerned directly with one another.[37]

Certainly Christians do associate with one another in these activities and experiences, but Paul's emphasis is upon their participation *alongside* one another in such things, not *in* one another as the term 'fellowship' suggests. Paul does talk about fellowship with one another in this more personal and intensive sense, but uses words other than *koinōnia* to express it — as we are about to see.

34. 1 Cor. 10: 18ff.; 2 Cor. 1: 7 and 8: 23; Philem. 17
35. Rom. 15: 27; Phil. 4: 15 and see Eph. 5: 11
36. Phil. 2: 1; 2 Cor. 13: 13; Philem. 6; Phil. 3: 10; 1 Cor. 1: 9; Phil. 1: 5; Gal. 2: 9; Rom. 15: 26
37. 1 Cor. 10: 14ff. (3 times); 2 Cor. 6: 14, 8: 4 and 9: 13

CHAPTER SIX

The community as a body

Through the description of the Christian community as a 'family', Paul says something about the basis and character of the relationships that either exist, or should exist, within it. His comparison of the commmunity with a *sōma*, 'body', on the other hand, seems more concerned with the nature and exercise of the various gifts that are present in the community and with the source from which they come. Yet it would be misleading to distinguish too sharply between the application of the metaphors, for it is one of Paul's basic convictions that the two cannot really be separated. We shall see this as we go along.

PAUL'S EARLY USAGE OF THE BODY METAPHOR

Description of the Christian community as a 'body' first takes place in the latter half of 1 Corinthians, though this is preceded by mention of Christians as individually 'members' of Christ earlier in the letter (1 Cor. 6: 15). The first two references are quite cryptic in character and occur in Paul's discussion of 'the Lord's Meal'. They emphasize the *unity* of the members with one another, and through that their unity with Christ, rather than the *gifts* exercised for each other's welfare. 'Because there is one loaf', he says, 'we who are many are one body, for we all partake of the one loaf' (10: 17). Here the unity of the community, despite the multiplicity of its members, is pictured and, in the surrounding verses, the community of all with Christ.

Again Paul says that 'any one who eats and drinks without discerning the body eats and drinks judgment upon himself (11: 29). Although this has been generally interpreted as a reference to Christ's crucified body, the community itself is almost certainly in view as well, if not exclusively. By means of it, the need for the members of the community to recognize their unity by 'receiving' one another (this is preferable to the RSV's 'waiting' for one another) is stressed (v. 33). The fact that there are many members of the community should not lead to the assertation of individualistic attitudes, nor to the formation of cliques within it, but instead to a continuing affirmation of its solidarity.

This problem of unity and multiplicity is given more extended and vivid treatment in the following chapter. Here Paul treats the human body in parabolic, almost allegorical, terms drawing analogies between it and the Christian community at a number of different levels (12: 12-30). In this passage, the following points deserve special notice:

(a)   It is the local community at Corinth which is described as 'the body of Christ'. *You* are the body of Christ', insists Paul, 'and individually members of it.' (v. 27) We must avoid two possible misunderstandings here. First, it is not so much the *ekklēsia* which is described in these terms as the community. This means that the *sōma* metaphor and *ekklēsia* terminology do not completely overlap, since the former has a wider reference than the latter. The term 'body' can apply to relations between the members outside church as well as to those which take place within it. Yet even so, it is primarily by *assembling* that the responsibilities of members to one another are fulfilled. The 'body' most clearly and fully finds expression as 'church', even if it is not only visible when it assembles together.

Secondly, the community at Corinth is not said to be *part* of a wider body of Christ nor as *a* 'body of Christ' alongside numerous others. It is *'the* body of Christ' in that place. This suggests that wherever Christians are in relationship there is the body of Christ in its entirety, for Christ is truly and wholly present there through his Spirit (v. 13). This is a momentous truth. We find here further confirmation of the high estimate Paul had of the local Christian community.

(b)   Each member of the community is granted a ministry to other members of the community. This means that no person, or group of persons, can discount on the basis of their particular gifts other contributions to the 'body' or impose a uniformity upon everyone else. The community contains a great diversity of ministries, and it is precisely in the differences of function that the wholeness and unity of the body resides. God has so designed things that the involvement of every person with his special contribution is necessary for the proper functioning of the community (vv. 14-21). This means that each member has a unique role to play, yet is also dependent upon everyone else.

(c)   It is precisely those members who render the less obviously spectacular services who should be accorded the greatest respect. The most outwardly attractive or dramatic ministries are not necessarily the most fundamental. Care must therefore be exercised in assessing the importance of certain gifts, e.g. *glossolalia,* for the welfare of the community. Others less striking in character, exercised in a less ostentatious, more private manner, may contribute more substantially to the community's well-being and growth (vv. 22-25).

(d)   So close is the link between members of the community that what affects one necessarily affects all. Paul's language must be carefully noted here. He does not say that the experiences of individuals within the community, both pleasurable and sorrowful, *should* be shared by all the others who belong to it. He says instead that they *are* so shared, whether others consciously experience them or not. The 'body' has a common nerve. There is a common life within it in which each is identified with the other — all in one, as it were, and one in all (v. 26). The interrelationship of the individuals of whom the community is made up could scarcely be more strongly emphasized.

(e)   The closeness of the relationship between the community and Christ is underlined, but its character is not really specified. Although at the beginning of the passage Paul appears to identify the community with Christ *in toto* (v. 12b), at its close the community is unambiguously spoken of as his *body* (v.27). Does this mean that Christ is its head or that the community is wholly his body? Presumably, since no qualification is given to the contrary, the latter. This does not mean that it is his form in some literal or physical sense, as some have suggested. Paul states at the start of the passage that he is united to the community through the Spirit (v. 13), and the relations between the members themselves are said to take place through the same agency (vv. 4-11 and 14: 12).

Reference to the community as a 'body' next appears in Paul's letter to the Romans (Rom. 12: 4ff.). Here again it reinforces the principle of unity-in-diversity, though from a slightly different angle to that found in the Corinthian correspondence. Paul has in mind here not only the over-valuation of some gifts at the expense of others, but also the over-estimation by some members of the gift which they actually possess. Unlike the earlier situation, he is not reacting to an error that has already occurred, but guarding against a possibility that might emerge in the future (compare Rom. 1: 11-13). Despite his statement that 'we', rather than 'you' (as in 1 Corinthians), are 'one body in Christ', he is probably referring to the Roman community. The plural simply means 'we Christians' (wherever we are), though just possibly he is including himself among the members of the community in view of his projected participation in it. Since, as we have already noted, the Christian community there probably gathered in different groups throughout the city, the broader reference of the 'body' metaphor to more than a single church is again present.

The primary application of the body metaphor to the exercise of gifts is also clear. It is precisely through the *variety* of the various members' contributions that the unity of the community becomes manifest (12: 6a), as well as in their proportionate strength (v. 6b). In Romans 12 Paul describes the relationship of the community to Christ in more intimate terms than in 1 Corinthians. They are not just 'the body *of* Christ', but are now 'one body *in* Christ' (v. 5a). This way of putting it stresses the fact that Christ is the source of its unity; the means by which this takes place, and the precise nature of the link between the two, are not identified.

PAUL'S LATER USAGE OF THE BODY METAPHOR

In Paul's later writings certain developments in his use of the 'body' metaphor may be found. These arise from the different situations encountered by the communities. Religious ideas from a number of sources — Greek, Jewish and Oriental — have coalesced and threaten to penetrate the small Christian enclaves. According to these foreign ideas various cosmic powers, which are themselves emanations of divinity, can assist people in their contact with God. This being so, believers need to supplement their reliance upon Christ by an acquaintance with such powers. In his letter to the Colossians, Paul deals with this threat by explaining that everything in creation owes its life to Christ (v. 16), that he triumphed not merely over sin, the Law and death but over these cosmic forces as well (v. 20), and that he is not merely one emanation of the divinity among others but the one in whom 'all the fulness of God was pleased to dwell' (v. 19). As such, he and he alone is 'the image of the invisible God' and is 'pre-eminent' over everything and everyone else (v. 15). This includes his *ekklēsia*. At this point Paul reintroduces the notion of the 'body', describing Christ as 'the head of the body, the church' (v. 18). This idea is repeated three times elsewhere in the letter. A little later in this chapter he speaks of 'his body, that is the church, of which I became a minister' (v. 24); in the next of Christ as 'the head, from whom the whole body, nourished and knit together, through its joints and ligaments, grows with a growth that is from God' (2: 19-20); and in the following chapter simply of its members as being 'called in the one body' (3: 15).

In Ephesians as well similar ideas come to the fore. The priority of Christ at every level of reality is once again reaffirmed, and his pre-eminence over the cosmic powers and the church are particularly singled out for mention. He is 'far above all rule and authority and power and dominion' (Eph. 1: 21) and 'head over all things for the church, which is his body, the fulness of him who fills all in all' (vv. 22-23). Further on in the letter, the metaphor refers to the new unity between Jews and Gentiles that exists in the church as a result of Christ's reconciling work (2: 16 and 3: 6). Later still, it emphasizes the fact that there is only 'one body' (4: 4), but then goes on to note the diversity of 'gifts' that exist within it, all of which have Christ as their author (vv. 7-8). These are given to equip the saints 'for the work of ministry' (i.e. to stimulate the exercise of other gifts in the community), and to build up the body of Christ. Speaking the truth in love, 'we are to grow up in every way into him who is the head, into Christ, from whom the whole body, joined and knit together by every joint by which it is supplied, when each part is working properly, makes bodily growth and upbuilds itself in love' (vv. 12 and 15-16). This is a very compact description indeed. It employs the stark image of the body growing up into the head and suggests that the conformity of the church to Christ should become ever more complete. The final references to the metaphor in this letter occur in the list of obligations for husbands and wives. Here again Christ is spoken of as 'the head of the church, his body' (5: 23), and Christians as 'members of his body' (v. 30) which he nourishes and cherishes.

(a) Its development

How has usage of the metaphor developed?
i.   In the earlier correspondence 'the body' refers to wider relations in the local community, whereas later it refers to the *ekklēsia*. (When the terms 'body' and 'church' occur together in Ephes-

ians, it refers to 'the church, his body'.) This means there is a broadening rather than narrowing of its application, for it is the heavenly church that is brought before us in these later letters, not the local gatherings which are its earthly manifestations.

ii.   The relationship between the church and Christ is more fully defined than in the earlier writings. There the community formed the whole body, head included; here Christ occupies the chief position. This signifies that he is both the source of its life and centre of its unity. Although he receives no mention in Colossians, Ephesians speaks of the Spirit as the one who establishes Christ's pre-eminence in the church and brings this life and unity into being (2: 18 and 22, 4: 3-4).

iii.   The extension of the metaphor to cover the racial composition of the church, or rather the new 'humanity' that has been created out of its Jewish and Gentile components, also takes place in these letters. Here we have a variation of the unity-in-diversity theme, one that focuses on the members' religious backgrounds instead of their individual gifts.

iv.   In talking about the mutual contributions of the members, the emphasis is on the necessity for their corporate growth, rather than on the interdependence that follows from this. That growth is defined as an ever-increasing integration into Christ himself and as a maturity of an intellectual and moral kind for which he provides the standard. This occurs through their enlightenment of, and actions for, one another — through their 'speaking the truth in love' as the writer puts it (4: 15).

(b) Its limits

All these references to the 'body', as well as those in Paul's earlier writings, speak only of the internal relations between Christ and the community, and between the members of the community. While the heavenly 'church' is viewed as the fulfilment of men's social/political aspirations, the relation between that community and the world is not directly considered by the term 'body'. Though today the metaphor is frequently applied in this direction, Paul does not think of the 'body' as a world-oriented entity, nor of Christ as dependent upon it for his visible expression in the world. The local *ekklēsia* in particular has no 'face' to the world as such. The world sees only Christians and sees them when they are not, as a matter of fact, in church. Nothing in Paul's writings suggests that the gathering of believers has a *direct* function *vis-à-vis* the world. Though the 'body' metaphor also has the community of Christians in view when church is not taking place, it basically refers to the interaction of the members with one another, not with outsiders.

This does not mean that individual members of the community, or groups of members, lack responsibilities towards the world around them, but simply that the metaphor of the 'body' is never used to refer to such. Of course the church and the wider Christian community does have a function within the world, viz the integration of the members more firmly into one another and into Christ. Since this involves their growth not only to corporate but also individual maturity (resulting in a greater understanding and fulfilment of their wider obligations in the world), church and community do make an *indirect,* though fundamental, contribution to the life of the people around them. Indeed, if Paul's letters are any indication, much of the content of the Christians' meetings must have concerned their responsibilities to others and to society in general. Some passages on the internal relations of members for instance stand side by side with discussions of the external obligations of individual Christians (e.g. Romans 12).

(c) Its application

Much of what Paul says about the community as a 'body' is framed in response to the possibility of disunity severing it. While, as we have seen, unity in the local church is a reality to be acknowledged rather than a potential to be realized, Paul frequently appeals for such unity to be maintained in the face of possible or existing dissensions.[1] When divisions occur, schism is present within the community. It was precisely this that had occurred at Corinth, and threatened to take place in Rome and Colossae.[2] Rather than meaning divisions between churches, schism for Paul designates division within a single community. It results, he says, either from a lack of agreement with one another or from a lack of care for one another (1 Cor. 1: 12 and 11: 21), and is one of the works of the 'flesh' (Gal. 5: 20).

This does not mean that all differences of opinion within the church are schismatic in character. As Paul says, 'there must be different views (*haireseis*) among you in order that those who are genuine among you may be recognized' (1 Cor. 11: 19). Only when such differences are combined with a lack of acceptance of others, so that a section of the church hardens itself against the rest and behaves as if it were self-contained, does schism rend the body. Even doctrinal differences e.g. whether or not the resur-

1. 1 Cor. 1: 10; Rom. 15: 5; Phil. 2: 1; Col. 3: 12-14; Eph. 4: 3
2. 1 Cor. 11: 18; Rom. 16: 17-20; Col. 2: 16-19

rection has yet taken place (15: 12-58), or lifestyles that vary greatly from one another, e.g. the extent to which one may participate in some of the practices of the surrounding society (10: 23-31), do not lead to schism within the community, unless accompanied by coercive or careless attitudes on the part of some members towards others. But when something at the heart of the gospel is affected, such as insistence on an additional requirement for salvation (Gal. 1: 9), the infiltration of idolatrous ideas (1 Cor. 10: 14-22), or the exhibition of flagrantly immoral behaviour (5: 1-7), the schism created by such actions must lead the church to disassociate itself from the persons involved. In order to avoid schism, Paul does not require subscription to a detailed doctrinal confession or comprehensive moral code so much as the expression, by the members of his communities, of their common *acceptance* by God in Christ through the Spirit, and their *quest* for a unity of purpose and love in the light of the gospel they have received.

(d) Its originality

How original is Paul's use of this metaphor? It has no exact parallels in Jewish literature. Although the notion of 'corporate personality' is present in the Hebrew Bible, it was the Greek translation of the Old Testament which introduced the term 'body' into Jewish thought for the first time (e.g. Lev. 14: 9; Prov. 11: 17). Yet neither here nor in the literature of the intertestamental period was the term used in any metaphorical sense.[3] The rabbinic speculations on the grossly-inflated size of Adam's body (containing all of mankind in embryo) come from a later period and are quite literalistic in character.[4]

Gnostic thought recognizes the idea of the saved community as the body of the heavenly redeemer, but only in writings which are later than the New Testament. In any case Paul's initial use of the metaphor, in which the community is represented by the whole body and the emphasis is upon the interdependence of its members, has no parallel in Gnostic sources.

In Stoic literature prior to and contemporary with the New Testament, we do find the cosmos (including humanity) depicted as the body of the divine world-soul,[5] and the state as a body in which each member has a different party to play.[6] But then Paul refuses to portray the universe as Christ's body and rejects any

3. Compare 2 Macc. 8: 11; Wisd. 9: 15
4. R. Meir (c. AD 150)
5. Seneca, *De Ira*, II, 31: 7-8
6. Epictetus, *Dissertationes*, II, 10: 3

idea of the society to which a member belongs having priority over the individual members themselves. For him, the individual and the community are equally objects of his concern; neither is given priority over the other. One can only be an individual in a community and a community can only function properly when each individual is playing his own distinctive role within it. He also has a more restricted and, at the same time, more personal community in view than the *polis* — one that is linked to a person and involved in his ongoing personal history. Seneca's reference to the emperor as the 'soul' of the republic and the latter as his 'body' provides a closer parallel to this.[7] But Paul, a good Hebrew here, does not think of soul and body in these dualistic terms and therefore cannot describe the relationship between Christ and the community in this way.

While none of these usages yields an exact parallel to his ideas, they do indicate the extent to which the metaphor was 'in the air' in Hellenistic circles.[8] While the term 'body' did not originate with him, Paul was apparently the first to apply it to a community *within* the larger community of the state, and to the *personal* responsibilities of people for one another rather than for more external duties. We see again how a quite 'secular' term is used by Paul to illuminate what Christian community is all about.

7. Seneca, *De Clementia*, I, 4: 3-5: 1; II, 2: 1

8. See also *Livy, History*, II, 32; Josephus, *The Antiquities of the Jews*, IV, 406; Dio Chrysostom, *Orationes*, XVII, 19

CHAPTER SEVEN

Intellectual elements in growth

THE GOAL: MATURITY

Paul's description of the community as a 'body' indicates that its goal is not just the creation of harmony between the members — that is more the emphasis of his family terminology — but also their development towards maturity. Paul stresses the need for individuals to progress towards maturity on a number of occasions,[1] though generally in contexts where the corporate maturity of the community is in view.[2] God's intention is not merely the fashioning of mature individuals, but of mature communities as well. The Christian community doesn't exist just as a means to individual ends, though a mature community is an influential factor in shaping the individual maturity of its members.

This maturity is further defined in a number of passages throughout Paul's writings. He views it as an ever-closer approximation to the 'likeness' of God, so that there is an increasing reflection of his attitudes and concerns and an increasing participation in his activities.[3] Since Christ is 'the image of the invisible God' in whom 'all the fulness of God was pleased to dwell' (Col. 1: 15 and 19), Paul can also describe Christian maturity as a call to the 'imitation' of Christ and as a following of his 'example'; as

1. 1 Cor. 2: 16ff. and 13: 9-12; Phil. 3: 12ff.; Col. 1: 28
2. 1 Cor. 1: 10 and 14: 20; 2 Cor. 1: 13-14; Col. 1: 21-22 and 4: 12; Eph. 4: 11-16 and 5: 25-27
3. Col. 3: 10; Eph. 4: 24 and 5: 1

a possession of the 'mind' of Christ and bearing in one's 'person' the marks of Jesus; as a 'clothing oneself' with Christ, allowing Christ to be 'formed' within; and as the transformation into his 'glory', i.e. the unique quality that characterized him.[4] It is essentially an attaining of all to 'the knowledge of the Son of God, to mature adulthood, to the measure of the stature of the fulness of Christ' (Eph. 4: 13). Although this goal will only be fully realized in 'the age to come'[5] in God's perfected universe, we should now seek to attain it. Paul discusses this not only in passages which specifically mention the need for 'progress'[6] or 'growth'[7] but also, more obliquely, in metaphors drawn from athletic contests[8] and military life.[9] While he emphasizes throughout the indispensability of human effort,[10] it is the activity of the Spirit which alone makes this growth possible. Paul affirms this in a way that cannot be improved upon. Immediately following his statement that 'the Lord is the Spirit, and where the Spirit of the Lord is, there is freedom', he adds, 'We all, with unveiled face, reflecting the glory of the Lord, are being changed into his likeness from one degree of glory to another; for this comes from the Lord who is the Spirit.'[11]

THE ROLE OF FAITH

How exactly does this transformation and growth take place? In what *way* does the Spirit interact with individuals in the community so that they mature? In order to understand this properly we must turn back for a moment to the beginning of Christian experience.

The key word for Paul is faith. It is by faith, says Paul, that one embarks upon the Christian life in the first place.[12] Exertion of one's own willpower through energetic attempts at moral or spiritual reform, scrupulous observance of personal or corporate religious rituals, or involvement in various pious or mystical exer-

4. Gal. 4: 19; 1 Cor. 11: 1; 2 Cor. 3: 18; Rom. 13: 14 and 15: 7; Phil. 2: 5
5. 1 Thess. 2: 19-20, 3: 13 and 5: 23; 1 Cor. 1: 8 and 15: 49-57; Rom. 8: 28-30; Phil. 1: 6 and 3: 12-21; Col. 3: 1-4
6. Phil. 1: 25; compare Roms. 5: 3b-4
7. 1 Cor. 3: 6-8; 2 Cor. 9: 10; Col. 1: 10 and 2: 19; Eph. 4: 16
8. Gal. 2: 2; 1 Cor. 9: 24-27; Phil. 2: 16 and 3: 12-14 (compare also Col. 1: 29 and 2: 1)
9. 1 Thess. 5: 8; 2 Cor. 6: 7 and 10: 3-4; Rom. 13: 12; Phil. 1: 30; Eph. 6: 10-17
10. Rom. 8: 5-7; Phil. 2: 12; Eph. 6: 10-20
11. 2 Cor. 3: 17-18; compare Gal. 5: 16-26
12. Gal. chapters 2-3; Rom. chapters 3-5 et al.

cises cannot achieve this.[13] It begins only through faith, faith itself being a manifestation of the grace of God, however much human activity is engaged in it.[14] How does faith come? According to Paul, 'Faith comes through hearing, and hearing comes through the presentation of the message about Christ.'[15] This involves 'persuading men' and 'commending . . . the truth to every man's conscience' (2 Cor. 5: 11 and 4: 2). When this persuasion is effectual — when a genuine reception of the message that has been imparted takes place — faith is born. Because the association between faith and knowledge is so close here, Paul can even speak of his converts having 'learned' Christ (Col. 1: 7; Eph. 4: 20).

So it is through faith alone that the process of becoming a Christian begins and it is knowledge about Christ that alone makes it possible. The crucial role played by knowledge comes through in Paul's numerous descriptions of his apostolic work — essentially imparting knowledge or declaring the truth whereever he goes.[16] Yet this ministry is not simply a matter of speaking, informing and convincing, even when we see in it the persuasive power of the Spirit rather than mere human reasoning. Paul and his companions shared with their audiences 'not only the gospel of God but also our own selves' (1 Thess. 2: 8). Their message was as much embodied in their *actions* as formulated in their words. It was through both word and action that their hearers learned the meaning of the message, and on both that they modelled their response. Since the message was at its heart a message about suffering, it involved affliction for the preachers as well, just as the message did for those who accepted it.[17] It could not be otherwise if they were genuinely presenting and receiving it.

Paul's ongoing work, as exemplified in his visits and letters,[18] continues to revolve around the communication of knowledge by word and life. According to Luke he did not fail to declare 'the whole counsel of God' during his extended stay in Ephesus (Acts 19: 27). His letters contain reminders of things already said, amplification of earlier teaching, responses to questions on which his advice has been sought and instructions about problems with which the communities have to deal. All are conveyed in a personal way, with an emotional openness that shows his total and

13. See especially Rom. 10: 1-10; Col. 2: 16-3: 4
14. Rom. 3: 21-38 (compare 4: 16-20); Eph. 2: 8-10
15. Rom. 10: 17 (compare Gal. 3:5)
16. See Gal. 2: 5; 2 Cor. 2: 14 and 7: 14; Eph. 3: 7-10
17. 1 Thess. 1: 4-7; Gal. 6: 14-17; 2 Cor. 1: 3-8 and 4: 7-12; Col. 1: 24 et al.
18. E.g. 2 Thess. 2: 5; 1 Cor. 14: 6; Rom. 15: 14-15

not just intellectual involvement in what he is saying. They also reveal his vulnerability (as opposed to his self-sufficiency) when his words are brushed aside. Within all this, the centrality of knowledge to the ongoing life of his communities is specifically mentioned. This can be illustrated in a quite striking way by simply setting out side by side a number of relevant statements on this theme.

THE CENTRALITY OF KNOWLEDGE

Paul says that growth takes place within the community only insofar as its members are 'increased with', 'enriched by', 'renewed through' and 'filled with' knowledge.[19] Elsewhere he speaks of its occurring via 'the renewal of their minds'[20] and it is on this basis that he urges them to 'set their mind', 'be thus minded' and 'have a mind' on certain things.[21] When they have neglected to do so he insists that they 'come to their right mind'; on matters of indifference he advises 'everyone to be fully convinced in his own mind'; on issues where there should be no dispute he encourages them 'to be united in the same mind and in the same judgment'.[22] Indeed, the members of the community are to 'judge all things' and 'weigh all things' — especially in church. There they should 'judge for themselves' and 'weigh' what is said.[23] In all their thinking they are to 'bring every thought into captivity', to 'think upon whatever is' of real worth, to 'fix their thoughts on things' of real value and to 'beware lest their thoughts be led astray from a sincere and wholehearted commitment to Christ'.[24] As regards society in general they are to be 'naive toward that which is evil and wise towards that which is good', to 'behave in a wise manner' toward those who are outside the Christian circle, and to have an acquaintance of God's will 'in all spiritual wisdom and understanding'.[25] In sum, they are to 'understand' the significance of all that has been 'bestowed on them by God', to 'not be childish in their understanding but mature' (1 Cor. 2: 12 and 14: 20).

This pastiche of quotations demonstrates the *frequency* with which Paul refers to rational activity of some kind, the wide *variety*

19. Phil. 1: 9; Col. 3: 10; Col. 1: 9-10
20. Rom. 12: 2 (compare Eph. 4: 22-24)
21. Col. 3: 2; Phil. 2: 5 and 3: 15
22. 1 Cor. 15: 34; Rom. 14: 5; 1 Cor. 1: 10
23. 1 Cor. 2: 15; 1 Thess. 5: 21; 1 Cor. chapter 13 and 14: 29
24. 2 Cor. 10: 5 (compare Eph. 5: 6); Phil. 4: 8; Rom. 8: 6; 2 Cor. 11: 3
25. 1 Cor. 14: 20; Rom. 16: 19; Col. 4: 5 (compare Eph. 5: 15); Col. 1: 9

of contexts in which mention is made of it and the fundamental *place* he obviously accords it in the process of growth towards maturity. When other passages concentrating on the content of this understanding are taken into account, we find Paul using a large number of terms to bring out different aspects of what is involved, e.g. *nous* — mind (compare *noēma* — thought); *gnōsis* — knowledge (compare *epignosis*); *sophia* — wisdom; *sunesis* —understanding; *alētheia* — truth; *phronein* — to think (compare *phrēn*); *logizein* — to consider (compare *paralogizein*); *anakrinein* — to discern; *peithein* — to persuade; and *dokimazein* — to test. On occasions he can run several of these together in order to emphasize the importance of what he is saying. So, for example, he expresses his desire that his readers at Colossae will experience 'all the wealth of the fulness of understanding *(sunesis)*, the knowledge *(epignōsis)* of the mystery of God, even Christ in whom are hid all the treasures of wisdom *(sophia)* and knowledge *(gnōsis)*'. 'This I say', he adds, 'that no one may deflect your thinking *(paralogizomai)* with persuasiveness of speech' (Col. 2: 2-4). Throughout his writings Paul also frequently uses other terms, especially in passages where he is dealing less with the general process of growth than with specific issues encountered in its pursuit, e.g. *ginōskein* — to know; *mē agnoein* — not to be ignorant or uninformed; and *anamimnēskein* — to remind.

ITS RELATIONSHIP TO FAITH, HOPE AND LOVE

The significance of knowledge for Paul can be brought into focus through further consideration of its relationship to faith, hope and love, for it is these above all which are the most enduring elements in the community's experience (1 Cor. 13: 13). We have seen that one not only begins the Christian life through faith, but also makes further progress through it. What happens at the beginning thus sets the precedent for all that follows (Gal. 3: 1-5). Initially certain fundamental knowledge about God in Christ was conveyed and received. Through the aid of the Spirit people came into a new relationship with God. The way to further growth lies in the development of a deeper understanding of God and the consequent realignment of one's ways to him.

Such knowledge goes beyond the fundamental components of the gospel message. It deals with matters of a more comprehensive and detailed kind, e.g. those of a doctrinal, moral, communal, social and even political nature (e.g. Rom. chapters 9-15). We show faith in this knowledge by acknowledging its truth and internalizing its contents, that is, through a wholeminded and wholehearted commitment to it (Rom. 10: 9-10). Since God himself is always at the heart of this truth, this commitment results in a growing relationship with God through Christ in the Spirit. Knowledge therefore is both the vehicle through which faith comes into being and is increased. Without knowledge there can be no genuine faith — only superstition on the one hand or speculation on the other.

Paul can summarize this ongoing Christian life in terms of 'faith working through love' (Gal. 5: 6). Although for him love surpasses knowledge (1 Cor. 13: 8; Eph. 3: 19), and knowledge without love leads to self-centred pride rather than self-giving service (1 Cor. 8: 1 and 13: 2), knowledge alone can introduce one to love and reveal its full dimensions (Eph. 3: 18-19). Only if love is informed by knowledge as to what love itself really is, and its proper application is discovered by discernment, can there be a right evaluation of what is the most loving course of action (Phil. 1: 9-10). On occasions this will lead to the sharing of some truth, i.e. love is sometimes best expressed through the imparting of knowledge. Paul also believes that, within the Christian community, the presence of loving relationships between the members provides the most conducive environment within which fuller understanding of God — itself further outworking in love — can be gained (1 Cor. 12: 31ff.; Col. 2: 2). Though love ultimately surpasses it, and sometimes issues in its transmission, understanding alone provides the entrance to it, comprehends its range and meaning, and directs its concrete application.

Similarly with the communities' hope. Through 'the word of the truth of the gospel',[26] the basic elements of their hope are well-known to them. Nevertheless further instruction about aspects of it on which they should not be 'without understanding' is still in order.[27] In view of the threat posed by those who are pressing contrary versions of this hope upon them, Paul urges them to 'remember' the content of his initial teaching and to 'be not quickly shaken from (their) mind'.[28] While it is only through the 'enlightenment' of the Spirit that a person can have knowledge of this hope, it should be the aim of all seeking maturity to strive for it, remembering that 'though our knowledge is partial now, then it will be complete' (1 Cor. 13: 9-11). Hope certainly goes beyond understanding, but understanding helps introduce it and is one of the consequences of it. Understanding is the instrument through

26. Rom. 15: 4; Col. 1: 5; Eph. 1: 18
27. 1 Thess. 4: 13ff.; Rom. 13: 11ff. et al.
28. 2 Thess. 2: 2 and 5; compare Col. 1: 23

which further appreciation of hope takes place and false interpretations of it are rejected.

ALTERNATIVE PATHS TO KNOWLEDGE

So far as faith, love and hope are concerned then, knowledge
occupies a key place, and therefore a central place in the life of
Paul's communities. This makes the danger of false knowledge all
the more real, and it is from this perspective that we must
approach the various attacks upon knowledge in his letters.

(a)   The mystery cults

The mystery religions claimed to reveal the true character of the
supernatural world and insisted that it could be attained only by
non-rational means. Their *gnōsis* had its climax in a 'vision of the
divine', i.e. in a mystical, indeed ecstatic, illumination in which
the participant was taken quite outside his normal mind — even,
it was held, his physical body.[29] Paul warns his hearers against
being deceived by this promise of revelation and by the false persuasiveness it appears to possess (Col. 2: 4 and 8a). It is a purely
human creation and, for all its apparent piety and wisdom, is
essentially specious in argument and sensual in its appeal (vv. 8b
and 18). The true *gnōsis* for which it is searching is located 'in
Christ' and the genuine conviction for which it is aiming is an
allegiance of 'mind' and 'heart' (i.e. will) to the teaching about
him (vv. 2b-3 and 7).

   This does not mean that Paul rules out such experiences altogether. In one place he refers to a vision he experienced many
years before. While not denying its legitimacy (a) he draws attention to it unwillingly — it is forced upon him by his opponents'
line of argument; (b) he nowhere suggests that it resulted in a
significant change in his own nature or outlook; (c) he regards it
as an experience of secondary importance so far as his life and
calling in Christ are concerned (2 Cor. 12: 1-10). In each of these
respects Paul shows himself to be at odds with the values of the
mystery religions.[30] It is true that in a number of other places he
does talk openly about 'receiving an illumination' or 'knowing a
mystery', but this has to do with understanding the full implications of Christ's death and resurrection, not some mystical vision,
and he stresses the fact that God has now made this knowledge

29. Apuleius, *Metamorphoses,* XI, 23: Plutarch, *Isis and Osiris,* 77-78
30. Apuleius, *Metamorphoses,* XI, 22-24; Plutarch, *Isis and Osiris,* 68

openly available to all.[31] It is in the name of genuine knowledge, then, that Paul dismisses the alleged knowledge of the mysteries.

(b) Stoics and Cynics

This does not mean that Paul is arguing for a rationality of the Stoic or Cynic kind. He regarded this as also missing the mark so far as true understanding of divine things was concerned and as similarly facile in its appeal to men's minds (1 Cor. 1: 20-21). Over against it he emphasizes revelation as the source of divine knowledge and its straightforward presentation as the means by which it is impressed upon his hearers (2 Cor. 4: 1-6). He is probably closest to the Stoics in the way in which he does this. One does not have to read very far through Paul's writings to see that they are principally given over to various arguments in support of the instruction he wishes to convey. Particularly in the question-and-answer method that he employs from time to time (for example in Romans 6) does his kinship with Stoic practice become apparent. But frequently the newness of what he says breaks through the formal methods of argument he is using, just as his continued insistence on the revealed source of all his knowledge sets him apart from his Stoic counterparts. This insistence explains Paul's emphasis upon the need for *pistis,* faith, a notion that was fundamentally at odds with the Stoic or Cynic approach to life. But this should not obscure the fact that what divides them is their view of knowledge and how men receive it.

(c) Judaism

At this point Paul stands closer to the Jewish teachers of his day. Yet although they have the advantage of possessing in the Law the very 'embodiment of truth and knowledge', a 'veil lies over their minds obscuring its real significance' from them (Rom. 2: 17-21; 2 Cor. 3: 14-15). They undoubtedly 'have a zeal for God' but 'it is not enlightened', for they are too preoccupied with the 'letter' of the law at the expense of its 'spirit' (Rom. 10: 2-3; 2 Cor. 3: 5-6). Though he does not comment on it, the approach to knowledge within the Qumran community would have been regarded by him as similarly misdirected. While in its reformulation of the prophets (applying them to the present) it preserved the Old Testament understanding of knowledge somewhat more faithfully than the Rabbis, the Qumran viewpoint also contained foreign elements, frequently speaking of knowledge as an esoteric

31. 2 Cor. 4: 6; Rom. 16: 25-26; Col. 2: 2-4 (compare 1: 27); Eph. 3: 4-5 and 9-10

affair and freely using the language of mystical enlightenment.[32]
Paul's understanding of knowledge corresponds much more to the
Old Testament, especially the prophetic, outlook. In this, knowledge of God comes neither through human speculation nor
mystical illumination, nor primarily through rational deductions
based on God's past revelation, nor through circumstantial
present applications of it. Knowledge of God arises from a personal transaction between the dynamic word of the Lord and the
prophet's mind, with human insight, visionary experience,
scriptural exegesis and situational discernment playing a
subordinate role.

So then it is knowledge which the community needs for its
growth — knowledge whose content is the 'whole counsel of God'
and whose only source is in God. Such knowledge — which is
transmitted as much by life, especially suffering, as it is by word
— can only be communicated to members of the community by
the Spirit. 'The Spirit', says Paul, 'searches everything, even the
depths of God. For what person knows a man's thoughts except
the spirit of the man within him? So also no one comprehends the
thoughts of God except the Spirit of God. Now we have received
. . . the Spirit which is from God, in order that we might understand all that has been bestowed upon us by God of his own free
grace' (1 Cor. 2: 10b-12). Although intimations of that truth are
revealed by God to men as they reflect on the character of their
external environment (Rom. 1: 19-20), absorb the deepest insights of their culture (e.g. Acts 17: 28; Phil. 4: 8), or listen to
their most basic intuitions (Rom. 2: 14-15), it comes to clearest
expression within the Christian community itself and most characteristically in the gathering of its people together. The way in
which this happens must shortly concern us, but before we can
turn to that a further basic element in community life must be
considered.

32. IQS 4: 6 and 11: 3-6; IQH 18: 19-20 and 25-31

CHAPTER EIGHT

Physical expressions of fellowship

Paul singles out understanding and communicating as especially important for the community's progress to maturity, but emphasizes that these do not only involve its thinking and speaking. The members are to live out these things for which they will inevitably suffer. Only knowledge that has been translated into action and tested by affliction has the stamp of genuineness about it. Until that happens it has not really grasped the person who claims to possess it. Any knowledge to which he lays claim is only superficial or counterfeit. Paul's insistence that thoughts and words be embodied in his readers' lives and actions springs from his belief that man is essentially a physical being — not, as the Greeks thought, an imprisoned intellect, spirit or soul. He does not just *have* a body, he *is* a body; he does not live *in* a physical form, he exists *as* a physical form. This being the case, it comes as no surprise that physical actions have a place in Paul's communities alongside mere verbal activities.

BAPTISM

The best example of a physical action being important to Christian experience is baptism. This was really an individual, not a community, affair. However although Paul did not always personally baptize his converts (1 Cor. 1: 16) and regards baptism as only a secondary feature of his apostolic work (v. 17), baptism gives visible expression to the change from the old way of life to the new. Paul talks about this in a number of places in his letters where he elaborates upon the significance of baptism for his readers.[1] But we must be careful here. Despite the general assumption that Paul always has water baptism in mind in these passages, he may sometimes be employing the word metaphorically to refer to conversion. Novel though this suggestion may seem, a metaphorical use of the term (or cognate expressions) already occurs in the Gospels (Mk. 10: 38-39; Luke 12: 50), as well as in Paul himself.[2] The passages certainly make excellent sense if interpreted along these lines. Metaphorically the word signifies an overwhelming experience of some kind, so it provides a very appropriate and vivid shorthand description of regeneration. It also makes more sense of those places where baptism is juxtaposed with other metaphors, e.g. death and burial (Rom. 6: 3-4), putting on clothing (Gal. 3: 27). The combining of literal and metaphorical elements can be awkward, whereas the mixing of metaphors is a common (and quite Pauline) procedure. Certainly the allusion to baptism by the Spirit in 1 Corinthians 12 fits more naturally into this interpretation (1 Cor. 12: 13), while the isolated mention of baptism in Ephesians (Eph. 4: 5) — alongside such spiritual realities as 'faith', 'hope' and the heavenly 'body', and unaccompanied by any reference to the Lord's 'meal' — looks less out of place.

Yet clearly water baptism still took place. Paul mentions in passing some instances of it (1 Cor. 1: 16-17) and Acts adds others.[3] These passages indicate that baptism was often a family occasion, signalling the introduction of a whole household into the Christian way of life (Acts 16: 33 and 18: 8). In view of the distinction generally drawn in the ancient world between children and household,[4] the close association between faith and baptism in both Acts and Paul,[5] and the special status accorded to children simply by birth into a family where at least one member is Christian (1 Cor. 7: 14), the probability of infants being involved seems minimal. This argument is strengthened by Paul's identification of the seal of the new covenant with the *Spirit*,[6] and his conviction that circumcision has its fulfilment in the *death* of Christ, and

1. Gal. 3: 27; 1 Cor. 12: 13 and 15: 29; Rom. 6: 3-4; Col. 2: 11-12; Eph. 4: 5
2. 1 Cor. 6: 11 and 10: 2; compare Eph. 5: 26
3. Acts 16: 15 and 33, 18: 8 and 19: 5
4. Compare 1 Tim. 3: 4 and 12, and earlier Gen. 18: 19, 36: 6, 47: 12 and 50: 7; 1 Sam. 1: 21
5. Acts 8: 12, 16: 31 and 18: 8 (compare 16: 14 and 19: 4); Gal. 3: 23-25; Col. 2: 12; Eph. 4: 5
6. 2 Cor. 1: 22; Eph. 1: 13 and 4: 30

perhaps the convert's death to sin in him (Col. 2: 11-12), not in
Baptism.

What then does water baptism signify? Paul does not regard it
as a solely symbolic action, nor as an inexplicably magical one. It
is not an outward representation of an already concluded inner
decision, i.e. God's covenantal election of the person involved[7]
and the latter's individual commitment to God (Acts 16: 33-34),
nor is it the mechanism by which God's benefits are automatically
guaranteed to whoever undergoes it. Paul's linking of faith with
baptism suggests that it was by means of baptism that the individual *actually committed* himself to God.[8] It is precisely because man is
not simply a soul imprisoned within a body but a physical being,
and because God's relations with him do not take place within a
vacuum but within the framework of a physical environment, that
the whole man (not merely his inner self) and water, an element
of God's material creation (not merely God's invisible power), are
involved in this most important decision. Baptism, therefore, is
neither a symbolic nor a magical act, but a genuinely dynamic
affair. Through it a person becomes an individual in the full sense
for the first time — by becoming aware of his own true position
vis-à-vis God and being drawn into relationship with him.

This means that baptism is in the first instance something between the individual or, given the household baptisms in Acts,
between the family and God. This does not mean that it has no
wider communal dimension at all. As we have already seen, a
person's entrance into God's freedom, or salvation, while an
existential affair for the individual concerned, also marks his
introduction into a wider community. Baptism, which dynamic-
ally embodies and effects this translation from one way of life to
another, necessarily involves a transferral from one community to
another, from that 'in Adam' to that 'in Christ'. But so far as the
action itself is concerned the *ekklēsia*, church, does not strictly
come into view. Nowhere in Luke's account of Paul's activities or
in Paul's discussions of baptism, do we find a hint that baptism
has anything to do with the church. The context of baptism is the
preaching of the gospel, not the *gathering* of the community.

LAYING ON OF HANDS

Although, contrary to much that has been written, the giving of
the Spirit is not necessarily tied to baptism itself — the giving of

7. Compare Acts 18: 10 and 16: 33-34
8. Compare 1 Pet. 3: 21-22

the Spirit may precede baptism, though more often follows it[9] — a close link between the two naturally exists. But then a different physical action from baptism normally accompanies the gift of the Spirit — the laying on of hands.[10] Once again we do not have here a merely symbolic movement on the one hand or a quasi-magical one on the other. As its Old Testament background indicates (e.g. Gen. 48: 14ff.), the laying on of hands was essentially an enacted prayer — one that achieved what it was requested. The action did not just *accompany* the prayer; it *was* part of the prayer itself.

As such the action lent itself to a wide variety of situations. Those, according to Acts, in which Paul is involved include commissioning of mission-workers (Acts 13: 3, compare 6: 6), healing of the sick,[11] and recognition of leaders[12] — as well as conveying of the Spirit. It would be a mistake to see in the third of these anything approaching 'ordination' in the modern sense. Like the others it is simply an acted prayer and does not carry any special significance over and above the content of the prayer itself. The Book of Acts confirms this. There the phrase 'the laying on of hands' is equated with 'commending to the grace of God'.[13] While we should not overlook the fact that Paul makes no mention of this action anywhere in his letters, there does not seem any reason to doubt the authenticity of Luke's account in this matter. With the laying on of hands we have a physical sign which potentially involves not only the individual, as in baptism, but members of the community as well (Acts 13: 1-3). Insofar as it does this, it expressed not merely the prayer of the members to God for the person before them but their fellowship with him in the matter concerned.

THE COMMON MEAL

The most visible and profound way in which the community gives physical expression to its fellowship is in the common meal in which the members share. Only in two places does Paul talk about this, while Acts associates him with it just once. It is certainly extraordinary, on the face of it, that so little should be said by Paul about a practice that has been so much at the heart of

9. Compare Acts 10: 44 and 2: 38
10. Acts 8: 17-19, 9: 17-18 and 19: 6
11. Acts 28: 8 (compare 9: 17, 19: 11 and 20: 10)
12. Acts 14: 23 (?)
13. Compare Acts 14: 26 with Acts 13: 3

corporate Christian activity throughout the centuries. This is especially so when, apart from four brief references elsewhere, two in Acts, one in 2 Peter and one in Jude, Paul says all that there is to say in the New Testament on the subject. This means that we have very little to help us in reconstructing his views on the matter, though there is sufficient evidence for us to discern the basic outlines of his approach.

There can be little doubt that the sharing of a meal together in the Lord's name was a Christian practice before Paul's churches appeared on the scene. From the evidence in 1 Corinthians 10-11 it is not fully clear whether the Lord's Supper accompanied every gathering of the 'whole church' (1 Cor. 11: 18, compare 14: 23) or whether the community sometimes met especially for this purpose. The phrase 'when you come together to eat' (11: 13) certainly suggests the second, but it is impossible to be certain. No mention is made of holding the meal in the smaller house-church meetings, but then little is said specifically about the content of these anyway. One would most naturally expect the Lord's Supper to be part and parcel of what took place. The setting of the Lord's Supper, even in the larger gatherings, was of course the home.[14]. The word *deipnon* (1 Cor. 11: 20), generally but not very aptly translated 'supper', tells us that for Paul it was not a token meal (as it has become since) or part of a meal (as it is sometimes envisaged), but simply the meal itself. The term indicates that we have here rather the main (normally evening) meal, the one to which guests were generally invited. Its character as an ordinary meal is assumed throughout; its significance has been heightened through the new meaning given it. Paul's injunction to the 'hungry' to eat before they leave home (vv. 22 and 34) does not represent the beginnings of a separation of the Lord's Supper from the meal itself. He is merely trying to avoid abuses that had entered into the meal at Corinth, not introduce a fundamental alteration in its celebration. As we shall see in a moment, its character as a meal is quite essential to it.

Nowhere does Paul suggest that the Lord's Supper has any cultic significance. With the exception of the words that accompany it, it was in no respect different from the customary meal in a Jewish home at which guests were present. The breaking and distribution of the bread was the normal way of commencing such a meal, just as the taking of a cup was the usual way in which it was brought to a conclusion — prayers of blessing being attached to both.[15] Though commentators have generally assumed that the

14. Compare Rom. 16: 23; Acts 20: 8
15. See Jer. 16: 7; compare Ber. 7: 1 and 6: 1

Christian meal included a formal recitation of the words uttered at the last meal Jesus shared with his disciples, this may not necessarily have taken place. While the recalling of the the events of that night probably follows normal practice in his churches, in reciting the words of institution Paul may simply intend to remind his readers in what *spirit* the meal should be conducted (1 Cor. 11: 23-26). Elsewhere in his writings similar references to sayings or actions of Jesus are introduced by him in order to recall his audience to the real nature of their responsibilities,[16] though, it must be admitted, these do not contain anything so explicit as Jesus' 'do this in remembrance of me'.

The character of the meal could be affirmed in other ways, e.g. through the prayers which commence and conclude it. No priestly celebrant is in view in any of the contexts where the meal is discussed; indeed there is no suggestion that its management was in the hands of officials of any kind. Most probably general arrangements were in the hands of the 'host' in whose home the meal was held, though the Corinthian practice of some going ahead without others (plus the fact that Paul addresses his remarks throughout to the whole church rather than one member or group within it) indicates that responsibility lay upon all for its proper conduct. The presence of children in the regular meetings of Christians (Col. 3:20; Eph. 6: 1-3) suggests that at least those of a reasonable age — Paul's direct addresses to children indicate that they were more than infants — naturally participated in it. A precedent here would be the Passover Feast, also held in the home, which included education of the young in the fundamentals of their religious heritage (Exod. 12: 21-27).

The meal itself was a visible proclamation of the death of Christ to all who participated in it, and therefore a call to discipleship by him. In what way this was so we must now consider more carefully. For Paul the words, 'This is my body' (1 Cor. 11: 24) mean, 'This is me, the one who gave up his life on your behalf'. The words, 'This cup is the *new covenant in my blood'* (v. 25 — not, as in Matthew and Mark, 'This is the blood of the covenant') mean, 'This is the new relationship established between God and you through my death' (the term 'blood' being for Paul a shorthand way of referring to Jesus' crucifixion.[17]) References to the 'body' and 'covenant' of Christ (by means of the 'bread' and 'wine') are not simply two ways of referring to the

16. E.g. 1 Cor. 7: 10-11 and 15: 1ff.; 1 Cor. 8: 8-10; Rom. 6: 1-11 and 15: 7-13; Phil. 2: 5-13
17. Rom. 3: 25 and 5: 9; Col. 1: 20; Eph. 1: 7 and 2: 13

same thing, viz Jesus' death for others' sake. The term 'body' obviously describes the death of Jesus, but the term 'covenant' goes on to identify the great benefit that results from that death, a new relationship with God and one another. The taking of bread at the beginning (1 Cor. 11: 23) and drinking of wine at the end (v. 25) of the meal now become all the more appropriate, for between them lies the experience of that new relationship in the course of the meal itself. This is really vital, since it is as the members of the community *eat and drink together* that their unity comes to visible expression. The meal is therefore a truly social (and possibly gastronomical!) occasion, providing the opportunity for this unity to take place in reality, and not just sacramentally. The sharing of the wine at the close of the meal is appropriate for a further reason as well. This action anticipates the time when they shall all 'drink' (i.e. 'fellowship' together) with Christ in God's kingdom in a more direct way. What could be a more fitting note on which to conclude the meal? It is not only a truly social but also a truly eschatological event for those who participate in it.

Thus the meal that they shared together not only reminded the members of their relationship with Christ and one another but actually deepened it, much as participation in a common meal by a family or group not only symbolizes but really cements the bond between them. This explains why Paul does not direct his criticisms against the attitudes of people to the elements of bread and wine, or the quality of their individual relationships to God, but rather against their attitudes and behaviour *towards one another.* When these do not reflect that Christ-like pouring out of their lives for each other that lies at the heart of the meal, they are 'guilty of drinking the cup and eating the bread in an unworthy manner' and of 'profaning the body and blood of the Lord' (v. 27). This is the significance of Paul's warning that 'anyone who eats and drinks without discerning the body, eats and drinks judgment upon himself (v. 29). Here, as in the previous chapter (10: 17), the community is in view. The emphasis is upon participation, not the elements of bread and wine, and upon the unity of the community, as symbolized in the 'one' loaf that is distributed among them.

A similar thought lies behind Paul's comments, a few paragraphs earlier, about the behaviour of the 'strong' towards the 'weak'. There he urges the former to 'take care lest this liberty of yours somehow become a stumbling block to the weak'. This not only destroys the weak man, the brother for whom Christ died, for 'Thus sinning against your brethren and wounding their conscience when it is weak, you sin against *Christ* (8: 11-12). So seriously does Paul consider all this, that for him a meal in which the members are not sensitive to the physical needs of the community is not the 'Lord's meal' at all. He also explains that, if unchecked, wrong attitudes between individuals will result in physical weakness, even death, among the members. This is one more indication of the way in which physical and spiritual factors are intertwined in Paul's thinking.

Comparison of the meals in Paul's communities with the *haburah* meals allegedly characteristic of groups like the Pharisees is difficult, because there is no real evidence to suggest that these lay fellowships held regular community feasts at all. Apart from the annual Passover festival and the celebration of the New Moon, there are only meals in which 'fellowships for the observance of a commandment' took part, generally in the synagogue. These were essentially duty meals, such as those connected with circumcisions and betrothals, weddings and funerals, in which participation as a paying guest was regarded as meritorious. It was different at Qumran where the members came together twice daily for a common meal. Certainly this played an integral part in their community life and was a real expression of their unity. But it was also a cultic celebration, presided over by a priest, with the members sitting and participating according to a rigidly defined order of precedence. Novices were excluded until they had completed the second year of their probation and women were completely absent.[18]

Although there have been some ambitious reconstructions of the meals held in the cults, frequently emphazising their similarity with the Pauline Supper, it would be more accurate to describe these as feasts held in honour of the initiate on his entry into the mysteries (or as meals involving only the devotee and the god he worshipped), than as occasions for mutual fellowship and service.[19] We know more about the common meals held under the aegis of a god by the members of a guild, but here again we are dealing with cultic, specifically sacrificial, meals of a very different kind to those which Paul was advocating. The distinctive character of the Pauline meal, and of the idea of community embodied in it, remains even if at certain points there is overlap between them.

For Paul, as we have seen, man was not an imprisoned spirit but an embodied person, his physical frame being as much a part

18. IQS 6: 20-21
19. Apuleius, *Metamorphoses*, XI, 24-25; Josephus, *The Antiquities of the Jews*, XVIII, 73

of his created glory as any other aspect of his personality. Consistent with this Paul believed that the body itself is inhabited by, indeed is a 'temple' of, the Holy Spirit (1 Cor. 6: 19). Along with every other aspect of the personality, it should take its part in the life of the church. This is anticipated in the action by which a person joins the community — baptism — but comes to fullest expression in the central action by which the community maintains and deepens its life, the Lord's meal. Also, according to Acts, healing was conveyed through the laying on of hands, ministry endorsed, workers commissioned and even the Spirit communicated.

THE EXCHANGE OF KISSES

Two final physical expressions of fellowship remain. 'Greet all the brethren', Paul says to his first converts in Thessalonica, as later to the recipients of his letters in Corinth and Rome, 'with a holy kiss.'[20] To interpret this action as merely a formal procedure, or to regard it as merely a peripheral matter, would be to sadly underestimate its importance. Though not significant to the same profound degree as baptism and the Lord's Supper, like the laying on of hands it does play a quite important role in early communal life. By means of this action the bond between each member of the community was given real, and not merely symbolic, expression.

In itself the exchange of kisses in such a group is not particularly remarkable. While we have no direct evidence of its use in the synagogue or at Qumran, it was part of the everyday life of Eastern societies, especially among relatives, friends, and those giving and receiving hospitality (compare Luke 7: 45). In the mysteries it signified the type of relationship that existed between the initiate and the mystagogue (the one who initiates another into a mystery cult) and between the individual initiate and other members of the cult.[21] In Greek society generally it played much the same role as it did in the East. So it is the significance attached to it that differentiates its Christian use. Its communal character marks it off from its more individualized exercise in the mysteries — in church the members are all to 'greet one another'. And the breadth of the relationship to which it gives expression — it is the kiss of Christ's peace among people of different races, classes and

20. 1 Thess. 5: 26; 1 Cor. 16: 20; Rom. 16: 16; compare Acts 20: 37
21. Apuleius, *Metamorphoses*, VII, 9

families — gives it a more profound meaning than its practice in Judaism.

THE SHARING OF POSSESSIONS

For all his emphasis on these physical expressions of fellowship however, Paul never suggests that the members of his communities have 'all things in common' as, for example, took place at Qumran. The oneness of Christians in the gospel does not necessarily involve the pooling of all their material resources. Not that their attitude to property stays unaffected by their commitment to Christ and one another. They are to remember 'the grace of our Lord Jesus Christ, that though he was rich, yet for your sake he became poor, so that by his poverty you might become rich' (2 Cor. 8: 9-10). The model for their attitude is nothing less than the central gift in the gospel itself (9: 13). In practical terms this does not mean divesting themselves of all their property so much as the sharing of their 'abundance' and 'prosperity' with those in want (2 Cor. 8: 14; 1 Cor. 16: 2). This should lead to the situation where 'he who gathers much had nothing over, and he who gathers little had no lack' (2 Cor. 8: 15). In the spirit of the gospel such sharing should spring from a 'loving' and 'generous' heart.[22] Indeed without this voluntary response, even the total yielding up of one's possessions is worthless, an 'exaction' stemming from a 'command' (2 Cor. 8: 8 and 9: 5). Paul insists that 'each one must do as he has made up his mind, not reluctantly or under compulsion, for God loves a cheerful giver' (9: 7). And this opens up the possibility of people exhibiting a 'wealth of liberality', giving not only 'according to their means' but 'beyond their means, of their own free will' even though in a situation of 'extreme poverty' (8: 2-3).

Paul does not call for the abolition of private property, or for its transformation into joint ownership. But neither does he talk of people possessing a right to it. Any idea of rights is foreign to Paul. It cuts across all that he stands for. The gospel is not about the claiming of a right but the offering of a present. It is no accident that at the climax of his longest discussion on this subject he breaks off into the exclamation, 'Thanks be to God for *his* inexpressible gift (9: 15). All that the believer owns has to be viewed through the cross, to feel its imprint and become the basis for service to others. In some instances that will mean parting with

22. 1 Cor. 13: 3; 2 Cor. 8: 8, 9: 11 and 13

things, particularly when there is more than enough; in others it will mean parting even with some that are really less than enough. Just occasionally, as with Paul himself, it will mean parting with all and not even asking for recompense in return.

All this takes Paul's view of possessions beyond that characteristic of the Hellenistic associations. For Paul the physical expression of fellowship by the sharing of material possessions was to take place, but not-compulsorily. The principle of mutual financial support also lay at the heart of club life. But it was a carefully regulated affair and kept within calculated limits. In this respect it mirrored the practice of philanthropy in the ancient world generally at this time, with its desire for reciprocal returns.[23] If other motives sometimes surfaced, they lay in the expectation of official honour being awarded to the donor.[24] Even where gifts were distributed without anything being received in return, it often took place on a *quid pro quo* basis, with the most worthy of the disadvantaged gaining all or most of the charity dispersed.[25]

Unlike the Essenes[26] Paul did not found communes as he moved around the ancient world, but this does not mean that he did not challenge common attitudes to property. Those who became members of his communities could never look on what they owned with the same eyes again.

---

23. Cicero, *De Officiis*, I, 15 and 48; Seneca, *De Beneficiis*, II, 35
24. Pliny, *Epistulae*, I, 8 and 15
25. Cicero, *De Officiis*, II, 15: 54; Seneca, *De Vit. Beat.*, Pliny, *Ep.*, IX. 30
26. Compare IQS 6: 19ff.

CHAPTER NINE

Gifts and ministry

THE PURPOSE OF CHURCH:
WORSHIP, MISSION OR EDIFICATION?

One of the most puzzling features of Paul's understanding of
ekklēsia for his contemporaries, whether Jews or Gentiles, must
have been his failure to say that a person went to church primarily
to 'worship'. Not once in all his writings does he suggest this is the
case. Indeed it could not be, for he held a view of 'worship' that
prevented him from doing so.

This is crystallized in his plea at the beginning of Romans 12: 'I
appeal to you therefore, brethren, by the mercies of God to
present your bodies as a living sacrifice, holy and acceptable to
God, which is your spiritual worship. Do not be conformed to this
world but be transformed by the renewal of your mind, that you
may prove what is the will of God, what is good and acceptable
and perfect' (Rom. 12: 1-2). Paul certainly talks here in the language of the cult through which the Jewish worship of God was
offered in the Temple. Such language would have been familiar to
Gentile audiences as well, though their understanding of these
terms would not generally have possessed the same moral dimension. The striking feature of Paul's statement, however, is his
non-cultic use of this language — its metaphorical application to
the sphere of everyday behaviour. The spiritual or rational
'worship' *(latreia)* which Christians are called upon to make
requires them to offer *(parastēsai)* their whole selves, bodies

included, to God as a living sacrifice *(thusia),* dedicated *(hagia)* and
acceptable to him. The stress here upon obedience rather than
literal sacrifice, and upon the rational or voluntary rather than
ecstatic, distinguishes Paul's view from that of the Jewish or
Hellenistic cult. In practice this means behaving in such a way
that God's will, which is by definition good and perfect,
determines all their actions — something that can only be
achieved if their minds accept his standards, rather than those
characteristic of the times in which they live, as normative.

So worship involves the whole of one's life, every word and
action, and knows no special place or time. The remainder of this
section in Romans brings this out most forcibly. In turn, and
without marking them off from one another, Paul discusses
behaviour in the Christian community, among other social circles
and at the political level (12: 3-13: 4). Since all places and times
have now become the venue for worship, Paul cannot speak of
Christians assembling in church *distinctively* for this purpose.
They are already worshipping God, acceptably or unacceptably,
in whatever they are doing. While this means that when they are
in church they are worshipping as well, it is not worship but something else that marks off their coming together from everything
else that they are doing.

This 'something else' has often in the past been defined as 'mission'. According to this way of looking at things, the primary purpose of church is evangelism and/or social action. Now Paul says
a good deal about the importance of these but he never suggests
that they provide the basic rationale for church as such, the
regular gathering of Christians. He insists that Christians should
'conduct themselves wisely towards outsiders, making the most of
the time', and that this involves both their conversation with such
people and their behaviour towards them. They are to 'do good to
all men', providing food and drink even for their enemies, and are
to 'hold fast the word of life' by their uncomplaining and unargu-
mentative way of life.[1] But he envisages these things as taking
place outside church, as there is 'time' and 'opportunity' among
the contacts and circumstances of everyday life. This does not rule
out the possibility that one or other may occasionally happen
within the gathering itself, but when it does so it is only as a
byproduct of what is going on. He gives an illustration of this in 1
Corinthians 14. Having already defined prophecy as something
that 'edifies the church' (1 Cor. 14: 4), and as a gift for believers,
not unbelievers (v. 22), Paul says that 'if all prophesy, and an un-

---

1. Col. 4: 6 and compare Gal. 6: 10; Rom. 12: 14-21; Phil. 2: 14-16

believer or outsider enters, he is convicted by all, he is called to account by all, the secrets of his heart are disclosed; and so falling on his face, he will worship God and declare that God is really among you' (vv. 24-25). All this is a consequence of Christians sharing the word of God *with one another*, not directly with the outsider! We shall have more to say about this later, for in a variety of ways the church indirectly involves itself in mission to the world outside its meetings. But not in the first instance. The main reason for its activities lies elsewhere.

The purpose of church is rather the edification of its members through their God-given ministry to one another (vv. 12, 19 and 26). This, as we have seen, takes place as they share in a meal at which they remember and express Christ's service for them and renew their hope of their future with him. There are also other gatherings which revolve mainly around the sharing of gifts with one another through the Spirit. These two kinds of meetings may not always have taken place separately. On occasion one probably led into the other (e.g. Acts 20: 7-12), or the two were merged into a unified whole. The disciplinary meeting described in 1 Corinthians 5 appears to be simply part of the regular gathering (1 Cor. 5: 4-5), as does that involving the settling of disputes between Christians foreshadowed in the following chapter (1 Cor. 6: 5ff.). This is not to say that other meetings never took place from time to time for a specific purpose, for example gatherings for prayer during a crisis situation (compare Acts 12: 5) or gatherings of leaders when the calling together of the whole community was impracticable (Acts 20: 17ff.). Apart from the occasional coming together 'to eat' however, the most general form of meeting centred around the exercise of ministries by members for each other's benefit.

THE DYNAMICS OF CHURCH: GIFTS AND MINISTRIES

This brings us to a consideration of Paul's understanding of *charisma*, 'gift'. This is the main, though not the only, term by which Paul refers to this aspect of the Spirit's work. His use of it has little precedent in the ancient world of his time. Though it occurs twice in an apocryphal[2] and once in a pseudepigraphical work,[3] the textual tradition underlying the first is not very secure and the second is almost certainly a post-Pauline reference. Paul's near contemporary, Philo of Alexandria, also uses it twice in one

2. Ecclus. 7: 33 (cod.B) and 38: 30 (cod.S)
3. Sib. Or. 2: 54

passage, though for him the word means simply a 'token of favour' in quite an ordinary sense. This is also the case in the other references.[4] In classical Greek literature the term *charisma* does not occur at all, while in the papyri there are only a few occurrences, all of them later than the New Testament. In these it also means 'present' in the most general sense, without any religious significance attached. Though the word probably did not originate with Paul, he does appear to have been the first to give a technical meaning to it. Here we have not merely a further example of Paul's utilizing a common term to describe some aspect of community life, as with *ekklēsia* and *sōma,* but an instance of his stamping a little-used term with an altogether distinctive significance. This is something for which there does not appear to be any real parallel in the rest of his writings.

The importance of this term 'gift' lies in its expressing the basic principle involved in Paul's approach to the dynamics of church. Unfortunately this has all too often been neglected or minimized in scholarly treatments of Paul's idea of the Christian community, even in discussions of the term itself. Only in fairly recent times have attempts been made to emphasize its significance for Paul's thinking on this subject. But the term is not confined to passages in which the life of the Christian community is under discussion. The word has a wider reference, which gives a basic insight into its meaning and also provides the proper framework for understanding its other use. It describes those privileges which Israel received at God's hands and rejected,[5] the saving work of Christ and the acquittal from condemnation that has been extended to many as a result of it (Rom. 5: 15-17). It also describes the gift of eternal life which can be experienced now as the alternative to sin's 'wages' of death (6: 23). Paul's use of *dōrea* and *dōrēma* as synonyms for *charisma* in Romans 5: 15ff. suggests we can include the reference to Christ himself (as 'God's inexpressible gift'[6]) and to faith, 'which is God's gift' (Eph. 2: 8), not a reward for work done. So Paul can comprehend virtually the whole of God's saving activities vis-à-vis mankind in terms of gift: the sonship, the glory, the covenants, the giving of the Law, the worship and the promises which were granted to Israel. In addition there is justification, faith, eternal life — even Christ himself — extended to all men. Paul could do this because the word stressed for him, at one and the same time, the freedom of God in his relationship with mankind, the generous nature of his dealings and, as a con-

4. Philo, *Legum Allegoriae,* III, 78
5. Rom. 11: 29 (compare 9: 4-5)
6. 2 Cor. 9: 15 (compare Rom. 9: 5b)

sequence, a person's grateful dependence upon him for all that he enjoys. These *charismata* are the fundamental gifts of God and they undergird whatever other presents he may give to those who are in relationship with him.

Other gifts Paul mentions are also explicitly said to have God,[7] or alternatively Christ[8] as their author. The Spirit's task is to 'apportion' (1 Cor. 12: 11) them to every one and 'manifest' (12: 7 and 14: 12) them through individuals for the common good. As Paul's prepositions indicate, the gifts are given 'in accordance with', 'by means of', 'through' the Spirit, not 'by' him. Since he is only the medium of God's and Christ's action, to talk of the 'gifts of the Spirit' as if he were their source is misleading. The gifts are derived not from the Spirit, *pneuma*, but from God's grace, *charis*.[9] They are its concrete expression. The different terms used to describe them bring to the fore different facets of their character, e.g. their revelatory character (*phanerōsis:* manifestation), their dynamic quality (*energēma:* effectual operation) and their social purpose *(Diakonia:* service — 1 Cor. 12: 4-6). They are thus said to be specific and effective ways in which God communicates himself so that Christians may be corporately strengthened. Perhaps the words *charisma* or *charismata* themselves might be more appropriately translated as 'grace' or 'graces', thinking of these in a particular rather than general sense. The word 'graces', for all its old-fashioned associations, does catch more of the flavour of the term than our over-used and somewhat colourless word 'gifts'. So far as the duration of the *charismata* is concerned, they are clearly not temporary in character but permanent features of the community's life as long as this present age lasts. They are not given merely to help the churches get started but are intended as the main constituents of their gatherings so long as they continue to meet. According to Paul it is only when 'that which is perfect is come' (13: 10), when all communications between God and mankind of an intermediary character are abolished, that these gifts will come to an end.

Paul provides us with four main lists of the *charismata*, two within the same chapter. There are also some isolated references elsewhere to life outside the Christian community, which we will leave to one side for the moment.[10] We also have two other references — Paul's desire to share an undefined *charisma* with the

7. 1 Cor. 12: 6 and 28; Rom. 12: 3; Eph. 3: 7
8. 1 Cor. 12: 5; Eph. 4: 7, 8 and 11
9. 1 Cor. 1: 4ff.; Rom. 12: 6; Eph. 4: 7
10. 1 Cor. 7: 7; 2 Cor. 1: 11 and perhaps 1 Cor. 7: 17ff. (compare Rom. 11: 29)

Christians in Rome when he visits them ('undefined' because, until he has arrived, he does not know what contribution will be relevant — Rom. 1: 11) and his acknowledgement that the community in Corinth did not lack in *charisma* (1 Cor. 1: 7). The first list mentions the following: the utterance of wisdom (special insight into the profundity and implications of the gospel)[11] and knowledge (understanding of the Old Testament and Christian traditions and capacity to expound them concretely); faith (with respect not to salvation but to a specific circumstance), healings (presumably of various kinds in view of the plural, and of a non-miraculous character in view of the distinction from the following gift) and miraculous works (especially exorcisms); prophecy (knowing and speaking God's mind intuitively rather than, as with the teacher, deductively through the sacred writings) and discernment of spirits (whether they are of God, from a demonic source or merely reflect a human opinion, and what their significance is for the community); glossolalia and the interpretation of glossolalia (the speaking and explaining of unknown, non-human languages — 1 Cor. 12: 7-11). A reiteration of most of the items on this list occurs shortly afterwards, partly in terms of the persons to whom a gift has been given, partly in terms of the *charisma* itself. Also present are three additional *charismata*. This second list runs as follows: apostles; prophets; teachers; then miraculous works, healings, helps, administrations, various kinds of tongues and the interpretation of tongues (v. 28).

The remaining two lists are much briefer. One mentions prophecy, concrete acts of service, teaching, exhortation, financial aid (or the sharing of possessions), the ministry of guiding and the carrying out of merciful actions to those in need (perhaps including the giving of financial aid — Rom. 12: 6-8). In the other list *domata* rather than *charismata* are talked about and the persons who possess ministries appear to be themselves described as gifts. Here we have apostles, prophets, evangelists, pastors and teachers. The last two are bracketed together and probably refer to the one activity, as we shall see later (Eph. 4: 11). Outside these lists, two of the items mentioned, viz apostleship[12] and financial aid,[13] are independently related to God's grace. Elsewhere other gifts are referred to, but not designated specifically as gifts. These are: apostleship,[14] prophecy,[15] evangelism (2 Cor. 8:

11. Compare Rom. 11: 33-35; 1 Cor. 2: 6-10
12. Eph. 3: 7 (*dōrea*)
13. Phil. 4: 17 (*doma*)
14. 1 Cor. 3: 5; Rom. 16: 17; Phil. 2: 25; Eph. 2: 20
15. 1 Thess. 5: 19-20; 1 Cor. 13: 2, 14 passim; Eph. 2: 20

18), oversight (Phil. 1: 1), teaching (Gal. 6: 6; 2 Cor. 8: 7), exhortation (1 Thess. 5: 14), service,[16] miracles (Gal. 3: 1), faith (1 Cor. 13: 2; 2 Cor. 8: 7) and merciful actions (Gal. 6: 10; 1 Thess. 5: 14).

This last point raises the question of consistency in Paul's use of the term *charisma*. We can in fact detect a development in his understanding of 'gifts' and his employment of the word. The idea is present in the earliest of his writings but the terminology is absent. Thus already in the Thessalonian letters we find reference to the activity of the Spirit in fellowship, the importance of prophecy, the obligation upon all to contribute, the need to test ministries and so on. It is not till 1 Corinthians that Paul offers any extended teaching on the subject or uses the term *charisma* itself, perhaps prompted by the particular situation that had arisen there. After that he discusses the matter in his most systematic letters, Romans and Ephesians. (Although *doma* rather than *charisma* is used in Ephesians, this probably arises from its presence in the LXX quotation (Ps. 67: 19), not from any disinclination on the writer's part to use the word *charisma*.)

THE NATURE OF THE *CHARISMATA*

On the basis of these various lists, isolated references and accompanying remarks, the following conclusions may be drawn.

(a) Open-ended in character

To begin with, these lists contain *charismata* of both word and deed and are clearly intended to be open-ended. Neither individually nor as a group do they exhaust the possibilities for spoken and practical ministry within the community. The mention of particular *charismata* within the lists springs from the nature of the audience and the type of group to whom Paul is writing. The Corinthian community, as we are told elsewhere, met as a 'whole' church as well as in house groups, and favoured the more extraordinary gifts — both of these factors are reflected in the wide range and specific items in the lists given in chapter 12. In Romans we have a briefer list. At first this list appears to be more random in character, but perhaps it corresponds to the kinds of gifts most frequently exercised in the smaller house church (or domestic groups) in which Christians largely gathered in that city — the former being familiar to Paul through his previous associa-

16. 1 Cor. 16: 15; Rom. 16: 1; Phil. 1: 1; Col. 4: 7, 12 and 17; Eph. 6: 21

tions with Aquila and Priscilla. In Ephesians we have an even more restricted and structured list which, in accordance with the circular nature of the letter, mainly concerns itself with the more itinerant and significant local ministries. Thus Paul nowhere attempts to provide a systematic or full description of the gifts available to the Christian community. Indeed it is reasonable to assume on the basis of the gifts included in these lists, that any contribution by any member of the community of a constructive nature would be recognized by Paul as a gift.

(b)   Individually, but not evenly, distributed

Also each person within the community receives at least one *charisma* for the benefit of his fellows.[17] But not all have the same gift[18] and some have obviously been granted more gifts than others. The *charismata* are not distributed equally by the Spirit. Paul himself exercises a very large number of them — virtually all the gifts he mentions in his list.[19] Though there is a democratic element in the Spirit's way of proceeding to the extent that no one is excluded from a share in the gifts, no egalitarian principle is involved. Nor does Paul envisage the possession of a gift as a static affair, so that the type of contribution each member makes to the life of the community has a fixed character about it. Paul can encourage his readers to seek after gifts that they apparently do not as yet exercise (1 Cor. 14: 1). So, although the gifts are not distributed equally, they are not distributed in an inflexible, once-for-all manner.

(c)   Ranked according to their effects

This brings us to a further point. Paul describes the gifts to which people should especially aspire as 'higher' or more significant than others (12: 31). We have already seen that in two of the four lists there is a ranking of gifts or of the ministries proceeding from them. These are not graded according to their *form*, so that priority is given to the most extraordinary manifestations, such as glossolalia. This was the Corinthian error. Paul's lists demonstrate that quite ordinary, practical actions are more valuable than those the Corinthians prized. He wishes to eradicate any distinction between gifts made on this basis. Rather the gifts are graded on the basis of their *effect;* those which make the most

17. 1 Cor. 12: 7 and 11; Rom. 12: 3; Eph. 4: 7
18. 1 Cor. 12: 29-30; Rom. 12: 6; Eph. 4: 11
19. E.g. Paul in 1 Thess. 2: 7ff.; 2 Thess. 2: 15; Gal. 2: 2; 1 Cor. 1: 1; 2 Cor. 12: 1, 14: 6 and 18; Rom. 15: 19; Acts 20: 10 and 34

profitable contribution to the community's growth are accorded the highest importance.

One of the interesting things that results from this is that, generally speaking, certain gifts of speech predominate over those of deed. Understandably enough Paul gives first place to apostles, for without their preaching of the gospel and binding together of their converts the communities would not exist. Behind this ministry lies the possession of 'wisdom', which for Paul signifies special insight into God's saving plan and its benefits for his hearers. Yet despite its pre-eminent position, Paul never says that his ministry is derived from a particular *charisma*, e.g. apostleship, but only from *charis* in general (Rom. 12: 3; Eph. 3: 7). The reason for this could be that the apostle exercises all the basic gifts (see footnote 19). These form a necessary part of his equipment if his communities are to be founded on the broadest possible base and their members taught what is necessary for their continuing life. His leaving them then provides the opportunity for the same range of gifts to emerge or further develop within the communities themselves.

Second are the prophets, for they communicate to the community those things which it needs to hear directly from God for its concrete encouragement, admonition and direction. Teachers come next, for they are able charismatically to draw from what God has already done or said, specific insights and practical challenges for his people in the present. Behind these two stand the gifts of communicating 'revelation' and 'knowledge' respectively. But to some extent the importance of these 'higher' gifts is relative. A 'lower' gift, such as glossolalia, when complemented by another gift, the gift of interpretation, can become equivalent to a 'higher' one. This is the case with prophecy (1 Cor. 14: 5b). One can also infer from Paul's writings that, according to the specific needs of the community at a given time, a gift that is generally of slightly lesser value than another, for example teaching in comparison with prophecy, may be temporarily more relevant to the situation at hand.

(d) Regularly and occasionally contributed

The existence of these 'higher' gifts reminds us that some exercise a *charisma* in a regular fashion, providing the basis for a continuing ministry, while others only exercise it in an intermittent or occasional manner. All, according to Paul, ought to and can prophesy,[20] but only some have an ongoing ministry of this kind

20. 1 Cor. 14: 5a and perhaps 14: 31

and can therefore be regarded as 'prophets' (12: 29). Paul does not see any qualitative distinction between members on the basis of their exercise of a gift, merely a quantitative difference in the *frequency* with which they exercise it and (perhaps) the scope of the message they communicate. Not only the 'higher' gifts but also those low on the scale of charismatic priorities can become the basis for a regular ministry — though Paul has no title by which those who perform them are designated, only a description of their function (v. 30).

(e)   Not only 'new' but renewed

As for the nature of the gifts themselves, Paul questions not only the priority of the more spectacular gifts, but any distinction drawn between more ordinary and extraordinary manifestations. In his lists both lie side by side, for example, 'miraculous works' and 'gifts of healing' alongside 'helpful deeds' and 'practical guidance' (1 Cor. 12: 28). This raises a related question: to what extent are these gifts to be regarded as natural phenomena and to what extent purely supernatural affairs?

The distinction really begs the question, for it is not one which Paul would have made. He certainly stresses the 'newness' of the gifts, i.e. their distribution by the Spirit whom the Christians are now experiencing. Paul talks elsewhere about the 'newness' of the whole life of the converted person — 'If any one is in Christ he is a new creation; the old has passed away, behold, the new has come' (2 Cor. 5: 17). Paul does not mean that the Christian is a completely different person without continuity with his old personality. Rather he is pointing to the radical change that takes place when a person genuinely encounters God in Christ. This suggests that Paul's language about 'gifts' should not be taken to rule out altogether their connection with natural capacities, implanted by the prior creative activity of God, or by social advantages conferred by the circumstances of life. (It would not be difficult to demonstrate from Paul's own ministry certain continuities between his previous capacities and later gifts just as later we shall call attention to some links between people's social position and Christian ministry.) Such abilities are renewed (passing through their own 'crucifixion' and 'resurrection') along with all other aspects of the personality, as well as activated by the Spirit to achieve their full potential when there is a service to be performed.

(f)   Exercised on any appropriate occasion

Finally we must take note of the sphere within which the gifts are exercised. In all the writings where lists occur, the primary context for Paul's discussion of gifts is not the 'church' but the 'body', not the gathering of the Christians together but the local Christian community itself.[21] Though gifts are certainly, even pre-eminently, exercised in church, they are also exercised on other occasions when Christians are in contact with one another. It follows from this that those who have continuing ministries within the community not only engage in these while church is in progress, but would have opportunities to contribute these at other times as well.

There is another aspect to this. Since Paul has the local Christian 'body' in view in these passages, only when 'all' are assembled can the full range of gifts given to the community become evident. This does not mean that smaller gatherings are invalid, but it does mean that in the meetings of the 'house churches' there will not be as broad a representation of gifts as in the gatherings of the 'whole church'. On the other hand, the restrictions that Paul imposes on the number of people who can participate in the meetings of the 'whole church' (1 Cor. 14: 27-33) would not have been as necessary in the gatherings of the smaller 'house church' groups.

21. 1 Cor. 12: 12-27; Rom. 12: 4-6; Eph. 4: 4 and 12-16

CHAPTER TEN

Charisma and order

It is one thing to describe in theory the place of gifts in the community. How in practice are they to operate? To answer this we need to analyse the actual exercise of the gifts in the community and Paul's approach to *taxis,* or 'order'. We commence with a closer inspection of the purpose for which gifts are given, for this is the fundamental factor which controls their exercise.

THE IMPORTANCE AND BREADTH OF EDIFICATION

Paul insists that they were not granted to individuals primarily for their own enjoyment, but rather for the edification of the community (1 Cor. 12: 7; Eph. 4: 12). Though he recognizes the legitimacy of a private use of *charisma,* only in a very limited way is it appropriate in church (1 Cor. 14: 28). There the service of others, not oneself, should be in view. In fact it is precisely through seeking to fulfil the needs of others, rather than an individual quest for the *charismata* themselves, that various members of the community will come into a greater experience of the gifts (1 Cor. 14: 12). This reverses the procedure that was apparently in operation at Corinth where the charismatic aspirations of the individual, rather than the common good of the community, were paramount. So the basic principle that Paul lays down for the conduct of church is that 'all things should be done for edification' (v. 26). Only when a contribution has this as its object should it be exercised.

This idea of edification requires closer attention, for Paul has a much broader understanding of it than is generally recognized. Edification can take place in a number of different, though ultimately complementary, ways. This becomes apparent when the various aspects of community life which the gifts serve are identified. Though a particular *charisma* rarely falls into one category only, most tend to fit substantially into one of them.

Some are primarily directed towards the *growth of understanding* in the community — of God, of the community itself, outsiders, the world and so on. This cognitive aspect of the community's life is particularly served through the exercise of prophecy, teaching, exhortation, discernment of spirits and interpretation — though all of these also involve personal conviction and practical action, not just intellectual appreciation. Knowledge, as we have seen, is as much doing as thinking, as much commitment as reflection.

A second group of gifts is primarily directed towards the *psychosocial well-being* of the community, i.e. the integrity and harmony of the group and of its members. Important here are the gifts which have a pastoral orientation, for example, practical 'helps', 'acts of mercy' and the pastoral gift itself. As these gifts are exercised, the psychological needs of the members are met and the social cohesion of the group sustained.

A third group is primarily directed towards the *physical welfare* of the community. Paul never suggests that the *charismata* affect only the spiritual dimension of those whom they serve. The rendering of financial assistance, the exercise of gifts of healing and the occasional performance of miraculous works are all relevant here. The 'body' of Christ, or the gathering of the 'church', is not merely a 'communication of souls' but a fellowship of persons in contact with each other in their totality.

A fourth group of gifts appears to be directed towards what we might call the *unconscious life* of the community. There are things, says Paul, which our spirit wishes to communicate with God of which our conscious minds are unaware (Rom. 8: 26-27). It is the function of speaking in tongues and singing in the Spirit, its melodic counterpart, to make this possible. He who engages in either of these activities 'utters mysteries in the Spirit' (1 Cor. 14: 2) and 'prays with the Spirit' (v. 15), though he should seek for the interpretation of what he is saying so that his mind does not remain 'unfruitful' (vv. 13f.).

In a quite extraordinary way, therefore, the gifts have been designed by God to *encompass every aspect of the community's life.* Since the individuals within it are inextricably bound up with the relationships, obligations and structures of the world around them, the gifts must also *concern every aspect of the members' activities*. For that reason, the content of church must sometimes have been quite 'everyday' or secular'. Nor are the emotional and aesthetic aspects of people's personalities excluded from this process. The reference just made to 'singing in the Spirit' (spiritual songs) as well as other references to 'psalms' (sung teaching) and 'hymns' (sung prophecy)[1] remind us that the aesthetic dimension is not left out. In addition, the passionate enthusiasm (in contrast to logical detachment) characteristic of almost all Paul's thinking, and the depth of feeling invested in Paul's ministry to his churches — from his outpouring of love at one end of the spectrum to his agonies of anxiety at the other — emphasize the emotional involvement that could accompany exercise of the gifts. The breadth of charismatic activity in the community is very marked indeed, and the levels at which edification can take place very diverse in character.

THE EXERCISE OF GIFTS

(a)   In a balanced way

Paul consistently argues for a representative, rather than partial or one-sided, exercise of the gifts in the community's gatherings, though once again he does not do this on the basis of some egalitarian principle. Since he regards some gifts as more fundamental than others, he wishes more time to be given to these and less to the remainder. He has prophecy and teaching particularly in mind (1 Cor. 14: 6) and this suggests that the first group of *charismata* mentioned above, those directed to growth of the community's understanding, are for him the most important. But we have seen how teaching is closely associated by him with pastoral care (1 Thess. 5: 12-14), since it is through the discerning ministry of the word that personal help is frequently given. This indicates that the second category of gifts, those directed to the psychological and social harmony of the community, are not far from view.

Paul still insists that lesser gifts should not be ignored or slighted just because others are more inherently helpful. The higher gifts — he specifically instances prophecy (1 Cor. 14: 29) — should not dominate the meeting in too disproportionate a way. Partly for this reason he places a restriction on the number

1. 1 Cor. 14: 26; Col. 3: 16; Eph. 5: 19

of contributions of even the most important gifts that should be made during any gathering of the 'whole church'. Responsibility, therefore, devolves upon the individual possessors of gifts, as well as upon the community as a whole, to ensure that both a broad representation and a discerning balance of gifts are present, for only so can all aspects of church life grow and develop in proper relation to one another.

(b) Within an intelligible context

In view of Paul's emphasis upon those gifts which deepen under-standing within the community, it comes as no surprise that one of the main criteria by which the value of contributions are judged is their intelligibility. This introduces us to a further determining feature of the order that should characterize the gatherings. His reaction to the view that glossolalia was the most important *charisma* of all provides a good illustration of this principle at work. 'If you speak in tongues that are unintelligible,' he says, 'how will anyone know what is said? For you will be speaking into the air' (v. 9). It is the new member and interested outsider who are particularly at a disadvantage here, and likely to receive the wrong impression as to the purpose of church (vv. 16, 23). He does not wish to prohibit the *charisma* itself, for it is a genuine gift of the Spirit and is, for the individual, an edifying way of communicating with God (vv. 2, 39). In fact the gift is not without rational content; it is just that this content is *hidden* from the mind of the person giving expression to it. That is why Paul directly encourages those who exercise the gift to pray for the ability to interpret it (vv. 13 ff.) and speaks of others within the community who have a particular ministry of interpretation (vv. 27-28). Its *incommunicability*, not its irrationality, makes its presence inap-propriate in the gatherings of the community. The whole spirit of Paul's outlook on this matter is crystallized in his statement: 'I thank God that I speak in tongues more than you all; nevertheless, in church I would rather speak five words with my mind in order to instruct others, than ten thousand words in a tongue' (vv. 18-19).

(c) Evoking a discerning assessment

Paul identifies the practice of discernment as another regulative feature of the community's gatherings, especially in relation to the extent and value of the gifts that have been granted. Each individual must think his way through to a proper estimate of the kind of contribution he can make to the community's life. No one should overestimate his abilities here, i.e. conclude that he has a gift when he does not have one (Rom. 12: 3; Eph. 4: 7) or exercise one out of proportion to the extent to which he does possess it (Rom. 12: 6). It is also through discernment that the truth and value of contributions are to be gauged. This is something in which the prophets particularly, but in fact all the members, should be involved. They are, says Paul, to 'test everything' (1 Thess. 5: 21) and 'weigh what is said' (1 Cor. 14: 29), even if uttered by someone claiming to be under prophetic inspiration. This involved bringing all that is said or done to the bar of the original gospel (Gal. 1: 8), the apostolic tradition (2 Thess. 2: 15), practice elsewhere (1 Cor. 14: 33), previous experience (Phil. 3: 16), the spirit which accompanies it (1 Cor. 13: 1ff.), and its general constructive character (14: 26). So recognition of the gift or gifts one has, realization of the limits of one's own gift or gifts and evaluation of the quality of those exercised by others provide further linked criteria by which the structure of community gatherings is determined.

(d)   Under the individual's self-control

All these principles of 'church order' presuppose the importance of self-control on the part of those exercising the gifts. It is a mark of the genuine operation of the *charismata* that they do not compete with one another but follow one another in an orderly sequence (vv. 27b, 30-31 and 40). All this is quite within the control of those making contributions to the meeting, even with respect to the more spectacular gifts which were considered by some to be outside a person's control. Paul insists that 'the spirits of the prophets are subject to the prophets' (v. 32). The timing of their contributions lies within their power; they are also quite able to contain them if another has a more relevant contribution to make (v. 30). Similarly, with glossolalia. If no interpreter is present, those who have this gift are to refrain from giving expression to it (v. 28). If however an interpreter is present two or three may exercise the gift in turn, not all at the same time as tended to happen to Corinth (v. 27). Clearly for Paul, neither prophecy nor glossolalia are ecstatic phenomena over whose utterance the speaker had no control. On the contrary, both can be integrated in an orderly way into the conduct of the gatherings.

(e)   Within a framework of love

Finally, all the contributions must take place within the frame-work of loving behaviour between the members of the community. Here we come to the most basic principle of all, one to which Paul gives expression in all his discussions of gifts.[2] Exercise of one's gift, however wholehearted, is quite non-productive if love is absent (1 Cor. 13: 1-3). In the well-known passage of 1 Corinthians, Paul defines love in terms of the fruit of the Spirit as outlined in his letter to the Galatians (Gal. 5: 22). Since love is not 'rude', does not 'insist on its own way' and is not 'jealous or boastful', it is easy to see its relevance to some of the criteria we have already identified (1 Cor. 13: 4ff.). Such things as allowing others to contribute their gifts without interruption, submitting one's own revelations to the testing of others and having a proper estimate of one's own abilities, have their roots in a loving attitude towards other members of the community. This means that the gifts of the Spirit and the fruit of the Spirit are inextricably bound together (so inextricably in fact that the same term can occur in both, i.e. *pistis,* faith, though certainly with a different emphasis).[3] Exercise of the one without the presence of the other leads to chaos in the gatherings, unfruitfulness in understanding and derision on the part of outsiders. Only when the two occur simultaneously is there proper order in the gathering and genuine edification of its members.

THE SPIRIT AND ORDER

Although I have so far viewed the gifts chiefly from the perspective of those who exercise them, the sovereign control of the Spirit over the order which results from their appropriate expression should now be brought into focus. The gifts are and remain his to direct. This means that the fellowship of Christians is through and through a divine 'gift' rather than a human 'work'. Although this could open the door to a quite random and fluctuating distribution of the gifts, leading to uncertainty within the community as to the functions different members have within it, the character of the Spirit does not allow this to happen. He acts as the agent of a God who is 'not a God of confusion but of peace' (1 Cor. 14: 33). His sovereignty over the gifts results in a relatively stable, though not inflexible, distribution within the community and in their orderly, though not rigidly liturgical, interplay in the course of its gatherings. In so working the Spirit does not arbitrarily or coercively force his gifts upon the persons with whom he is dealing

2. 1 Cor. 13 passim; Rom. 12: 8-9; Eph. 4: 15
3. Compare Gal. 5: 22; 1 Cor. 12: 9

but at all times works through their wills in a way that safeguards their integrity and freedom. In the same way he does not signal the moment of their exercise by means of an overwhelming experience over which they have no control. Intimations there may be of the gifts which individuals have and indications of the time when they should share them, but throughout this whole process the Spirit respects and does not violate the wills of the persons involved.

So then, provided certain basic principles of the Spirit's operation are kept in view — a comprehensive, but properly-proportioned, representation of the gifts; their intelligible communication; a right recognition and evaluation of them; their orderly expression and fusion with the fruit of the Spirit and above all love — Paul sees no need to lay down any fixed rules for the community's proceedings. There is no one order proper for its meetings: any order is proper so long as these criteria are observed. Paul therefore has no interest in constructing a fixed liturgy. Anything of this sort would restrict the freedom of the Spirit and lessen the variety of his communications. Each gathering of the community will have its structure, but that will emerge naturally from the particular combination of the gifts that comes to expression in it and the order in which they are exercised.

This structure will vary from gathering to gathering, let alone from community to community. Within this, fixed liturgical elements such as psalms, doxologies, blessings, responses (e.g. amen, maranatha), credal statements, traditional formulae, scripture passages, hymns and so on may have their place, as they obviously did in Paul's churches.[4] However there is no suggestion that the reading of the Old Testament *per se,* as opposed to its being drawn into charismatic evangelizing, prophesying and teaching, was a stable element in the community's gatherings. The main speaker at the gatherings, e.g. an apostle who was in the vicinity, and certain decisions as to form of the meeting, were also obviously sometimes decided beforehand.[5] So while the proper working of the Spirit could not be safeguarded by the creating of a fixed liturgical structure, neither was it maintained by a purely spontaneous exercise of the gifts. Since the Spirit indicates some of his intentions in advance, the form and content of the early Christian gatherings were partly determined beforehand and partly during the occasion itself.

4. 1 Cor. 14: 26; Col. 3: 16; Eph. 5: 19; also Rom. 15: 9ff. and 16: 25-27; 2 Cor. 13: 13; 1 Cor. 16: 22; Gal. 6: 18; Rom. 1: 3-4; Gal. 6: 4; Eph. 4: 8 and Phil. 2: 6-11
5. Compare Acts 20: 7-11

Paul's notion of *charisma* cuts across the distinction so commonly drawn between formal and extempore elements, since for him contributions of both kinds should be equally charismatic in character. Yet the possibility of a fresh word from the Spirit interrupting the proceedings is always present and those exercising gifts must ever be alert to its occurrence (1 Cor. 14: 30). Taking all this into account, it becomes clear why the notion of *taxis* could never become a central idea in Paul's understanding of community life. The word, in fact, only occurs twice in all his writings.[6] Order for him is important but it is essentially a by-product, not a primary concern. If the basic principles of Christian ministry and behaviour are observed, then order naturally follows. Where order is lacking, it is not remedied by liturgical rearrangements of one kind or another but rather by attending more seriously to those principles that have been transgressed.

OTHER CONTEMPORARY APPROACHES TO *CHARISMA*

In drawing this section to a close, something must be said about the significance of Paul's understanding of *charisma* in comparison with Jewish and Greek approaches in his day. Though Paul first gave the word *charisma* a technical meaning, both Judaism and Hellenism were familiar with aspects of the phenomenon itself.

In apocalyptic and rabbinic Judaism the conviction that the Spirit had temporarily departed from Israel[7] and at Qumran a somewhat Hellenized view of the Spirit's operation,[8] tended to push charismatic concerns to the periphery of their life. Insofar as the rabbis considered God to be in some respects still active in Israel's life,[9] and Essene groups and some Galilean rabbis[10] possessed stronger charismatic interests (e.g. in prophecy, healing etc.), some common ground with Paul existed. But the centrality Paul gave to the *charismata* in the fellowship of the community and the insight he demonstrates into their operation have no parallel in contemporary Jewish circles.

A different picture presents itself in Hellenistic religious circles. Interest in the more extraordinary charismatic phenomena,

6. 1 Cor. 14: 40 and (in a different sense) Col. 2: 5
7. Sot. 9: 15
8. IQS 3 and 17ff.; 4: 18ff.
9. Josephus, *The Antiquities of the Jews.* XIII. 46-49: XV. 373-379. XVII 345-348
10. Ber. 5: 5; Taan. 3: 8: Sot. 9: 5; Josephus, *Ant.* XIV. 22-24; compare XVII, 43 (?)

particularly those of an ecstatic kind, was widespread in both the mystery cults and certain aspects of traditional religion. Always however, they were restricted to certain individuals and were not a community experience. An excellent example of this is the philosopher-wonderworker Apollonius of Tyana, who was frequently said to prophesy and heal. A large number of Greek terms was utilized to describe such happenings, among them *ekstasis, entheos, empneusis, enthusiasmos.* The term *pneumata* mentioned by Paul in 1 Corinthians[11] should probably be numbered amongst them. (In using that term, Paul is almost certainly echoing, not endorsing, the Corinthian way of talking about ecstatic manifestations, e.g. prophecy that so overwhelms the person engaged in it that he is compelled to say 'Jesus be cursed' rather than 'Jesus is Lord' — 1 Cor. 12: 3.)

Paul describes these experiences in terms of their participants being carried away despite themselves to idols incapable of true communication so that they had no control over what they said or did. For him, what marks off the Christian exercise of the *charismata,* including prophecy and Christian glossolalia, from these pagan counterparts, is their basis in a free commitment to one who communicates intelligibly to them through gifts subject to the control of those who receive them (v. 2). His desire to distinguish such gifts from their Hellenistic counterfeits leads Paul to avoid every one of the customary Greek words for ecstatic experiences and turn the Corinthians' attention away from the term *pneumata.* He uses instead almost uniformly throughout 1 Corinthians his own term *charisma.* Just occasionally he employs the term *pneumatikos.*[12] This may have been another term the Corinthians used in reference to these gifts, but Paul can take it up because elsewhere he uses it of other aspects of Christian experience.[13] Even so it is not the term he prefers and his own use of it would emphasize the divine source of such gifts rather than, as with the Corinthians, their ecstatic character.

PAUL'S IDEA OF COMMUNITY: ITS DISTINCTIVENESS

We are in a position now to identify more precisely the basic difference that marks out Paul's view of community from that of his contemporaries. We have already seen that by his integration of the notions of 'commonwealth' and 'household' into his under-

11. 1 Cor. 14: 12 and note especially 12: 10
12. 1 Cor. 12: 1 and 14: 1 (compare 14: 37); Rom. 1: 11
13. E.g. 1 Cor. 2: 13, 9:11 and 15: 44; Rom. 15: 27; Col. 3: 16; Eph. 1: 3

standing of 'church', Paul's view encompasses a broader range
than that found in its Jewish and Graeco-Roman counterparts.
Also his understanding of identity and unity within the church, of
the meal through which they come to expression, and his idea of
ministry and order contain a distinctive accent compared to other
approaches at that time.

But there is a further divergence between them. For the members
of Jewish religious associations, such as at Qumran and among
the Pharisees, participation in the fraternity centred primarily
around a *code,* as embodied in the Torah.[14] This lay at the basis of
the blessings, readings, expositions, confessions and prayers that
formed the content of the synagogue services. For the members of
the Hellenistic religious associations, participation in the
fraternity centred primarily around a *cult,* with dramatic rituals
and processions, as well as mystical overtones.[15] This cult
provided the basic rationale for its activities. According to Paul's
understanding, participation in the community centred primarily
around *fellowship,* expressed in word and deed, of the members
with God and one another. It demonstrates concretely the
already-experienced reconciliation between the individual and
God and the individual and his fellow-men: the gifts and fruit of
the Spirit being the instruments through which this is expressed
and deepened.

This means that the focal point of reference was neither a book
nor a rite but *a set of relationships,* and that God communicated
himself to them not primarily through the written word and tradition, or mystical experience and cultic activity, but *through one
another.* Certainly fellowship is not altogether lacking in these
other groups, ranging as they do from the comparative in-
dividualism of the mysteries to the strong community at Qumran,
nor are the Old Testament scriptures and various corporate
activities absent from the Pauline churches. But a real difference
lies at the heart of their respective gatherings. This makes it
impossible for Paul's approach as to what happens in church to
have been derived in any fundamental way from the practice of
the synagogue or of the cults. For him something quite new has
broken into human experience, and this is nothing less than the
'first fruits' or anticipation of that community between God and
his people that will be ushered in at the Last Day. Paul's view
arises from his understanding of the gospel and the Spirit and has

14. Philo, *Embassy to Gaius,* 156, *De Somniis* II, 127; *Vita Mosis,* II, 215-216;
Josephus, *The Jewish War,* II, 301; *Ant.,* XIX, 300 and 305; Yom. 7: 1; Meg.
3-4; Sot. 7: 7-8; Ab. 1: 1-2
15. Apuleius, *Metamorphoses,* XI passim; Plutarch, *Isis and Osiris,* 2ff.

only secondary points of overlap with either the synagogue or the cults, though more with the former than with the latter. But since even the synagogue's worship has its basis in an order that is 'passing away' (2 Cor. 3: 4-11), Paul does not begin with the synagogue and 'Christianize' it. Nothing in his writings suggests that the order of the synagogue service, which was clearly defined, or the central features of its worship, i.e. the Shema, Eighteen Benedictions, Old Testament readings, translation and exposition or Priestly Blessing, played a part in the meetings of his communities. Instead he develops his own views out of Christ's sacrificial service to mankind on the Cross and impartation of his resurrected life through the Spirit, integrating elements of synagogue practice only insofar as it is appropriate to do so and frequently altering their emphasis and presentation.

Paul's approach is really a quite revolutionary phenomenon in the ancient world. In view of subsequent developments — in which Catholicism increasingly followed the path of the cults and made a rite the centre of its activities, and in which Protestantism followed the path of the synagogue and placed a book at the centre of its services — it would be true to say that in most respects it remains no less revolutionary today.

CHAPTER ELEVEN

Unity in diversity among the members

We have seen that individual Christians come together as a church to share gifts with one another and to join in certain corporate activities. Within this each member of the gathering has his particular contribution to make. Since all have some function or responsibility to perform, there are no mere spectators in church but only active participants. In turning now to look more closely at the participants themselves, we need to enquire whether the early churches preserved the various distinctions that were drawn between people in the ancient world at that time. In this chapter and the next, Paul's attitude to these will occupy our attention.

THE OVERCOMING OF RACIAL, CLASS AND SEXUAL DISTINCTIONS

(a)   Tendencies in Graeco-Roman society

In the Roman Empire of Paul's day distinctions along national, social and sexual lines existed but they were also in the process of being blurred. The members of one's own nation with outsiders who became citizens of it, the class of free citizens especially those with an aristocratic background, and the male element in the population both young and old, theoretically had advantages that were denied to those who did not share their position. Without doubt those who held Roman citizenship possessed real privileges, if also additional responsibilities, over those who did not.

However, at the practical level a broadening of the notion of citizenship was gradually taking place — Paul's own position is a good indication of this. Though some degree of class shift can also be observed, social status still remained the principal criterion by which people were evaluated and treated. Still the conditions by which freedmen were frequently bound could outweigh the social, civil and financial advantages of manumission, especially when viewed against the high degree of security and responsibility that many slaves enjoyed. By and large women were regarded as second class citizens during this time. But in some parts of the Empire, particularly in the Eastern provinces and also to an extent in Rome, women were able to participate alongside men in public, commercial and religious life, own property and have a considerably independent existence. Among the philosophers, whose attitudes (together with various social and economic realities) helped turn thinking and practice in a more tolerant direction, there was advocacy of a universal republic embracing all men,[1] recognition that legal slavery and freedom had little to do with inward bondage or liberty,[2] and occasional pleas for a large measure of equality between men and women.[3]

(b)   The breakthrough in Paul's letters

Paul's thinking does not begin with the distinctions that divide people from one another, but from that which is common to them all — their distance from God and degree of response to him. He goes on to describe the Christian community as consisting of those (irrespective of nationality, social position or sex) who acknowledge the death and resurrection of Christ, experience the power of the Spirit in their lives and look forward to God's kingdom which will be ushered in at the Last Day. These all share in a common salvation. This has its roots in certain historical events, its reality in the present experience of liberation and its culmination in a future life of a qualitatively new kind. So far as anyone's entry into this new relationship with God and one another is concerned, expressed as it is through their visible gathering together in church, no distinctions can be made. What they now have in

---

1. Plutarch. *De Alexandri Fortuna,* 1, 6; Philo, *De Josepho,* VI, 28-31; Seneca, *De Otio,* IV (31); compare Marcus Aurelius, *Meditations,* VI, 44
2. Epictetus, *Dissertationes,* II, 1: 27; IV, 1: 1-5 and 89; compare Dio Chrysostom, *Orationes,* XIV, 18 and XV; 29-30
3. Especially by Musonius Rufus, *Fragments,* III-IV

common has been given freely and fully as a gift to all who have shared in it.

So, for example, an individual's *national identity* or heritage gives no advantage here. 'God shows no partiality' at this point, says Paul. Since 'all have fallen short' of his ideals, 'no distinction' can be made between people on grounds of this sort (e.g. Rom. 3: 22b-23). The fact that some belong to a nation with a higher religious tradition than others, e.g. the Jewish nation (vv. 1-2a; 9: 4-5), is of no account here. At the level of their response to the gospel message 'there is no distinction between Jew and Greek', for 'everyone' who declares his allegiance to Christ will be accepted by him.[4] In fact non-Jews who follow this course are said to inherit all that the Jews have in the past received. They have been grafted in, says Paul, to the Jewish olive tree (11: 17ff.). They can claim Abraham as their ancestor and have become heirs of all that was promised to him (Gal. 3: 29; Rom. 4: 16-17). Their introduction to the Christian community also bypasses national differences. 'By one Spirit we were all baptized into one body — whether Jews or Greeks . . . — and all were made to drink of the one Spirit' (1 Cor. 12: 13). Membership in the community takes note only of an individual's identity in Christ, not his nationality (2 Cor. 5: 16; Gal. 3: 11), and through the Spirit this is equally shared by all who turn to him.

The same principle applies to an individual's *social position*. In these matters 'there is . . . neither slave nor free', says Paul, 'for you are all one in Christ Jesus' (Gal. 3: 28), all recipients of the one Spirit (1 Cor. 12: 3) and consequently all members of the one community (Col. 3: 11). In a sense there has been a reversal of conditions, for 'he who was called as a slave is a freed man in the Lord, while he who was free when he was called is a slave of Christ' (1 Cor. 7: 22). In fact the free are to regard the slave 'no longer as a slave, but more than a slave, as a beloved brother . . . both in the flesh and in the Lord',[5] i.e. not only as a Christian but as a man, not only in the religious sphere but at the level of everyday social interaction as well. This principle also relates to such other indicators of social prestige as intellectual ability, political authority or aristocratic rank. Though some people in the community possessed advantages of this kind, such did not place them in any privileged position vis-à-vis God (1 Cor. 1: 26-29). According to Paul, God's action in Christ is the real expression and criterion of wisdom, power and dignity (as opposed to the

4. Rom. 10: 12-13; compare Rom. 2: 11
5. Philem. 16; compare Col. 4: 9

way in which these are evaluated by the world and their possessors accorded prominence in it) (v. 30). Rather than thinking in
terms of such distinctions, members of the community should
recognize that they are all simply 'brethren' (v. 26, 2: 1 et al).
Intellectual, political or familial status are irrelevant so far as
one's membership in the community is concerned.

This same principle also operates in the area of *sexual differentiation*. Regarding entry into the community 'there is neither male
nor female; for you are all one in Christ Jesus' (Gal. 3: 28). If, as
is most likely the case, this phrase recalls the very similar wording
in Genesis 1: 27, it forms a climax to what precedes it. In this case
Paul is arguing that in Christ not only the conventional distinctions of religious allegiance or social rank are banished, but even
the primeval distinction of sex has ceased to be relevant. Does this
have any implications for the homosexual/heterosexual distinction that exists between people? Though Paul does not discuss this
issue in the kind of context we are considering here, it would seem
that a homosexual background was no bar to membership in the
church or ground for being regarded in a different light to others
(1 Cor. 6: 9-11). His remarks elsewhere indicate that he would
not have tolerated continuing homosexual relations on the part of
such a person (Rom. 1: 26-27). But then he does not tolerate
'adulterers . . . the greedy, nor drunkards, nor revilers' in the
community either.[6]

(c)   Comparisons with other religious groups

So concerning their ground of membership in the community all
are in the same position. We have an advance here upon contemporary attitudes in Judaism. Only by becoming a full citizen
could a non-Jew find entry into Jewish religious groups. Even the
synagogue with its open-door policy to Gentiles who embraced
monotheism and the commandments but were unwilling to
become circumcised, regarded Gentiles only as second order
members of their assemblies.[7] The mystery-cults were more
flexible here and generally became quite cosmopolitan in
membership once transplanted to foreign soil.

What about slavery? While slavery was nowhere as common
among the Jews as elsewhere, the more wealthy and politically influential members of the population practised it[8] and even Jewish
subjects could for a period not exceeding six years undergo

6. 1 Cor. 6: 9-10; compare Rom. 1: 29-32
7. Acts 10: 28; compare 10: 22
8. R. Sh. 1: 7; Josephus, *The Antiquities of the Jews*, XX, 205 and 207

slavery as a way of paying off their debts.[9] But most slaves were aliens and, so that their masters could associate with them without infringing the law, soon became Jewish citizens. In fact their religious obligations were the subject of special legislation, particularly in the Temple.[10] The mystery-cults appealed strongly to slaves and freedmen and welcomed them openly. But these people remained a minority in such religious associations and the cost of initiation procedures prohibited many from being fully involved in them. Still, for members of this disadvantaged group in society, they provided a less class-conscious group with which to identify. (It should not be forgotten that due to the increasing number of slaves born within households during this period, many were treated as members of the family and could sometimes rise to positions of considerable responsibility. On the whole they expected to be manumitted at a relatively early age in life.)

Within both Jewish and Graeco-Roman religion, women generally possessed a secondary importance in comparison with men. Among the Jews this was mirrored in the fact that, though women and daughters were included within the covenant, the basic rite of circumcision was something that only males could undergo.[11] While it may not necessarily reflect first-century attitudes, this estimate lingers on in the later rabbinic prayer, recommended for daily use: 'Blessed be God who has not made me . . . a woman'.[12] While the integration of elements from the mystery-cults in classical Greek religion, and the later wholesale importation of the cults themselves as rivals to the traditional religions, gave women a more recognized position, the records we possess nowhere contain so explicit a declaration as that in Galatians 3: 28: 'There is neither Jew nor Greek, there is neither slave nor free, there is *neither male nor female,* for you are all one in Christ Jesus'. Among the Cynic philosophers, we do find a corresponding insistence upon equality — of race, birth and sex — but their lack of interest in community meant that this was viewed too much in individualistic terms.[13]

With this saying of Paul, national, social and sexual distinctions that still partially separated individuals within the ancient world were cancelled. Fellowship with God and with one another was no longer to be limited by these things. But recognition of this should not lead us into a false impression of what he is asserting.

9. Josephus, *Ant.* IV, 273 and XVI. 3; compare Ex. 21: 2; Dt. 15: 12
10. Ber. 3: 3: Pes. 8: 2 and see B.M. 1: 5: Arak. 8. 4ff,: M.Sh. 4: 4
11. Compare Gen. 17; 10ff. et al.
12. T. Ber. 7, 18, 16
13. E.g. Diogenes Laertius, vi, 72

Paul's stress is not so much upon the *equality* of Jews and Greeks, free and slave, and men and women with one another as upon their *unity* in Christ. (The same emphasis can be found in the similar statements in Colossians 3: 11, though this does not include reference to the overcoming of sexual distinctions.[14]) This is an important point to grasp. While Paul's remarks imply that at the level of their relationship with Christ all so to speak are on an equal footing, the emphasis lies on their integration into Christ, not the new status disadvantaged groups have acquired vis-à-vis others. Also, Paul's remarks do not imply that differences between groups disappear as a result of what has now happened. As his comments elsewhere indicate,[15] even within the new community forged by Christ, Jews and Greeks continue to exist alongside one another as Jews and Greeks, as do slaves and free, men and women. He does not deny the continuing legitimacy of national, social and sexual differences — Paul is no advocate of a universal, classless and unisexual society — he merely affirms that these differences do not affect one's relationship with Christ and membership in the community. There is an egalitarian strain in Paul's pronouncement, but it is secondary. He is more interested in the unity the gospel brings than in its equality, and in this unity diversity is preserved rather than some uniformity created.

THE REDIRECTION OF RACIAL, CLASS
AND SEXUAL DISTINCTIONS

This diversity can be demonstrated by considering ways in which the differences between each of these groups continued to play some part in the life of Paul's communities.

(a)   Jews and Gentiles in the communities

Most of them contained a reasonable proportion of Jews. As long as Paul's preaching in the cities began in the synagogue, this was bound to be the case, though God-fearers probably responded more freely to his message and formed the numerical base of his churches. In some places, such as Philippi, a Gentile Christian community seems to have existed from the start, but this was the exception.[16] Although, as we have seen, the Jews possessed no

---

14. See also Eph. 2: 11ff.
15. Rom. 16: 3ff.; 1 Cor. 1: 14 and 16: 15; Col. 4: 10, 11; Acts 13: 43, 14: 1, 16: 1, 17: 4 and 12, 18: 2 and 8, 19: 9
16. Acts 16: 11-40 and see too Acts 18: 4

special advantage so far as their acceptance into the Christian community was concerned, Paul can speak of their being favoured over others by virtue of their divine education in God's historical programme for mankind's salvation.[17] In this respect Paul does not view the Christian community, with its predominantly Gentile membership, as altogether replacing Israel in God's purposes. In the first place it is only because they have been 'grafted on' to the Jewish olive tree that they can share in them at all (Rom. 11: 17). And though they have temporarily become the locus of God's saving work in the world, he still reserves a future role for Israel.[18] Even in the present, converted Jews play a prominent part in communicating the message of Christ, not only to other Jews but non-Jews as well (Rom. 11). All this lends weight to the suggestion that within the newly-found Christian communities themselves Jewish converts, because of their knowledge of the Old Testament, had an important teaching function in the initial stages of church life.

In a more general way differences also emerged between Jewish and Gentile Christians within Paul's communities. As a result of their distinct religious and cultural backgrounds, converted Jews and Gentiles tended to carry over into their new way of life patterns of behaviour from their past. Jews in particular, in the Dispersion as well as in Jerusalem, continued to adhere to certain revered customs of their people, such as observance of the sabbath day and abstinence from particular kinds of food and drink. The distinction Paul draws between the 'strong' and the 'weak' in Romans probably reflects this difference in life-style (chs. 14-15). There he distinguishes between 'one who believes he may eat anything' and 'esteems all days alike' and the other who 'eats only vegetables' and 'esteems one day as better than another'. This is not to say that some Jews did not win through to a freer attitude on such matters or that on occasions Gentiles did not maintain habits that would have been adopted by them when they were attached to the synagogue. The distinction between 'strong' and 'weak' does not in all respects correspond to that between 'Gentile' and 'Jewish' Christians, but there must have been a considerable overlap between the two.

Rather than agitating for a consensus on these questions and a uniformity in behaviour among his readers, Paul allows such cultural differences to co-exist within his communities provided each person acts with integrity before God and does not put pressure

17. Rom. 9: 4-5 and 11: 28-29
18. Rom. 11: 11-15, 25-27 and 30-32

upon others to adopt his ways (14: 20-23). The 'strong' — among whom Paul counts himself — have to be particularly sensitive here (15: 1). But when Jewish Christians turn what is a matter of lifestyle into a criterion of salvation by insisting that circumcision and observance of the Law are obligatory for Gentiles, the time for mutual toleration is past and the legalists must be shown the error of their ways.[19] Or, to take another example, when the pursuit of different life-styles prevents Jewish and Gentile believers from sharing a common meal together, a trap into which both Peter and Barnabas had fallen at Antioch, hard words must be spoken in order to restore the breach of community that has occurred (Gal. 2: 11-16). Here 'weakness' has turned into harshness, vulnerability into self-righteousness, and to such 'Pharisaism' one must not yield. By the same token, when Gentile Christians flaunt their freedom before weaker, more vulnerable brethren, whether Jewish Christian or sensitive Gentile converts, so that their faith is put at risk, then a voluntary foregoing of their freedom must take place (1 Cor. 8: 7-13). If no 'weaker' person is in view however, the 'stronger' may pursue his own convictions to whatever practical conclusion they might have (1 Cor. 10: 23-30). In all this the basic principle is one of 'peace' among and 'acceptance' of one another despite their differences.[20]

(b)   The socially eminent and socially disadvantaged in the communities

Although distinctions were not to be made within the community on grounds of intellectual, political, social (or commercial) prestige, Paul's writings suggest that the advantages possessed by people in such positions often led to their making a contribution to the community which others, because they lacked these advantages, could not make. Acts attests the presence of such people in many places Paul visited.[21] Even at Corinth where 'there were not many . . . wise according to worldly standards, not many . . . powerful, not many . . . of noble birth' (1 Cor. 1: 26), a significant number of people in the church came from the more respected levels of society. No fewer than eight or nine people named in the letters to the community were members of the wealthier class, as hints about their occupation, dependents and/or possessions demonstrate. Stephanas, Crispus, Gaius, Erastus, Aquila, Priscilla, Titius Justus, Phoebe and perhaps

19. Gal. 1: 6-8. 4: 8-10, 5 1, 2 and 6: 12-15
20. Rom. 15: 7; compare 14: 17
21. Acts 16: 14, 17: 4, 12 and 34, 18: 7

Sosthenes all come into this category.[22] What is more, these are clearly the most prominent figures in the congregation. Gaius, for example, acted as 'host to the whole church', i.e. extended hospitality towards it and placed his premises at its disposal for such larger gatherings as it required, and also accommodated visiting apostles or their delegates (perhaps for months at a time) while they worked among churches in the vicinity.

Most probably this would have occurred at the 'house church' level as well. Given the cramped quarters in which many people lived, for example the tenement dwellers in Rome, and the subordinate position of slaves who may sometimes have formed a considerable proportion of the church — it has been estimated that approximately one third of the population in Corinth at this time were slaves — the owners of homes naturally became the focus around which church developed. Aquila and Priscilla, and also Lydia, all engaged in commerce and trade, illustrate this principle at work. Other men and women of their position also probably featured amongst those who were able to give substantial financial help to those in need. So differentiations of a social kind were not treated as if they did not exist; nor were they subjected to an indiscriminate levelling process. Social privileges, no longer a mark of *distinction between* members of the community, could become an occasion for *service to* them.

We have seen that a basic unity also existed within the community at the sexual level. But here too Paul envisages women functioning in some respects differently from men. Due to the greater volume of evidence, the divergences in its interpretation, not to speak of the wide contemporary interest in this question, we must go into it in more detail. The next chapter has been reserved for that purpose.

22. 1 Cor. 1: 14-16 and 16: 15-17; Rom. 16: 1, 2 and 23: Acts 18: 2-3, 6-8 and 17 (?)

CHAPTER TWELVE

The contribution of women in church

What part did women play in Paul's churches? This question is customarily answered by reference to those passages in his writings where the activities of women in church come in for explicit comment. In order to see these in proper perspective we need to look first at other details in Paul's letters that throw indirect light on the issue. These are all too often overlooked and yet they provide the necessary framework within which his more specific remarks should be considered.

WOMEN AS FULL MEMBERS OF THE CHRISTIAN COMMUNITY

We begin with the fact that Paul addresses his letters to all the members of the communities to which he was writing, not just to the men alone. This includes those sections where he deals with the conduct of the churches' affairs. For example, in response to situations that had developed at Corinth, Paul outlines his views on the ordering of their meetings (1 Cor. chapters 12-14), arranging of their meals (ch. 10-11), settling of their disputes (ch. 5-6), and so on, simply directing his remarks to all 'the brethren'[1] rather than to any one person or group within the church. Use of this term does not mean that Paul speaks here to the male members of the church only, for in his writings this term embraces 'the

---

1. 1 Cor. 11: 33, 12: 1, 14: 6, 20, 26 and 39; compare 5: 11

sisters' as well. Compare the proximity of the term 'brethren' to such comments as 'When you are assembled . . . ' (i.e. as a church — 5: 4), 'When you come together . . .' (compare in the following verse, 'When you come together as a church' — 11: 27), and, 'If, therefore, the whole church assembles . . .' (14: 23). He confirms this by the use of such other terms as 'all',[2] 'whoever' (11: 27), 'everyone' (12: 6), 'anyone'[3] and 'each one'.[4] So women as well as men not only participate in these aspects of the community's life but can contribute to the good order and well-being of its gatherings. (For this reason, among others, it is unfortunate that the RSV inserts the word 'men' in its translation of these passages where there is no basis in the Greek,[5] or where the word *anthrōpos* is used generically — 11: 28; 14: 2-3).

In his explicit remarks on the contribution of women in church, Paul underscores both their freedom to do so at a number of levels and also certain restrictions placed upon them. It is not always clear which kind of women Paul has in mind, i.e. whether married, single or women generally. The usual Greek terms for 'men' and 'women', *anēr* and *gunē,* serve also for 'husband' and 'wife'. Only the context can determine in which sense these words are being used. We begin with Paul's advice in 1 Corinthians 11 where it is wives and husbands who seem to be primarily in view (11: 3), though women and men in general are also present in the background.[6] His opening comments indicate that women normally prayed and prophesied in the gatherings at Corinth (11 :5) and his closing reference to the practice of other churches suggests that this was the custom elsewhere as well (v. 16). (Though in that verse he primarily discusses the way in which women should appear in church, we have independent evidence that Paul moved amongst other churches in which women prophesied, e.g. Acts 21: 19). His mention of female prophets is most significant for, as we have seen, Paul believed that prophecy was the most important activity that could take place in church.[7] This ministry of sharing a direct word from God with others had precedence over the activity of the teacher. (The reversal of this order throughout the succeeding history of Christianity, or the conviction that prophecy no longer occurs, have obscured the

2. 1 Cor. 10: 17, 12: 26, 14: 5, 18, 23, 24 and 31
3. 1 Cor. 11: 29 and 34, 14: 9, 16, 27 and 37-38
4. 1 Cor. 11: 21, 12: 7, 11 and 18, 14: 26
5. 1 Cor. 5: 9, 10: 15, 11: 33, 14: 21, 16: 16 and 18
6. Compare 1 Cor. 11: 8-9 and 11-12
7. 1 Cor. 14: 1-5, 20-25, 30, 31 and 39, 40; compare 1 Thess. 5: 19-20; 1 Cor. 12: 28; Rom. 12: 6; Eph. 4: 11; Acts 13: 1 and 15: 32

significance of Paul's remarks here.) Since for him women have as
much freedom to participate in this as men, Paul would presumably agree with Luke's view that Joel's prophecy had now become
a reality: 'In the last days it shall be, God declares, that I will
pour out my Spirit upon all flesh, and your sons and your
daughters shall prophesy . . . yes, and on my menservants and
maidservants in those days I will pour out my Spirit; and they
shall prophesy.'[8]

RESTRICTIONS PLACED UPON WOMEN BY PAUL

(a)   *Concerning dress*

In spite of this freedom Paul argues that certain restrictions apply
to the way in which women appear in church. He talks about the
length of hair that women should have. The wearing of veils is
probably not an issue here. With the exception of one verse
(1 Cor. 11: 10) where the word translated 'veil' in the RSV is, as
the marginal note indicates, the Greek term for 'authority', Paul
throughout uses a word which simply means a 'covering'. The type
of 'covering' is not described in the early part of the passage but
later we are told explicitly that a woman's hair is given her for
a 'covering' (v. 15). But in this matter he does not lay an obligation only upon the women. When he required the women to wear
their hair at a certain length in church, i.e. long, he also required
the men to wear theirs at an appropriate length as well, i.e. short.
This appears to be in keeping with the custom in Paul's time, as
his own remarks suggest (v. 14). Presumably at Corinth women
in the church were tending to disregard this custom, perhaps as
part of a wider movement towards liberation in their recently re-
constituted and highly mobile city, perhaps as a consequence of
their experience of freedom in Christ, or both.

(b)   *Within marriage*

Certainly the wife's appearance marks her subordination to her
husband: 'For a man ought not to cover his head, since he is the
image and glory of God; but woman is the glory of man' (v. 7).
Yet in some sense it also signifies her own 'authority' (v. 10), even
if we cannot be sure exactly what Paul intended to cover by this
word (or what he understood by his accompanying words to the
effect that it is 'because of the angels' that the wife must so

8. Acts 2: 17, 18; compare Joel 2: 28, 29

appear.) So the wife has a legitimate sphere of authority alongside her husband, perhaps the right to have a ministry in church, even though she also stands under his authority.

Paul's argument for wifely subordination stems from his interpretation of the Genesis narratives. From them he draws the conclusions that man is the source of the woman (which is why though both are stamped with the image of God, man reflects the 'glory' of God while woman reflects the 'glory' of her husband) and that woman was made for man (vv. 8, 9). But to prevent the male members of his audience gaining a false sense of their own importance, Paul immediately qualifies these remarks by adding that 'in the Lord woman is not independent of man *nor man of woman;* for as woman was made from man *so now man is born from woman*'. Most important of all to remember is the fact that 'All things are *from God'* (vv. 11, 12). That is why, at the commencement of this whole passage, he can pronounce that 'the head of every husband is Christ, the head of a wife is her husband, and the head of Christ is God' (v. 3), playing on the dual sense of the term 'head' in Greek which can mean both 'source' and 'preeminence'. Supporting arguments for the way in which women (and men) should appear in church are also drawn from nature (v. 14), custom (v. 14) and church practice (v. 16). It is tempting at this point, as at the end of the following paragraph, to enquire into the legitimacy of the reasons given by Paul for his position on this subject. The question of interpretation or hermeneutics, becomes very pressing here but, as throughout this treatment of Paul's view of community, we cannot pursue it now. Yet it would not be out of place to observe that there are three kinds of arguments employed by Paul, only one of which has a fundamental significance: the argument from church practice is dependent on the other two and cannot stand without them; the arguments from nature and custom are in fact one (since Paul assumes that current practice exhibits a natural state of affairs) and depend on customs of dress or appearance remaining the same; the 'argument' from christology is in fact an analogy consequent upon the basic justification from the Genesis narratives, the continuing force of which depends upon one's estimate of the historical way in which Paul reads them.

(c) *During church*

At first sight, Paul's endorsement of women praying and prophesying in church seems to conflict with his later statement that 'the women should keep silence' in the gatherings (14: 34). Attempts to overrule his earlier endorsement by this statement, or to elide these verses from the text, should both be avoided. There is no justification for the first and scarcely any manuscript support for the second, while an appreciation of the wider and immediate context of Paul's advice renders such solutions unnecessary. The injunction is the third in a series (vv. 20ff.), all of which are directed against the existence of chaos in church, first through all speaking in tongues together and secondly through all jointly prophesying. The precise nature of the women's (more strictly wives') offence becomes clear in the following verse: 'If there is anything they desire to know', he says, 'let them ask husbands at home' (v. 35). The wives have been interrupting the meeting with questions about things said within it. If more than that were involved why does Paul single out this one problem without any reference to others? The injunction to 'keep silence' does not itself necessarily possess an absolute sense and must always be interpreted by the context in which it occurs. The situation presupposed by Paul's remarks is perfectly understandable. Women for the most part did not receive any substantial education in religious matters, yet in Christian gatherings they could not only be present throughout the whole meeting but also contribute in a number of ways to it. Particularly in a church like that at Corinth, where Christian liberty was prized so highly, it comes as no surprise that wives felt free to query things they did not understand as meetings were in progress. In ruling against this, Paul reminds them again of its contravention of prevailing custom (v. 35) — after all in Greek cities it was only the *hetairai*, courtesans, who engaged in public discussions with men — and of the practice of other churches (v. 36) and even of the Old Testament (v. 34).

PROMINENCE ACCORDED TO WOMEN BY PAUL

At this point we can return to the mention of Phoebe in Romans 16: 1. Paul there describes her as a *diakonos,* deacon (the RSV translation is misleading since it suggests our distinction between deacons and deaconesses existed then). The term *prostatis* (generally translated 'helper') in the following verse may explain what this means. While it could, as we will see, refer to her involvement in Paul's mission as a patroness, it has been pointed out that cognate terms from the same root are used elsewhere to describe the activities of those who exercise important functions in the churches. This could suggest that Phoebe was engaged in 'teaching' and 'leading' in her local church at Cenchreae.

Paul's statements elsewhere imply that women had some share in teaching and exhorting in his communities. In the first place, if Paul permitted women to prophesy in his churches, and considered prophecy as more important than teaching, why should participation in the latter be denied them? It could be argued that their lack of sufficient education in the Old Testament makes it improbable that they did. This would certainly help to explain the apparent absence of references to such, though note in Acts the case of Priscilla in her home (Acts 18: 26), but if so it means that a cultural circumstance, not a theological principle, lay behind this state of affairs. Secondly, in other passages Paul envisages that all 'God's chosen ones' should not only be full of the Spirit in their behaviour but also 'let the word of God dwell in (them) richly, as (they) teach and admonish one another in all wisdom, and as (they) sing psalms and hymns and spiritual songs with thankfulness in (their) hearts to God' (e.g. Col. 3: 16). Paul probably has in mind here the informal teaching and exhorting of one another that went on throughout the Christian meetings rather than some formal exhortatory address. However this does suggest that women as well as men, and women who were not necessarily deacons as well as those who were, were involved in these activities. Since these two activities are the basic elements in 'pastoral' ministry, this indicates that for Paul all Christians to some extent function in these ways.

Paul may even refer to women involved in this work at the fullest level. 'The household of Stephanas', which the Corinthians were to respect and recognize, almost certainly included women as well as men and both may be the object of his remarks (1 Cor. 16: 15). He also mentions 'Nympha, and the church in her house' (Col. 4: 15). If, as seems most natural, Nympha was a relatively wealthy woman who, like Gaius at Corinth, acted as host to a local group of believers, it seems unlikely that she, presumably a widow who conducted her family, managed her slaves and welcomed her friends all week, would take an insignificant part in the proceedings in favour of socially inferior male members who were present. To do that would be socially unacceptable whereas, in the absence of a husband, it would be perfectly legitimate in the eyes of others for her to behave in home and church *as her husband would have done* if present. Most probably male heads of other households also belonged to this church and had an influential role in its activities but, given her position, Nympha would have functioned alongside them in similar sorts of ways, not in a subordinate capacity. This acts as a reminder that Paul generally talks about the relation of wives to husbands: where no husband is in view, quite different arrangements become possible.

THE POSITION OF MINORITY GROUPS
IN OTHER RELIGIOUS COMMUNITIES

Once again we need to look at the wider social environment in which all this was taking place. The degree of involvement of people from different national backgrounds in religious associations has already been noted. While participation by Gentile god-fearers in the synagogue was limited, the fact that such people were occasionally their principal benefactors (e.g. Luke 7: 5) led to their grateful recognition by full members. But this was merely a formal honour, though certainly one to which some prestige was attached and for whose services appreciation was given. In the mystery cults a more flexible situation existed. While the initial impetus for their spread in foreign countries generally came from citizens from their land of origin, e.g. soldiers, tradesmen and people involved in commerce, over a period of time the dominant positions in the cult passed into the hands of local supporters.

We do not know a great deal about the activities of slaves in religious associations during this period. Since along with women and minors, they were not obliged to observe all the requirements in the Law,[9] their involvement in the synagogue may have been circumscribed in some ways as well. This probably did not affect their participation in its prayer or, if the slaves were men, the synagogue's instruction but would most likely have prevented them from holding any of the offices associated with it. In the mystery religions, slaves initiated into the mysteries became priests of the cult alongside their social betters. But it does not appear that the higher priestly grades were open to them and the expenses involved in becoming even an initiate must have hindered many from proceeding even this far.[10]

Unfortunately little is known for certain about the position of women in the synagogue at this time.[11] Practice was almost certainly less rigid than the later records suggest. According to these women and girls sat separately from their menfolk and were only permitted to be present during the liturgical part of the service. The second part of the service involved instruction in the Law and

---

9. Ber. 3: 3; Sukk. 2: 1 and 8
10. Apuleius, *Metamorphoses*, XI, 17, 23 and 27-28
11. But see Philo, *De Specialibus Legibus*, III, 171; *De Vita Contemplativa*, 69; Josephus, *The Antiquities of the Jews*, XIV, 260-261

this they were not allowed to receive. As a result women could not teach in the synagogue, though before the Fall of Jerusalem they could be asked to read the Torah. In later times they continued to be called but it was customary for them not to respond. A synagogue itself could be only constituted by ten Jewish males coming together: women did not count for this purpose, no matter how many.[12] In the Diaspora, by reason of surrounding influences, women later played a more prominent part in certain aspects of synagogue life, even formally occupying the position of *archisunagōgos.*

Qumran of course was virtually a male society though, unlike Essene groups generally, women do seem to have existed on the margins of its community life.[13] Outside Judaism the rites and experiences at the heart of the mystery religions, along with the kinds of rewards which they promised to their adherents, led to their possessing a strong and widespread attraction to women, especially among the middle and, later, upper classes. At least in the cult of Isis, when she began to dominate her consort Serapis, women took part fully in the various ceremonies that were at the core of their activities.[14] They also became priestesses on their in-itiation, and occasionally rose to considerable prominence within the cult. Even so, if the cult of Isis is any guide, the proportion of men involved in the cult continued to exceed that of women — though in Athens and Rome female devotees may have comprised about half the membership — and the very highest positions within it were uniformly reserved for them. On the other hand, in more private, family, mystery cults women do appear at times as priestess-leaders.

CONCLUSION

So while the position of foreigners, slaves and women in Paul's communities generally went beyond that which they possessed in Judaism, it converged more closely with their situation in the Hellenistic mystery cults. There too the distinctions between such groups and their more privileged counterparts were in the process of being transformed, though they do not seem to have articulated this in as principled a way as Paul. Also, since participation in the cult was pre-eminently an individualistic affair, the impact of this new state of affairs on the personal relationships of members of

12. Meg. 4: 3
13. CDC 7: 6-9, 14: 16 and 16: 10
14. Apuleius, *Met.,* XI, 6ff.

the cult could not have been as marked as in the early Christian communities. But we have seen that, for all his insistence upon equality at one level within the community, Paul does recognize the legitimacy of continuing national, social and sexual differences at other levels of its operation. This creates genuine diversities within the community. Although these differences do not give rise to *formal demarcations* between its members and the granting of special powers to some at the expense of others, they provide a springboard for *helpful service* within the community from which all may benefit. So equality of religious status, which in any case should be subordinated to the new unity all experience with one another, does not rule out the possibility of functional diversities within the community. This principle has further ramifications which we must now go on to explore.

CHAPTER THIRTEEN

Participation and its responsibilities

Paul's approach to community partly abolished and partly preserved distinctions that divided people in the ancient world during
his time. Yet what it preserved was also *transformed*. Distinctions
were no longer to be the means by which some maintained an
advantage over others, but instead be the means by which some
had the opportunity to serve others. We can now go on to see
whether the new gifts individuals received, and the new
responsibilities they undertook, introduced a *different* set of distinctions into the community which once again separated people
on the grounds of privilege or status.

To answer this we must first discover whether any of the traditional religious distinctions maintained a place within Paul's
churches. Do we find here a persistence of distinctions between
priesthood and laity, between officials and ordinary members,
between holy men and common people, or not? In considering
these we will look briefly at each in turn, even though in many
cases these three categories coalesced in the one person or group,
i.e. were different aspects of the one set of arrangements rather
than alternative ways in which personnel were distinguished.

PAUL'S DISSOLUTION OF TRADITIONAL DISTINCTIONS

(a)   Between priests and laity

We begin with one of the most noticeable features of Paul's writings, *viz* the absence of the term *hiereus*, priest, a strange phenomenon from the standpoint of contemporary religious practice. A religious community without a priest! Certainly the term *leitourgia*, priestly-service, or one of its cognates does occur, though only seven times in all. But each time Paul uses it in a quite non-cultic sense, e.g. the service rendered to God by the apostolic preaching of the gospel (Rom. 15: 16) and the commitment of faith which arises out of it (Phil. 2: 17); the service rendered to others by sharing fellowship with those who are lacking it (Phil. 2: 25 and 30) and giving financial aid to those in need (Rom. 15: 27; 2 Cor. 9: 12); and the service rendered to society at large by the Roman political authorities in the exercise of their power (Rom. 13: 6).

We also find the term *latreia*, worship, (and verb *latreuein*). In the Septuagint this refers to not merely religious, but specifically ceremonial actions. Paul employs it himself in this way of both Jewish (9: 4) and Gentile (1: 25) worship (compare his use of *thrēskeia* only of heretical worship) (Col. 2: 18). His application of the word to the Christian community describes the dedication of its members to God and to Christ in the Spirit (Phil. 3: 3), as well as the total life-service of both the individual (Rom. 1: 9 and 15: 16) and the whole fellowship (12: 1). He also employs such other terms as *prosphora*, priestly-offering,[1] *thusia*, sacrifice,[2] *aparchē*, firstfruits (compare *prosagōgē*, access),[3] but here too the offerings are decidedly non-cultic in character. Those who present them are Christians in general, not a selective group among them.

So, although Paul uses the language of priesthood, priestly service and priestly cult, he never refers to a particular caste, activity or object of a sacral kind. Instead, the individual believer, the community as a whole or the secular authorities are 'priests' in his sense. Religious commitment, charitable actions and apostolic vocation are all 'priestly functions'. Faith, love and the total dedication of one's life are for him the 'priestly actions' that God now requires to be performed. This means that within the church distinctions between priest and layman, mediatorial and common service, cultic ritual and secular activity do not and cannot exist.

1. Rom. 15: 16; compare Eph. 5: 2
2. Rom. 12: 1; Phil. 2: 17 and 4: 18; compare Eph. 5: 2
3. 2 Thess. 2: 13; 1 Cor. 16: 15; Rom. 16: 5 (see also Rom. 8: 23) and Rom. 5: 2; Eph. 2: 18b and 3: 12

Confirmation of this comes from another quarter. For Paul not only transfers sacred language from its cultic domain to the sphere of everyday life, but also utilizes ordinary terms to describe the basic features of church life. We have already come across several examples of this and now we can draw them together. We have seen that Paul describes the actual coming together of Christians by such terms as *sunerchomai* and employs the word *ekklēsia* for the assembly that results. He characterizes the members who belong to it by use of the terms *oikeioi* and *sōma* and refers to its central activities by means of the words *charisma* and *deipnon*. While terms like *sōma* and *ekklēsia* very occasionally turn up in cultic contexts outside the New Testament,[4] all these words are essentially non-cultic terms. Even when they do occur in connection with a cult society, they do not necessarily have cultic significance themselves, e.g. *ekklēsia* appears two or three times in inscriptions simply because a word is needed to refer to the fact of meeting. And Philo's use of *charisma* to refer to God's gifts in creation, which in any case would not have been known to Paul, does not mean that the word had an inherently religious meaning: the few occasions where it turns up in the papyri suggest otherwise. Although *deipnon* does here and there signify a cultic meal, Paul's discussion of the Lord's Supper shows that he certainly did not use the term in that way. So alongside Paul's non-cultic application of specifically religious terms, we find that everyday words are consistently called in to express the fundamental aspects of church life. This dramatically highlights his refusal to work with the usual sacred/secular dichotomy.

The metaphorical use of cultic language sometimes occurs in the later prophetic books of the Old Testament[5] and in intertestamental Judaism[6] but, apart from certain anticultic tendencies in Hellenistic Judaism and partially Qumran, it is never associated with a rejection in principle of the cult.[7] But in Paul official priesthood, which exists to mediate between God and man, is shared by the whole community and never by any one member or group as distinct from others. Here we have a common priesthood, with no distinction between clergy and laity.

To a large extent Pharisaism and the synagogue anticipated this approach. The former was essentially a lay movement, and the latter were popular assemblies belonging to the local community and organized by it rather than by the priesthood. Yet

---

4. E.g. Josephus, *The Antiquities of the Jews*, XVIII, 73
5. E.g. Ps. 51: 17; Is. 58: 3ff.; Mic. 6: 6-8
6. E.g. Jud. 16: 16; Jub. 2: 22; Apoc. Mos. 33; Test. Levi 3
7. Dan. 3: 38-40 (LXX); 1 En. 45: 3; Arist., 170 and 234 and see IQS 9: 3-4

both sought to supplement the cultic life of the Temple, not replace it. Though it just may reflect post AD 70 practice, both also preserved a residual role for members of the priestly caste who associated with them. Among the ten men required to found a synagogue there had to be at least one priest. Some procedures within the synagogue required the priest's presence and validation, and certain prayers in the service were customarily reserved for them.[8]

Despite its broad membership, the priestly element is stronger at Qumran for, alongside its commitment to the Law, this group saw itself as the guardian of an alternative, if as yet (until the Temple fell into their hands in the coming Messianic war) incomplete cultic system. Priests were therefore essential to the conduct of its religious life and played a prominent part in its council, worship, admission procedure, common meals and disciplinary actions.[9] The various mystery cults were fundamentally, and hierarchically, sacral in character. A clear distinction was drawn between the initiates, who automatically became priests of the cult, and all those who had not yet been favoured by the god with a revelation of his mysteries. Between the initiates themselves there existed a graded series of priestly orders which one might ascend.[10]

Despite partial parallels with Pharisaism and the synagogue, Paul's abolition of the distinction between priest and people, sacred and profane, cult and ordinary service has no full precedent among his contemporaries. While it has a parallel in certain Stoic statements rejecting sacrifices (more often they are criticized for not springing from a moral intention), the 'spiritual' worship that replaces them is more an individual than communal affair.[11] While it has its basis in certain attitudes of Jesus, Paul was the first to give explicit expression to it and work out its communal implications in the most thoroughgoing fashion.

(b)   Between officials and ordinary members

Paul also rejects any formal distinction between official figures and ordinary members in the community. Had he wished to draw attention to the existence of offices as such, there were any

8. Meg. 4: 3 and 6
9. IQS 5: 2 and 21-24, 6: 2-5 and 8, 8: 1-4, 9: 6-7; compare IQS 1: 21, 2: 11 and 19-23, 7: 2-3; CDC 10: 4-6 and 14: 3-6
10. Apuleius, *Metamorphoses*, XI, 10, 12, 16-17 and 22; Plutarch, *Isis and Osiris*, 4ff.
11. Seneca, *Fragment* 123

number of Greek terms he could have used. However the title *archē* (compare *archōn* or *archēgos*), ruler, head or leader — often possessing in Greek a sense of legality or rank — never refers to individuals within the communities, but significantly only to Christ himself[12] or various subsidiary supernatural powers.[13] The term *timē,* which emphasizes dignity of office, and the term *telos,* which stresses the power inherent in such, are also absent from Paul's ecclesiastical vocabulary. Instead, as a general term for the service of individuals within the church, he uses almost uniformly throughout his writings the word *diakonia,* 'service', or one of its related forms. Paul chooses a word that is not only quite everyday in character, but also one never associated with a particular dignity or position. The word only occurs twice in the Septuagint and then in a quite general and secular sense.[14] In Philo and Josephus it refers to 'waiting at table' and 'serving' in general,[15] both meanings being present in ordinary Greek usage as well. In almost all cases it denotes an activity of an inferior kind, certainly one from which rights and privileges are absent, at least in the sense in which these are normally conceived. (Compare Plato's 'How can a man be happy when he has to serve someone?[16]) Paul can designate any service of any kind by any member of the community by the term, from the most insignificant to the most important. He uses it of the service rendered by apostolic delegates (Col. 4: 7; Eph. 6: 21), including himself;[17] more prominent figures within the church,[18] including women (Rom. 16: 1); any believer to his community (1 Cor. 12: 5; Eph. 4: 12) or to the members of another.[19]

Significant for understanding the meaning of *diakonia* is Paul's use of the word to describe the work of the Spirit and Christ (2 Cor. 3: 8; Rom. 15: 8). Its association with the Spirit confirms what has already been said about the Spirit's facilitating work within the community. This takes place neither by compulsion nor force. The use of *diakonia* to refer to Christ gives us an excellent illustration of the character of the word. Jesus himself had said that he did not come to be served but 'to serve and give his life as a ransom for many' (Mk. 10: 45). Paul elaborates upon this in a well-

12. Col. 1: 18 (compare Rom. 15: 12)
13. 1 Cor. 2: 6 and 8; Eph. 2: 2 and 6: 12
14. 1 Macc. 11: 58; Est. 6: 3
15. Philo, *De Vita Contemplativa,* 70; Josephus, *Ant.,* II, 65; XI, 163 and 166
16. Plato, *Gorgias,* 491e
17. 2 Cor. 4: 1, 6: 3ff., 11: 8 and 23; Rom. 11: 13
18. 1 Cor. 16: 15; Phil. 1: 1; Col. 1: 7 and 4: 17
19. 2 Cor. 8: 4 and 19-20, 9: 1 and 12-13; Rom. 15: 31

known passage (where, however, he uses the term *doulos,* slave, rather than *diakonos,* servant): 'Do nothing from selfishness or conceit, but in humility count others better than yourselves. Let each of you look not only to his own interests, but also to the interests of others. Have this mind among yourselves, which was in Christ Jesus, who, though he was in the form of God, did not count equality with God a thing to be grasped, but emptied himself, taking the form of a servant . . .' (Phil. 2: 3-7). Because of this service he rendered, and its continuation through the Spirit, he is the *archē* (Col. 1: 18) of the community. With his deliberate and consistent choice of this word, Paul rejects the idea of certain people in the community possessing formal rights and powers and the division within its ranks between officials and ordinary members.

This renunciation of offices, and of the titles and honours that belong to them, radically departs from first-century attitudes to religious organization. The synagogue had its officials, beginning with the *archisunagōgos* who has already been mentioned. Also there was the *hazzan* who was chiefly responsible for the conduct of public worship.[20] The reciting of the prayers and the announcing of the *Shema,* however, were functions not offices,[21] as were the reading of the Scriptures and the preaching of the homily (Lk. 4: 16-17; Acts 13: 15). Members of the congregation could fulfil these responsibilities in turn, though only when summoned to do so by the officers over them.

The Gospels also note the Pharisees occupying the chief seats in the synagogue (Matt. 23: 6). Distinct officials also existed at Qumran and among the Essenes. The *mebaqqerim,* or guardians, distributed in the community and throughout the camps, assessed candidates applying for membership,[22] received reports about transgressions that had occurred,[23] acted as the recipients and distributors of charitable gifts, and instructed those in their care in the maxims of the Law and the rules of the community.[24] Whether or not these were identical with the priests whose functions we have already noted is not altogether clear. In the mystery-cults also, various grades of officials were attached to local shrines and temples. These looked after the administrative and financial aspects of the cult's operations. Most probably those who held

20. Sot. 7: 7-8; Yom. 7: 1; compare Mt. 9: 18; Mk. 5: 35ff.; Lk. 4: 20, 8: 41, 49 and 13: 14; Acts 14: 15, 18: 8 and 17
21. Ber. 5: 5, R.Sh. 4: 9 and Tam. 5: 1
22. IQS 6: 13-14; CDC 13: 7-13
23. CDC 9: 16-20 and 14: 9-10
24. IQS 6: 19-20; CDC 14: 12-16

official positions were themselves priests who belonged to the higher orders of their sacral hierarchy.[25]

(c) Between holy men and common people

Paul also refuses to draw distinctions between members of the community according to the measure of 'holiness' they possess. The exclusion of any leading caste in the community of a priestly or official kind extends to a rejection of any spiritual aristocracy within it as well. For a start all genuine members of the community possess the Spirit. 'Through one Spirit' they were all introduced into it (1 Cor. 12: 13); 'in one Spirit' they all have equal access to God (Eph. 2: 18); 'from one Spirit' they all draw the same resources (1 Cor. 3: 18); 'by the (same) Spirit' all are to direct their lives (Gal. 5: 25). Since it is the same Spirit who dwells in them all, all share in the qualities of character that the Spirit produces (Gal. 5: 22-23) and all participate in the gifts of ministry that the Spirit distributes (1 Cor. 12: 4-11). All who belong to the community, therefore, are fundamentally 'spiritual'.

Paul's use of the terms *laos,* people, and *hagios,* holy, confirms this. Apart from its occurrence in Old Testament quotations[26] and in direct references to the Jewish nation (Rom. 11: 1-2), *laos* refers only to Christians as a whole, as those upon whom the promises of God concerning the creation of a 'people' of his own have fallen (2 Cor. 6: 6). Nowhere does the term refer to only part of the community, or in opposition to *klēros,* clergy. (It was only in the third century that the words for clergy and layman came into Christian usage.) Nor does any one member of the community, or group of members, possess a particular 'holiness' denied to others. Though, because of its Old Testament associations, Paul does sometimes use the plural of *hagios* with reference to the Jewish Christians in Jerusalem,[27] elsewhere all who are believers in a particular region or who are members of a particular community are specifically referred to as 'saints'.[28] In so describing them, Paul does not mean they possess or have received some inherent personal quality which sets them apart from others. In Old Testament terms he simply refers to their having been 'reserved' for, 'set aside' by, or 'dedicated' to God. Since all members of the

25. See footnote 10
26. 1 Cor. 10: 7 and 14: 21; Rom. 9: 25-26. 10: 21 and 15: 10
27. 1 Cor. 16: 1; 2 Cor. 8: 4, 9: 1 and 12; Rom. 15: 25-26; Eph. 2: 19
28. 1 Cor. 1: 2, 14: 33 and 16: 15; 2 Cor. 1: 2 and 13: 13; Rom. 1: 7, 16: 2 and 15; Phil. 1: 2 and 4: 22; Col. 1: 2, 3, 12 and 26, compare 3: 12; Eph. 1: 2, 15 and 18; 3: 18, 5: 3

community share equally in this, there cannot be different grades of holiness within the community.

As the presence of the Spirit was not a central theme among the Pharisees and the Essenes, little likelihood existed of figures within them who could claim superior charismatic status to others. Still, as we have seen, a small succession of charismatic rabbis emerged outside the main body of adherents in Jerusalem, especially in Galilee, and the Essenes had something of a name for their charismatic capacities, particularly with their prophetic prediction and interpretation of dreams. These apart, it does seem that grades of achievement existed within Pharisaism, while at Qumran the council of the community ranked its members according to their level of spiritual attainment and enforced strict rules concerning participation in the community.[29] In spite of this, there was a real participation by each person in the Qumran community since all 'eat in common, bless in common and deliberate in common', though only according to rank and under the supervision of a smaller group of the more senior members.[29]

In Hellenism, a different atmosphere prevailed. Holy men who practised divination and performed miracles, or those socially disadvantaged, but charismatically gifted, individuals who were employed by others to practise their gifts for gain, existed in many places (compare Acts 16: 16-18). There were also smaller groups who banded together into monastic societies and, like the Essenes on Jewish soil, became noted for their lonely and virtuous way of life. Though Paul's view of a community of 'saints' has something in common with such groups, and though within it some exercised extraordinary powers, he rejects the idea of isolation from the world or possession of unusual abilities as a mark of greater holiness. On the contrary, such detachment from worldly concerns and absorption in unusual phenomena can easily coexist with quite profane attitudes (1 Cor. 3: 1-3). He has a different and less elitist understanding of 'spirituality' and 'holiness'. So alien is the later Christian notion of 'the saint' to his thinking, that reference to the apostle now almost uniformly as Saint Paul is ironical indeed.

Paul therefore has no place in his view of community for the traditional distinctions between its members along cultic, official or religious lines. This clears the ground for a more positive appraisal of his approach to responsibility in the community. We must now investigate the extent to which his elevation of its mem-

29. IQS 6: 25-27 and 9: 12-16; Hag. 2: 5-6; Dem. 2: 2-3
30. IQS 6: 2 and 6-13

bers to an equally high status affects their involvement in practical matters. In order to do this we look first at where the responsibility lay for the organization of church, including the common meal, the care of members, discipline and the direction of the community, at the level of both understanding and activity.

PAUL'S EMPHASIS UPON CORPORATE RESPONSIBILITY

(a) For organization

In several places in his letters, and notably in 1 Corinthians, Paul talks about specific aspects of the church's meetings, clarifies the principles upon which decisions in this area should be based and gives concrete advice on the sorts of arrangements that follow from them. But nowhere does he address his remarks to a group of persons (or to any one person) who alone have responsibility for dealing with these affairs. This consistent and quite remarkable feature of his letters, so self-evident when one reads them that it is apt to be overlooked, has already been noted. He constantly reminds the whole community of its obligations in these matters and calls upon every member to deal with them in a proper fashion.[31] His letters are uniformly addressed to the local groups as a whole rather than to any authorities within them, and the expression 'brethren' is constantly on his lips — not least in places where organizational matters are being discussed. Clearly all who belong to the community share in the responsibility for the general conduct of its proceedings.

(b) For welfare

They were also all responsible for each other's welfare. This involves both self-examination on the part of individual members as well as alertness to the needs of others. They are all to 'bear one another's burdens', 'have the same care for one another', 'look not only to (their) own interests but also to the interests of others', 'encourage one another and to build one another up'.[32] Appeals of this kind occur repeatedly in Paul's letters and indicate how fundamental a theme this was for him.

(c) For discipline

He also lays responsibility for the discipline of offending members

31. E.g. 1 Cor. 11: 33-34a, 14: 39-40 and 16: 2-3
32. Gal. 5: 2; 1 Cor. 12: 25; Phil. 2: 4; 1 Thess. 5: 11

squarely at the feet of the remainder. When one of the members
has a legal grievance against another, and it cannot be settled at
the personal level, someone in the community should resolve the
issue, not an outsider (1 Cor. 6: 1-6). If one of the members suc-
cumbs unwittingly to a course of action harmful to himself, those
who have not fallen into it should 'restore him in a spirit of gentleness', looking to themselves, however, lest they 'too be tempted'
(Gal. 6: 1). When an action detrimentally affects the life of the
community, anyone aware of this should bring the matter to the
community's attention: however there must be at least two, if
possible three, involved so that it may be substantiated by more
than one witness.[33] Only if the defendant refuses to listen and
deliberately continues to disrupt the community are the members
to 'take note' of him and 'avoid him', especially at the communal
meal.[34] If the person turns his back on all that he has experienced,
more dramatic steps become necessary.[35] Where, as in 1 Corinthians 5, the error is repugnant even by pagan standards and the
offender remains unrepentant about his behaviour, the community as a whole should assemble together to consider the
matter, recognize the presence of evil amongst them and 'deliver
the person to Satan' as executor of God's chastisement (1 Cor. 5:
3-5). This strange expression could mean that they are to disown
him, i.e. completely withdraw from all contact. Or, on the
analogy of the Ananias and Sapphira incident in Acts 5, it could
signify their calling down a 'death sentence' upon him, i.e. a
prayer for judgement to take place. Either way, the object of this
extreme form of disciplinary action is the person's ultimate salvation. This (if 2 Corinthians 2 refers to the same case as 1
Corinthians 5) may lead to a more immediate change of attitude
on his part. Both nurture and discipline within the congregation
should then arise spontaneously from the concern of every member for the quality of its life and the involvement of every member
in decisions affecting the whole.

(d)   For growth

This leads on to a consideration of the way in which the community deepened its Christian commitment and determined its
future development. We have seen that gifts were distributed to
every member of the community by the Spirit, and that through
their mutual sharing these were exercised amongst them. Guid-

33. 2 Cor. 13: 1; compare 1 Cor. 1: 11
34. 2 Thess. 2: 14; 1 Cor. 5: 11
35. 1 Cor. 16: 22; Rom. 16: 17

ance on matters affecting the community's life was principally granted to members when they met together to discern what God required of them. They received this guidance from the Spirit as he built up their corporate understanding, through their exercise of gifts of knowledge, revelation, wisdom and so on. In all this Paul never tires of insisting that every member of the community has the responsibility to impart the particular insights he has been given to his fellows. All are called to 'instruct one another', to 'speak God's word . . . so that all may learn and all be encouraged', to 'teach and admonish one another in all wisdom', for it is through 'speaking the truth in love' that they are to 'grow up in every way into him who is the head, even Christ'.[36] So the most characteristic setting in which the community received guidance was when Christians assembled to share and evaluate the gifts given to them. Here in a variety of complementary ways, guidance was conveyed through each to all, and through all to each.

CONCLUSION

With respect to each of the areas of community life we have been examining, responsibility lies with every member to play his particular part in the leadership of the community. Rather than being the task of one man (or a select group) with the remainder obeying their decisions, leadership is a corporate affair devolving in some measure upon all who participate in the community's gatherings. The principle of equality was, of course, deeply embedded in Greek legal and political thought generally and was important to a certain degree in social relations. It was also strongly emphasized in Stoicism which deduced the theoretical equality of all from the possession of reason by all. The Pauline approach differs from these formulations. Paul grounds equality in a divine act rather than some aspect of the human personality, and extends it into a more intimate conception of communal life. Even so, for Paul equality was subservient to the more fundamental idea of unity. He regards the former as only the gateway to the latter. For this reason the idea of equality itself could never become a leading motif in his thought. Within this unity, as we have already noted in our discussion of *charisma,* room exists for diversity — even inequality — within the Christian community as well. We must now explore this further.

36. Rom. 15: 14; 1 Cor. 14: 31; Col. 3: 16; Eph. 4: 15

CHAPTER FOURTEEN

Service and its recognition

Although all members of the community participate in its gatherings and are responsible for its affairs, some individuals do so more decisively than others. Examples of this have already been given in various areas of corporate life and can now be grouped together here. For example, people like Aquila and Priscilla (1 Cor. 16: 19; Rom. 16: 3-5), or for that matter Nympha (Col. 4: 15), must have had a special hand in arranging the affairs of the churches that met in their homes. Gaius too, as 'host' to the 'whole church' in Corinth, would have had practical responsibilities to perform (Rom. 16: 23). In the area of pastoral care we have the cryptic reference to a 'true yokefellow' who is to help two women at Philippi, Euodia and Syntyche, come to a common agreement in the Lord (Phil. 4: 2-3).

This reference is one of the few places in Paul's writings where he does not address his remarks to the whole church. There are exceptions — e.g. when Paul speaks in turn to husbands and wives, parents and children, slaves and masters in Colossians 3; or to the various groups of people in 1 Corinthians 7; or to Jews and Gentiles, weak and strong in Romans 1-2 and 14-15. But that is a different matter. Paul also envisages the presence in Corinth of a 'wise' person who could solve legal disputes between members of the community (1 Cor. 6: 5). In the discussion of *charisma,* we noted the distinction between the regular ministry of 'prophets' and 'teachers' (1 Cor. 12: 29) and the occasional prophesying and teaching in which all members of the community engaged. Our reason for not systematically taking up these refer-ences before is the common failure to realize that, whatever Paul may say about the role of particular individuals within the com-munity, his emphasis is on the responsibility of all. We now investigate terms used by Paul to describe the administrative, pastoral and directive aspects of the church's life. We shall also look at some accompanying remarks which throw light on the role played by people involved in these activities.

TWO CLASSES WITHIN THE COMMUNITY?

As a prelude to this, we may note Paul's broad distinction between those who are more spiritually-minded among his readers and those who are not. Earlier we alluded to Paul's state-ment that 'if a man is overtaken in any trespass, you who are spiritual should restore him in a spirit of gentleness' (Gal. 6: 1). In a number of other places, he also differentiates between those who are mature or strong and those who are worldly or weak in their Christian understanding.[1] These are not regarded by him as two levels of membership within the community. Some, because of their sinfulness, remain immature in their attitudes long after they should have progressed beyond them. Paul urges them to rectify this state of affairs. Others, because of their background, pass through an initial stage of immaturity. For a period Paul willingly accommodates his teaching to them. Spiritual growth, precisely because it involves intellectual and moral growth, is a gradual thing, even though some are able to get on the right wavelength, so to speak, in a relatively short period of time. Only when those capable of deeper spiritual insight and more consistent behaviour fail to develop spiritual maturity does the discrepancy between them and other members of the community become un-healthy. Maturity is the aim of all and Paul nowhere limits its achievement to an elite. In the meantime, those who have advanced furthest along the path towards maturity ought to assist those who still have some distance to travel. Such people must watch themselves lest they too slip back into immature patterns of behaviour (Gal. 6: 2). Instead they should be grateful for what they have been able to attain (Phil. 3: 15-16). Within this group, which in many of his churches may have been encouragingly large if in others disappointingly small, Paul singles out some who have more specific tasks to perform.

1. Compare 1 Cor. 2: 14-3: 4; Rom. 14: 1-15: 7

THOSE WITH SPECIAL TASKS IN THE COMMUNITY

We turn now to the terms Paul uses to describe such people and the functions they perform. When his letters are examined in order of composition, some interesting features emerge.

The first reference occurs in 1 Thessalonians 5: 12. No title is mentioned, nor does Paul identify any positions held. Instead we have three participles used to define three tasks in the community, viz *kopiōntes, proistamenoi* and *nouthetountes*. These are the ones who 'labour among you', 'give aid to you' and 'admonish you'. The RSV translates the second of these in Romans 12: 8, as 'those who . . . are over you in the Lord' (following the AV). However its translation of the word in 1 Thessalonians 5 as 'he who gives aid' is preferable. Though the term appears occasionally in the papyri for official persons in voluntary associations, religious as well as secular, it is unlikely to have that more technical force here. This is clear from the use of its participial rather than noun form, its positioning between the two other terms and the general meaning of the verb in the New Testament. Together these three words simply indicate the effort expended by such people in carrying out their tasks, the supportive character of their work and the note of exhortation and warning appropriate to it. Because those 'who give aid' in the Roman social system were those in a position to confer benefits upon others, we may have reference here to people who came from the more socially advantaged level of the Thessalonian community. Nevertheless what is in view here is not official positions within the community but special functions.

Turning to the list of ministries and gifts at the end of 1 Corinthians 12 we find two different terms, *antilēmpseis* and *kubernēseis*. Here, unlike 1 Thessalonians 5, we have nouns being used rather than participles, but they still describe functions rather than persons or positions. In Paul's list only the first three items — apostles, prophets and teachers (1 Cor. 12: 28) — have specific persons in view; the remainder, our two terms mentioned above amongst them, are applicable to any. For this reason, we must depart again from the RSV rendering of these words as 'helpers' and 'administrators'. Instead they simply mean the rendering of assistance and the giving of direction in a less personalized way. (It is difficult to think of words in the plural which could be used as more exact translations of their Greek counterparts: 'helpful deeds' and 'practical initiatives' are about as close as one can get.) Once again these terms are not technical in character. Certainly no official positions in the church are in view. Their application to functions rather than the persons engaged in them, their ranking so far down the list of gifts and, perhaps, their occurrence only here in the New Testament all support this.

Later in this same letter Paul recommends the household of Stephanas to the Corinthian community (1 Cor. 16: 15-18). He describes them as the *aparchē*, firstfruits, of Asia so far as the preaching of the gospel is concerned. But regarding their presence in the church, Paul just says 'they devoted (or appointed) themselves to the service *(eis diakonian)* of the saints'. Here we have the very general term for 'service' whose wide range of meaning we have already discussed. Nothing suggests that the word *diakonia* has any technical meaning here. The community's function is not to ordain such people but rather recognize the value of their service. Paul goes on to say that acknowledgement is due not only to Stephanas and his household, but also to every 'fellow-worker' and 'labourer' (in the Greek *sunergounti kai kopiōnti*) for the work they do. The participial form of these words and the broad way in which Paul alludes to these people again preclude the possibility that any formal position is involvd. Once again the RSV translation 'fellow-worker and labourer', is more personalized than the Greek which speaks of those 'co-operating' and 'labouring'. The reference to 'firstfruits' however, may suggest that the initial converts in a given locality became not only the nucleus around which a new community was established, but key participants in establishing the actual work itself. And the fact that Stephanas possessed a household — it has been suggested that Fortunatus and Archaicus were two of his slaves — indicates again that a more socially eminent group in the community fulfilled these pastoral functions.

Galatians has little to offer on this topic — only Paul's injunction that those who learn should display some generosity to those who teach *(katēchountes)* (Gal. 6: 6). Here again we have the participial construction; a specific title or position is not in mind. The exhortation to the beneficiaries to 'share all good things' with those who benefit them does not, as commonly stated, demonstrate that a paid ministry existed at this time. Certainly Paul establishes here the principle of recompense, as he does elsewhere. Of the Gentiles' debt to the Jews he says those who 'have come to share in their spiritual blessings . . . ought also to be of service to them in material blessings' (Rom. 15: 27). Or again, speaking of his own work, he asks, 'If we have sown spiritual good among you, is it too much if we reap your material benefits?' (1 Cor. 9: 11). The basic principle here, stemming from a commandment of the Lord, is that 'those who proclaim the gospel should get their living by the gospel' (v. 14), though this is not a right on which Paul himself insists (vv. 15-18). But in such passages Paul has only in mind his communities' debt to him or to the Jerusalem church — the two sources of the gospel message. Most probably his comment in Galatians has one or other of these in mind as well. The more general expression, 'all good things', may not even mean primarily material possessions but simply the expression of fellowship between receiver and giver.

In the list of gifts provided by Paul in Romans 12 we have reference to someone described as 'he who is giving aid' *(proistamenos)* (Rom. 12: 8). The participial form occurs again, though here with more emphasis on the person involved in the activity. The RSV translation 'he who gives aid' rightly catches the spirit of the Greek here. In 1 Thessalonians, though employing a different term, Paul mentions the vigour (here 'zeal') with which such work should be undertaken. So again no formal office is in view. The construction used, despite its more direct personal reference and its position (between references to those who make financial contributions and act mercifully) demonstrates this clearly. Paul uses two other words later in Romans when he endorses Phoebe, the traveller from Cenchreae. She is called a deacon, *diakonos* (16: 1), of the church at Cenchreae and a *prostatis*, helper (16: 2), of many, including Paul himself. This second term, which probably relates to her being a 'patron' of the Pauline mission rather than any specific activity by her in the local church, will be looked at more carefully in the following chapter. The other provides us with the first clear application of the noun *diakonos* (the word has the same form for masculine and for feminine) to a member of a local gathering. But it would be premature to conclude from this that Phoebe held some official *position* in the church. She has simply distinguished herself by her helpfulness, though (as the word *prostatis* hints) the social level she occupied may well have placed her in a position to do this. The nominal form of the term could suggest that a more precise terminology is developing in Paul's communities or in his own thinking about them.

Most frequently a basis for the idea of office is thought to be in Paul's greetings to 'bishops' and 'deacons' in Philippians and in the mention of pastors *(poimenes)* and Archippus' ministry *(diakonia)* in Ephesians and Colossians respectively. In Philippians names are used to distinguish two groups of people from the rest of the community (Phil. 1: 1). Yet the 'saints' have precedence over 'guardians' *(episkopoi)* and 'servants' *(diakonoi)* — a strange order if the latter were the chief officeholders in the church. Also, and this applies to the words in Ephesians *(poimenes* and *didaskaloi)* as well,[2] the Greek has no definite article with these terms. This means that they are *not* being treated as titles. Maybe only one group of people is in view. Further, with the sole exception of the reference to the 'true yokefellow' whose task is to settle a personal dispute (perhaps between people to whom he was related), in Ephesians, Philippians and Colossians Paul always addresses the whole community. Nowhere does he entrust special responsibilities to any single group vis-à-vis the remainder. True, certain individuals are singled out in Philippians on account of the gifts they have brought from the community to Paul (Phil. 4: 18), but this is a different matter (and will be treated more fully in a moment). Finally, the terms *episkopos* and *diakonos* themselves should be freed of the official ecclesiastical connotations they have for us today, for they are not essentially different from the various other pastoral terms Paul uses. No real evidence exists to suggest that these terms had any technical meaning at this time. This is confirmed by the fact that in the second century Ignatius and Polycarp know of no episcopal pattern in the church at Philippi. Certainly in Colossians, Archippus, who appears to be a member of another socially prestigious household, is charged to fulfil the ministry *(diakonia)* which he has received from the Lord (Col. 4 17). Though we have here the very general term for ministry, this is something to which Christ, not the church, appointed him. The community's task is rather to encourage him to exercise it.

The conclusions we have drawn from the kinds of terms used are reinforced by the thrust of the comments accompanying them. In 1 Thessalonians 5, the members should 'respect' and 'esteem very highly in love' Stephanas and his household, not because of any official position they have been granted within the community, nor, for that matter, any social position that most of them seem to have occupied outside it, but 'because of their work' (1 Thess. 5: 12-13) — on account of the way in which they have functioned within it. After saying this, Paul significantly goes on to speak to the wider church (some commentators take the word 'brethren' here to apply to the smaller group Paul has just mentioned but this is most unlikely) and exhorts *everyone* to 'admonish the idle, encourage the faint-hearted, help the weak, be patient with all' (v. 14). Pastoral responsibility can never remain the preserve of a select few but always exists as an obligation upon every member of the community — even if some have a more advantageous position or a greater gift for it, and so can devote themselves more energetically to the task. This is confirmed by the reference

2. Eph. 4: 11; compare 1 Thess. 5: 12 and 1 Cor. 16: 16

to Stephanas and his household in 1 Corinthians 16. These had not been appointed to any position in the church: their prominence in Paul's eyes arose from the way in which they had freely 'devoted (or appointed) themselves' to helping others (v. 15). The community is to 'recognize' and 'order itself under' such people because of this 'work' and 'labour' they have performed (vv. 16, 18). Only a few verses before we find Paul reminding all the members of the community that they too should be 'abounding in the work of the Lord, knowing that your labour is not in vain' (15: 58), just as here 'everyone who works and labours' (16: 16) should receive the same acknowledgement as that due to Stephanas and his household.

SOME RESIDUAL PROBLEMS

(a) The link between 'pastors' and 'instructors'

The relationship between the groups discussed in 1 Thessalonians and 1 Corinthians, and the prophets and teachers in these churches, is unclear. In view of their work of admonition mentioned in 1 Thessalonians, some link could be presumed, yet the list of gifts and ministries in 1 Corinthians 12 distinguishes those involved in prophecy and teaching from those involved in other helpful and practical activities. Not until Ephesians 4 do we find teachers and pastors closely linked with one another. Even there the term 'pastor' *(poimenes)* may be simply a metaphor whose content is defined by the following 'teacher' *(didaskalos)*[3] In any case the prophets remain in a group by themselves. So we must not assume that prophetic and teaching gifts on the one hand and pastoral contributions on the other were necessarily combined in the one person. The reason for this may well lie in the specifically charismatic basis of the first and the frequently social foundation of the second. (Not that these two categories should be set off against one another: we saw earlier how Paul embraces 'natural' capacities within his concept of what is charismatic, as well as 'social' advantages.) Also we need to remind ourselves again that *all* members of the church are called upon to prophesy and teach in some measure; those who have a special ministry of this kind are not to be listened to uncritically. Evaluation of the prophet's message comes explicitly into view in 1 Corinthians 14. The need to test the teacher's instruction follows from Paul's stress on the importance of clear and informed instruction and the warning to

3. Compare 2 Bar. 77: 13-16

disown false teaching when it infiltrates the community.[4] His acceptance by the community corresponds to the degree with which he genuinely speaks on God's behalf to it.

(b)   The question of 'ordination'

In none of these passages do we find Paul suggesting that people have undergone ordination of any kind to the ministries they fulfil. Of course Acts records that Paul and Barnabas 'appointed elders . . . in every church', with prayer and fasting (Acts 14: 23). This process of appointment probably took place through the laying on of hands, as it did elsewhere in Acts. But in these other references we find that, either through the word of a prophet in the assembly (13: 3) or the discerning choice of all the members (6: 1-6), people were chosen with a view to their fitness for the task. Hands were then laid upon them as a tangible sign of fellowship and prayer, not as a mechanism for the creation of a ministry or imparting of special grace. In the Acts passage quoted above, Luke mentions that 'elders' were appointed in this way.[5] However, Paul outside the Pastorals (see later) never uses this term *presbuteros* in his letters. Luke does once use the term *episkopos* to refer to such (20: 28), but what we have in his work is probably a later standardization of Paul's more fluid terminology.

(c)   The origin of 'eldership'

In view of suggestions that the notion of eldership was drawn from the synagogue, it should be noted that there is no evidence whatever for the synagogue having such positions. The Jewish sources mention no such group. The one reference in the New Testament that comes closest to doing so has the elders of the city in view, whose jurisdiction included religious meetings, not officeholders in the synagogue (Luke 7: 3). But as we have seen, Paul does not use the term 'elder' in his undisputed letters. (In secular Greek *presbuteros* simply meant 'senior man' — at least outside Egypt. Just possibly Luke understood it this way in Acts. If he did then Paul appointed some 'elders' to a particular responsibility, not some people to the position of elder.) The word *episkopos* served a wide range of purposes in non-biblical Greek, being applied to men and women overseeing various activities or other people, philosophers examining and testing their hearers[6] and, most rele-

---

4. 1 Cor. 14: 6-9; Rom. 16: 17-18
5. Acts 14: 23; compare 20: 17
6. Epictetus, *Dissertationes.* III, 22: 97, Plutarch, *De Solone,* XIX, 1

vantly here, officeholders in voluntary societies. However, the term never refers to any precise function. The positions held are always of a minor kind. Biblical Greek uses the word freely but knows no clearly defined office bearing that title.[7] In any case, Paul's understanding of 'oversight' grew out of his view of gift, service and work. This transformed the meaning of any terms he, or his communities, might have borrowed from the surrounding culture.

SUMMARY

Surveying these passages as a whole, we conclude that the varied and imprecise terminology used by Paul, its comparatively infrequent and unemphatic occurrence in his letters, and the thrust of the remarks that qualify them, all confirm the view that formal positions within the communities are nowhere in mind. We have noted a gradual move towards a more specific and personal, rather than general and functional, terminology. However, considering the small amount of evidence we have, this should not be overstressed. Since variations in terminology may at times reflect local usage in the communities (influenced perhaps by the backgrounds from which their adherents came) it would be unwise to generalize from, say, the appearance of *episkopos* in Philippians or *diakonos* in both Philippians and Romans. We cannot say, then, that Paul's communities were hierarchical in structure. He did not vest authority in one man, or in a group of men, over the remaining members who merely had to receive and submit. On the other hand his communities were not egalitarian either. He did not vest authority in all equally nor did his communities select or call certain people to act on their behalf in some democratic fashion. Paul's communities were instead theocratic in structure. Because God gave to each individual within the community some contribution for its welfare, there is a strong democratic note — everyone participates authoritatively in its activities. Because the Spirit distributes his gifts and advantages unequally, so that some have more to contribute than others, there is also an element of differentiation. But neither of these tendencies is given a formal structure. Instead they are transformed through their subordination to the charismatic and, if I may coin the term, 'diaconic' principle.

7. E.g. Neh. 11: 9; 2 Kings 11: 15; 1 Macc. 1: 51; compare Philo, *De Somniis*, II, 186; Josephus, *The Antiquities of the Jews*, XII, 254

So significant persons are present in Paul's communities. However their authority comes from the ministry discharged by them in the community, not from their status outside it or position within it, and certainly not as an unchallengeable possession. Insofar as all discharge a ministry through the exercise of the gifts they have been given or the advantages they have acquired, authority resides not only in the most prominent members but in everyone without exception. While there are some through whom God speaks or acts authoritatively more frequently than others, their authority does not differ in principle from that which accrues in some measure to all. We have here, in a real sense, *a participatory society* in which authority is dispersed throughout the whole membership. For all the democratic tendencies present in the synagogue and, to a lesser extent, in Qumran, nothing quite like it existed in contemporary Judaism or Hellenism. (Compare the earlier examination of authority figures in these communities and the cults.) But are there not figures outside it, *viz* its apostolic founder, his associates and others involved in apostolic activity, who have authority over it of a qualitatively different kind? As we consider this question the essential character of the authority present in all these ministries will come into clearer focus.

CHAPTER FIFTEEN

The structure of Paul's work

Who were the influential people in the communities founded by Paul? How did they achieve their influence? Prominent persons emerge in Paul's churches, but their authority does not stem from any special status or office so much as from the special gifts they have and their exercise of them. Well-known figures also exist outside the churches in Paul's mission who play a part not only in their foundation but in their continuing life as well. We must gain a clearer understanding of exactly who was involved in the mission, and on what terms. We must also obtain a precise definition of its charter, particularly with respect to the communities founded by Paul's mission. This will enable us in the following chapter to consider the role played by those involved permanently in local churches yet having some connection with Paul's work, as well as by Paul's hand-picked associates in the mission. Since neither Paul nor Luke discuss these matters in a systematic way, information about them has to be gleaned from passing comments on the activities of the mission, or distilled from passages dealing primarily with other matters.

PAUL'S FELLOW-WORKERS

Paul began his missionary work with a companion apostle and

assistant (Acts 13: 2-4), first as the junior partner[1] but later as the senior member (13: 13ff.). Relying upon his rabbinic status, Paul used synagogues as platforms for his message.[2] On the second journey he chose his own assistant (15: 40) and then broadened the membership of his mission by the recruitment of additional personnel, beginning with Timothy (16: 1-3). Although he continued initially to work through the synagogues,[3] his approach now took on a different character, one that was more in line with the methods of those who may be called the 'Sophists' of his time. Utilizing his Roman citizenship and operating more at his own social level, he gained an entrée into certain levels of the Hellenistic social elite. (Since citizenship in Tarsus was only given to those who had substantial property, Paul's family must have met this test. Their subsidizing his education in Jerusalem also suggests they possessed wealth and social status.) In the Eastern provinces, this group comprised members of the commercial and administrative classes more than, as in Rome itself, the traditional aristocracy. Such people were sometimes already sympathetic towards or connected with the local synagogue. It was from this base that Paul frequently communicated his message, made his converts and established his churches.[4] Unlike the 'Sophists' and the rabbis (who only in the second century exercised a trade alongside their teaching), he generally worked with his hands in the places at which he stayed, his earnings helping to support his colleagues as well as pay for his own needs.[5] Paul was essentially a part-time, not a full-time, missionary, carrying on his evangelistic and pastoral activities alongside the practice of his trade. This makes his achievements all the more extraordinary. But at times he could not work — when he was imprisoned, for example, or constantly on the move. In addition his group of assistants tended to increase.

At this point the extension of hospitality and financial support offered him along the way became not only important but necessary. From Paul's writings we can single out as many as forty persons who were actual or potential sponsors of his activities. His letters abound with thanks for the generosity of these people.

1. Acts 13: 2 and 7; compare 11: 25 and 30, 12: 25
2. Acts 13: 5 and 14, 14: 1 et al.
3. Acts 17: 1, 10 and 17, 18: 4 and 19, 19: 8
4. Acts 16: 15, 17: 4-7 and 12; 18: 5-7; Rom. 16: 2, 4 and 23; Phil. 4: 2-3; Philem. 7 (compare verse 22). See too Acts 19: 31; Phil. 4: 22
5. Acts 18: 3 and 20: 33-35; 2 Thess. 3: 6-9; 1 Cor. 9: 3-6; compare Ab. 2: 2 and 3: 21. See also Cicero, *De Officiis*, 1: 150, but compare Dio Chrystostom, *Orationes*, III, 123ff.

Through the exercise of hospitality and granting of financial aid, they enabled him to carry out his work freely in the new areas he entered, and they often aided him when he ran foul of the authorities or was imprisoned for his efforts. His writings also reveal a second group of people who constituted his retinue or staff. A number of these came and went from local churches, sometimes rendering particular services to him, e.g. bringing financial assistance (Phil. 4: 18), greetings from his churches,[6] appeals for his help (1 Cor. 1: 11), and sometimes undertaking return services to the groups from which they had come (Phil. 2: 25-30). Others were more or less permanent members of his entourage, either attending to him personally in a secretarial way (Rom. 16: 22) or medical capacity (Col. 4: 14), or being deployed by him to carry out specific and limited tasks vis-à-vis local churches which he, through lack of time or imprisonment, could not fulfil, e.g. carrying letters and/or verbal messages,[7] and overseeing the collection for the Jerusalem poor.[8] Though Paul on occasions was forced to deal with situations alone, most of the time he had a circle of colleagues around him. So we have a second group of persons who are Paul's colleagues or working associates. In contrast to his patrons, who (with one or two exceptions) were fixed local sponsors, these temporarily or permanently journeyed with him and actively participated in the work.

RACIAL, SOCIAL AND SEXUAL DISTINCTIONS

As we have done already with the composition of Paul's communities, we must now examine the way in which the traditional racial, social and sexual distinctions affected the membership of his missionary work.

(a)   Jews and Gentiles

Although among the forty or so persons mentioned as Paul's possible patrons we have only one or two Jewish Christians explicitly named, e.g. Crispus (Acts 18: 8), the majority of those more directly involved in his work are Jewish converts to Christianity. According to Acts, Paul begins his mission among the Gentiles with Barnabas and his cousin Mark, all three Jews of the Disper-

---

6. 1 Cor. 16: 17-18; Col. 1: 7-8 and 4: 12
7. 1 Thess. 3: 6; 1 Cor. 4: 17; 2 Cor. 7: 6-15; Phil. 2: 19-23; Col. 4: 7-9; Eph. 6: 21-22
8. 1 Cor. 16: 3; 2 Cor. 8: 16-23

sion, the latter two from Cyprus (4: 36; Col. 4: 10). After his break with Barnabas, Paul takes Silas with him, a distinguished member of the church at Jerusalem (Acts 15: 22, 40). On this second journey he also recruits Timothy who, though he has a Greek father, was raised by his Jewish mother in the religion of her forefathers (16: 1). At Corinth the party is enlarged by the addition of Aquila and Priscilla, the former from Pontus and the latter probably either from there or Rome (18: 1-2). On his third missionary tour we have first mention of a full Gentile, Erastus, the city treasurer from Corinth,[9] unless Luke who joined them at Troas on the previous trip is to be considered such (Acts 16: 10).

From this point on it becomes increasingly difficult to identify the racial origin of the people associated with Paul, viz at Ephesus — Gaius and Aristarchus (19: 29); on the return journey through Macedonia — Sopater, Secundus, Tychicus, another Gaius and Trophimus, as well as Timothy, Luke and Aristarchus (20: 4). The latter two also accompany Paul on his sea journey to Rome (27: 2). Others are mentioned at various points in Paul's letters, though once again it is not always easy to tell whether they are Jews or Gentiles. Among these 'fellow-workers', however, Lucius, Jason and Sosipater (Rom. 16: 21), and probably Sosthenes and Jesus Justus (1 Cor. 1: 1), were all Jews. We also find here that Aristarchus, mentioned above, was one of Paul's kinsmen. The declining Jewish-Christian membership in his mission is reflected in his regretful admission in Colossians — Aristarchus, Mark and Jesus Justus having just been named — that 'these are the only men of the circumcision among my fellow workers for the kingdom of God' (Col. 4: 10-11). But the predominance of Jewish Christians in the early days of the mission should not cause us to overlook the participation of Gentiles, notably Titus[10] and Tychicus,[11] on an equal level. Interestingly the three most active members in the work appear to have been Silas, a Jew, Timothy, a half-Jew and half-Greek, and Titus, a Greek. The increasing ratio of Gentile converts involved in the mission as it progresses has already been noted.

(b)   Slaves

Were slaves included among those accompanying Paul? Only in one instance can we be certain this took place, viz the celebrated

9. Acts 19: 22; compare Rom. 16: 23
10. Gal. 2: 1-5; 2 Cor. 2: 12-13, 7: 6 and 13, 8: 6, 16, 18 and 23, 12: 18
11. Acts 20: 4; Col. 4: 7; Eph. 6: 21

case of the runaway slave Onesimus.[12] Although Paul eventually
returns him to his master Philemon, he nowhere suggests that the
presence of Onesimus was inappropriate. What disturbs him is
that Onesimus left his master without permission. In his letter to
Philemon Paul clearly wishes to have Onesimus back (Philem.
13). He even hints that Philemon might exceed Paul's desire
(v. 21), presumably by freeing Onesimus from his service so that
he would be free to assist Paul.

This raises an interesting, if speculative, point. In many ways
the most unexpected aspect of Paul's mission in this area may
have been his refusal to either take or gain servants of his own, to
carry out the various practical arrangements that his missionary
enterprise involved. The Acts of the Apostles and Paul's letters
indicate that, by virtue of his family background and Roman
citizenship, he had been a person of some status who would
normally have his own servants with him on his extensive travels.

(c) Women

We can now turn to Paul's attitude to women as it comes to
expression in the course of his apostolic mission. Both his first and
second journeys begin with an all-male band. Not until Paul
crosses from Asia into Macedonia do women begin to feature in
the story in a positive way. At Philippi, a Roman colony where
apparently there was no synagogue, Paul and his colleagues
sought out Jews and Gentile 'god-fearers' who might be gathered
for prayer by the river. As a result of this encounter, Lydia, a
woman from Thyatira engaged in commercial activity, was converted, together with her household (Acts 16: 13-15). She not only
opened her home to the apostle and his assistants but also,
apparently, became host to the new church there (v. 40). From
this point on we find frequent reference to the adherence of
'leading women among the Greeks' to the apostle's cause, for
example, at Thessalonica (17: 4), Beroea (v. 12), and Athens
(v. 34).

At Corinth, he made the acquaintance of a couple who went on
to play an important role in his activities: Aquila and Prisca (or
less formally, Priscilla) who had been exiled from Rome by
Claudius' decree in AD 49-50 (18: 1-3). Paul and especially Luke
usually mention Priscilla first, perhaps because her status was
superior to her husband's.[13] (Possibly she belonged by birth or
manumission to the *gens Acilia,* an influential family among the

12. Col. 4: 8-9; Philem. 10ff.
13. Acts 18: 18 and 26; Rom. 16: 3

Roman nobility.) Rather than being confined to domestic duties, Priscilla is involved alongside her husband in the family business. In view of their later practice at Ephesus and Rome (1 Cor. 16: 19; Rom. 16: 3), they were probably hosts to one of the infant churches in Corinth. When Paul returned to Asia, they came with him as 'fellow-workers' in his mission,[14] so from this point on Paul's missionary party includes women as well as men. When certain deficiencies became apparent at Ephesus in the teaching of an itinerant Jewish-Christian, Apollos, both wife and husband (she again named first) are involved in setting him straight (Acts 18: 27). Priscilla's basis for doing this lay in her calling as a 'fellow-worker' with Paul.

This couple appears once more amongst the greetings at the end of Paul's letter to the Romans, where they are described as people to whom not only Paul 'but also all the churches of the Gentiles give thanks' (Rom. 16: 4). Another woman who has 'laboured' strenuously amongst them is Mary, mentioned in the following verse. Since Paul elsewhere uses the term 'labourer' in connection with 'fellow-worker' (1 Cor. 16: 16), and as a description of his own apostolic work,[15] she may have been independently involved in Christian mission. Two other women, similarly engaged in Rome, are 'those workers in the Lord, Tryphaena and Tryphosa', probably two sisters (Rom. 16: 12). Then, at the head of this list of greetings, Paul commends his 'sister' Phoebe who he says 'has been a helper of many and of myself as well' (v. 2).

Outside this list in Romans, Paul refers to two Philippian women, Euodia and Syntyche, who 'laboured side by side' with him in the gospel along with the rest of his 'fellow-workers' (Phil. 2: 2-4). So far as we can judge (unless Junias is a female apostle) (Rom. 16: 7), we have no instance of a female apostle or (unless Phoebe is an example) of a single woman acting as an itinerant apostolic delegate like Timothy and others. However we have in Priscilla an example of a married woman acting with her husband as an itinerant 'fellow-worker'. Also Mary, Tryphaena and Tryphosa (and perhaps Euodia and Syntyche) are examples of unmarried or widowed women acting as missionary 'workers' in a localized setting. If they do not occupy as prominent a place as men in Paul's missionary apparatus, women nevertheless play an important part within it and contribute significantly to the spread of Christianity in the early years of its expansion.

14. Acts 18: 18; compare Rom. 16: 3
15. Gal. 4: 11; Phil. 2: 16; Col. 2: 29

PAUL'S PRACTICE IN HIS SOCIAL CONTEXT

Little can be said about the social background to Paul's practice of combining Jews and Gentiles in his mission or his apparently preferring to travel unattended by slaves. Although Jews and non-Jews interrelated in various areas of daily life, particularly in more Hellenized upper class circles, so far as the propagation of religious ideas was concerned there does not seem to be any real precedent for their combining together. We have noted earlier the spread of the mystery cults through not only citizens from the cults' homeland but adherents from other lands as well. But we do not know of any attempt to do this along the lines of Paul's mission, with reliance upon a team of colleagues coming from different religio-national backgrounds. As for travelling unattended, it seems that itinerant teachers and miracle-workers were normally accompanied by servants — Paul's contemporary Apollonius of Tyana is an example — who were employed to carry out various secretarial and practical duties on the way. However the Cynics prided themselves on journeying without slaves.[16] So while Paul's practice appears to cut across the normal procedures of his day, it had some parallels.

More can be said about the role of women in various public activities. Among the later rabbis who composed the Mishnah this question was very easily settled: women were not permitted to engage in any real public activity at all. This attitude is reflected in earlier Jewish writings as well. Unmarried women especially were advised to stay within the borders of their house and not venture outside them.[17] Married women had to cover themselves when they went out so that they would not be observed by those with whom they might come into contact. Failure to comply with this placed the husband under an obligation to divorce his wife.[18] Conversation with anyone in public was also frowned upon (John 4: 27). (A notorious exception was Beruriah, the daughter of Rabbi Meir.) While stricter attitudes may have prevailed after AD 70 the principle, 'Talk not much with womankind', was enunciated a century and a half before Jesus. Since this applied to one's own wife, how much more should it govern one's relationship with another's![19]

Concerning women's attendance at meetings, Philo observes:

16. Philostratus, *Appolonius,* 1: 18 but see Epictetus, *Dissertationes,* IV, 22 and 45-47

17. Philo, *In Flaccum,* II, 89; compare Ecclus. 42: 11-12; 2 Macc. 3: 19; 3 Macc. 1: 18-19

18. Ket. 7: 6

19. Ab. 1: 5; compare earlier Ecclus. 9: 9

'Market places and council-halls, law-courts and gatherings, and meetings where a large number of people are assembled — in short all public life with its discussion and deeds, in times of peace and war — are proper for men. It is suitable for women to stay indoors, and to live in retirement, limited by the middle door (to the men's apartments) for the young girls (Philo has in view here the Hellenistic household of his native Alexandria) and the outer door for married women'.[20] While such may have been the ideal, at least in part of the Jewish Dispersion, in practice greater flexibility often existed. In Jewish towns women frequently had to assist their husbands in their craft or profession, at the point of sale as well as production.[21] As the Gospels indicate, women occasionally prophesied in the Temple, moved freely about Jerusalem, and (unless Jesus' presence provoked untraditional behaviour) also entertained visiting teachers and listened to instruction.[22] They seem to have caused no surprise as they followed Jesus around the countryside (Luke 8: 1-3; Matt. 20: 20). In the rural areas especially women travelled from one place to another, assisted in the fields, drew water from the village well, sold goods at the door, served at tables and were less concerned with the stricter urban proprieties of dress. Still, as the Gospels also attest, it was not customary for them to converse with a stranger.[23] Amongst the aristocracy even more freedom was permitted (e.g. Matt. 14: 6). Practice in the middle of the first century were certainly more free and less uniform than the later rabbinic writings suggest.

Among the Greeks prevailing attitudes to the public role of women were not dissimilar. Women had been traditionally disqualified from political life and daughters, until their marriage, were generally confined to the home.[24] But daughters certainly joined in such public activities as festivals, funerals, and the like, and married women attended civic speeches and religious rituals, went shopping and walking etc.[25] Yet discussion of moral and other matters was primarily a masculine pastime from which the women as a rule were excluded. When her husband had guests, a wife would retire to her own quarters, since it was only the *hetairai,* or courtesans, who participated openly in such activities.[26] Yet Acts suggests that women could participate in commercial

20. Philo, *De Specialibus Legibus,* III, 169   21. Ket. 9: 4
22. Luke 2: 36-38, 4: 39, 10: 38-42 and 11: 27-28; John 11: 20 and 12: 2
23. Luke 1: 39-40, 8: 19-21 and 43; John 4: 7; Ket. 1: 10; Yeb. 15: 2; Eduy. 1: 12, but see John 4: 27
24. Xenophon, *Oeconomicus,* 8: 10
25. Aristophanes, *Frogs,* 1346-1351
26. Sallust, *Bellum Catilinae,* XXIII, 3f., and XXVIII, 2

life, at least in places like Corinth, and move freely from one province to another (Acts 18: 3). In Roman life, this restriction did not apply, though in company the wife was expected to support her husband and not disagree with him.[27] This may have been the case elsewhere, especially in the Greek cities of the East.[28]

In both Rome and the East there existed wider opportunities for women to engage in public life. Roman noblewomen were able to move around more freely in public than their Greek counterparts, receive some education in moral and other subjects and belong to women's societies.[29] Some indirectly exerted considerable influence upon the course of political affairs.[30] In Macedonia, married and widowed women openly participated in commercial life, both inside and outside their native cities as the evidence from Acts demonstrates (Acts 16: 14-15). On occasion some received special honorific grants of full citizenship. They could also at times instigate judicial proceedings and, in some places, become magistrates. We have two examples of women who accompanied semi-itinerant philosopher or teacher/exorcists, though this practice seems to be most exceptional.[31] So free women in such areas were far from living secluded and subordinate lives.

CONCLUSION

As with the composition of his churches, Paul's mission in part contradicted, in part reflected and in part extended the various crosscurrents of national, social and sexual co-operation in his day. The Jewish/Gentile identity of his colleagues seems to have been his most adventurous practice, though his apparent refusal to be attended by slaves was also unusual, at least in Hellenistic circles, less so considering Paul's Jewish background. We have ample evidence of the prominent part played by women in the advancement of his mission, particularly on Macedonian and Roman soil. While this reflects the greater freedom enjoyed by women in such areas, it also testifies to Paul's flexibility of practice where that would not lead to offence. His approach resulted in the elevation of women to a place in religious work for which we have little contemporary parallel.

27. Plutarch, *Advice on Marriage*, 19, 32 and 48; Seneca, *Ad Helvium* XVII, 2-5
28. Compare Acts 18: 26; Rom. 16: 1
29. Livy, III, 44ff.; Pliny, *Epistulae*, IV 19: 1-5 (compare Plutarch, *De Pompeio*, 55: 1); Ovid, *Ars Amatoria*, III, 634-642
30. E.g. Sallust, *Bell. Cat.*, XXIV, 3, XXV, 5; Tacitus, *Annals*, 1: 3-14
31. Diogenes Laertius, vi, 96 (Crates and Hipparchia); Justin, *First Apology*, 26 (Simon Magus and Helena) if reliable

CHAPTER SIXTEEN

The work and the churches

We have seen enough already to conclude that Paul's work existed alongside the local churches founded and supported by it, as a separate entity with a life of its own. But just as Paul's apostolic career has a history which is independent of the communities fathered by him, the reverse is also substantially true. His communities tended to move away from close dependence on Paul. In fact, clear differences existed between the mission and the churches at the level of the principles upon which they operated. The precise points at which these differences occur can now be plotted.

At first sight, the structure of Paul's mission has certain *similarities* with that of the churches founded by Paul. So, for example, there is: (a) an extensive use of family terminology between those involved in the work, viz father (Phil. 2: 22), son (Philem. 10), brother[1], sister (Rom. 16: 1; Philem. 2); (b) a variety of gifts and ministries in evidence among the group, viz apostles (Gal. 1: 1 et al.), prophets,[2] evangelizing (2 Cor. 8: 18), serving (2 Cor. 8: 20), healing (Acts 28: 8-9); (c) a strong note of equality present among its members, indicated by Paul's way of referring to them, viz fellow-workers,[3], fellow-soldiers (Phil. 2: 25; Philem. 2), fellow-

1. 1 Thess. 3: 2; 1 Cor. 1: 1, 16: 12 and 20; 2 Cor. 1: 1, 2: 13, 8: 18, 22 and 23; Phil. 2: 25 and 4: 21; Col. 1: 1 and 4: 7-9; Philem. 1 and 20; Eph. 6: 21
2. Acts 15: 32; 2 Cor. 8: 23; Rom. 16: 7
3. 1 Cor. 3: 9 and 16: 16; 2 Cor. 8: 23; Rom. 16: 3, 9 and 21; Phil. 2: 25; Col. 4: 11; Philem. 1.

servants (Col. 4: 7), and the types of people represented, viz Jews and Gentiles, men and women, slaves and free. Alongside these similarities however exist some real *differences* between the work and the churches. We take each of the points mentioned above in turn in order to identify where these differences lie.

DIFFERENCES BETWEEN PAUL'S MISSION AND HIS CHURCHES

(a)   Character

In the first place Paul's whole operation has a specialized character. It exists for a specific and limited purpose. Unlike the churches, its basis lies not just in Jesus' death and resurrection and the Spirit's fruit and gifts. Nor is its goal primarily the welding together of its members into a common life, or the aiding of their growth to maturity. Like the members of the churches, members of Paul's mission must possess gifts and the maturity that goes with them. However experience of Christ and the Spirit are not in themselves sufficient to qualify someone for inclusion in the mission. Paul's mission is unique. It does not have a fixed geographical base, nor does it constitute itself chiefly by gathering. It is constantly on the move, more marked by the dispersion of its members than their united assembling. This does not mean that those involved in it never 'churched' together. In some measure that must have happened among those who were travelling together, especially when no local churches were in the vicinity. But this could never be the main purpose of the group.

(b)   Function

Secondly, nowhere do we find any hint of the 'body' metaphor being applied to this group. Those involved were not primarily participating in a common life — though that certainly did also occur — but rather sharing in a common task. Hence the description *ergon*, work, which lies at the root of so much of Paul's thinking about this.[4] The members were other-directed, not inner-directed. Paradoxically this may have led to their sharing 'all things in common' more than the communities founded by them. All that Paul earned at his trade seems to have gone into funding his missionary enterprise (Acts 20: 34); gifts from his churches were presumably treated in the same way (Phil. 4: 14-16). The 'work' may be viewed as a sort of mobile commune in which all

---

4. Gal. 6: 4; 1 Cor. 3: 13-15. 9: 1 and 16: 10; Phil. 2: 30

resources are pooled. Nevertheless unlike the churches, it has as its focal point not a *group* of people but a *man,* Paul himself. They were drawn into the orbit of Paul's own ministry and became an extension of it. So this work has as its basis Paul's commission and certain relevant gifts that can help fulfil it, and has as its purpose the preaching of the gospel and the establishment of churches. The churches in turn have as their foundation the message preached by Paul and the experience of the Spirit among their members, and as their goal the growing harmony and maturity of all who belong to them.

(c) Gifts

Thirdly, despite the variety of gifts represented, not all those listed by Paul as occurring in congregational contexts are present. Most prominent are those that can be directed towards outsiders rather than the Christian group. What we have here is a *concentration* of gifts, with the most significant ones present out of all proportion to others in his lists. Paul's entourage consists essentially of a group of specialists, whose gifts have to do with the most fundamental areas of religious life. *Evangelism,* rather than edification, is the primary task — even though, as churches are founded in various places, edification of their members also has its place. The activities of Paul's workers are directed outside the group to a different circle, being frequently exercised outside the home in places where the public gather, e.g. religious buildings, lecture halls, debating forums, market places etc. Others in the church had similar gifts for commending the Christian message to outsiders, but these were chiefly employed outside of the gatherings to which they belonged (Col. 1: 7). On a smaller scale their activities would run parallel to Paul's own work, related to the church from which they had come but not strictly 'church' activities. So, in both the kinds of gifts most in evidence in the work and the type of audience to whom they were directed, we find differences between the Christian communities established by Paul and the group centred around him, his mission.

(d) Authority

Finally, for all that he says about the co-operative nature of his work, Paul himself was not only the main influence in the group but the one around whose personal authority its activities centred. Paul regarded his ministry to the Gentiles as divinely granted and, after his break with Barnabas, assumed a position of authority among his assistants which he did not allow others in the churches subsequently founded by him. There were always several such figures in his communities,[5] so that a system of checks and balances always existed between them. But there is only one Paul. And whereas it is ultimately the whole congregation, including its apostle, in whom authority resides, in his work Paul under the Spirit appears quite definitely to be 'in charge'. So, for example, he is the one who 'sends' or 'leaves' his colleagues to engage in various activities.[6] Again throughout the journeyings of the group he generally seems to decide what the next step will be.[7] There are only two occasions where an exception to this appears to be involved. First Barnabas refused to comply with Paul's insistence that Mark should not come with them (Acts 15: 36-41). Because Barnabas had been the senior member of the duo, this disagreement resulted in the establishing of two separate missionary works. Secondly Apollos, having been urged by Paul to visit Corinth 'with the other brethren' declined to do so since 'it was not at all his will to go now' (1 Cor. 16: 12); but Apollos was engaged independently in evangelistic activity and did not come under Paul's authority. This does not mean that Paul was necessarily authoritarian in manner, nor that consultation with his fellow-workers was absent. The nature of Paul's relationship with his colleagues is beautifully captured in his exclamation: 'But thanks be to God who puts the same earnest care for you into the heart of Titus. For he not only accepted our appeal, but being himself very earnest he is going to you of his own accord'.[8]

INTER-RELATIONSHIP BETWEEN PAUL'S MISSION AND HIS CHURCHES

(a)   Through mutual participation

Despite their different orientations, the 'work' and the 'churches' do participate in each other's activities in various ways. Paul and those involved in other missions seek to nurture the small communities they have founded and lead them to Christian adulthood. They carry out this responsibility by making personal visits of longer or shorter duration, writing letters to help them

5. 1 Thess. 5: 12ff.; Phil. 1: 1; compare Acts 13: 1-2
6. 1 Thess. 3: 2; 1 Cor. 4: 17; 2 Cor. 8: 18ff.; Phil. 2: 19, 23, 25 and 28; Col. 4: 8-9; Philem. 12; Eph. 6: 22
7. Compare Acts 16: 9, 18: 1 and 18-21, 19: 21, 20: 13 and 16-17 et al.
8. 2 Cor. 8: 6 and 17, 9: 5, 12: 18; Phil. 4: 2

with their problems, sending emissaries as their personal representatives and praying constantly for their welfare and progress.[9] But always Paul is moving on 'making it (his) ambition to preach the gospel, not where Christ has already been named, lest (he) build on another man's foundation'.[10] For their part the churches seek to forward the pioneering work in which Paul and other apostles are engaged. They fulfil this in the following ways: by *transmitting* the Spirit's call of one of their members to the work of evangelism and *commissioning* that person to whom the Spirit has given the gift for the task (Acts 13: 1-3); by *participating* in the work that results, whether as members of the sponsoring church or of churches founded by the mission, through forwarding financial aid (Phil. 4: 14-16), praying for its success[11] and maintaining personal contact through letters or visit;[12] by *assembling* to hear from those involved in the work all that had taken place[13] and *sending* representatives to other churches to defend their activities when they come under suspicion (Acts 15: 1ff.). In all these ways they actually 'participate' in the apostolic mission, and are members of it. This provides the model for their involvement in any evangelistic work.

The principles upon which Paul's mission operated do not in all respects conform to those he impressed upon the churches which he founded. Some overlap occurs, but the basic divergence between them is quite deliberate. Though the 'churches' and the 'work' are integrally related, each has an ongoing life apart from the other. The purpose for which each exists, the skills upon which each depends and the authority through which each lives are not identical, even though they share a great deal in common. The two groups are interdependent and in a whole variety of ways assist one another in their work. This once again prompts the question: did the churches founded by Paul really possess as independent a life as his mission had apart from them? How subservient were the churches to him, his associates and other apostles? To answer this question we must compare the role of leading local members temporarily or intermittently caught up in Paul's missionary work, with the role of permanent colleagues

---

9. 1 Thess. 1: 2ff.; 2 Thess. 1: 3ff. and 3: 1ff.; 1 Cor. 1: 4ff.; 2 Cor. 1: 3ff. and 13: 9; Rom. 1: 8ff.; Phil. 1: 3ff.; Col. 1: 3ff.
10. Rom. 15: 20; compare 2 Cor. 10: 13-16
11. 1 Thess. 5: 25; 2 Cor. 1: 11; Rom. 15: 30-32; Phil. 1: 19-20; Col. 4: 18; Eph. 6: 18-20
12. 1 Cor. 1: 11, 7: 1 and 16: 17-18; Phil. 2: 25 and 4: 18; Col. 1: 17 et al.
13. Acts 14: 26-29 and 18: 22-23

chosen by Paul who have only an occasional contact with particular local churches.

(b)   Through local co-workers

The first group, the local members, comprises those instrumental in founding a church and maintaining personal contact with Paul as it developed. Since they engaged in these activities they were also involved in his work. That is why he speaks of them as 'fellow-workers' and 'labourers'. Participating in church is one thing; *commencing* a church is another: the latter quite possibly depended upon a prior call, either directly from God or mediated through the apostle. Stephanas and his household almost certainly fell into this category (1 Cor. 16: 15). So too Philemon, Apphia and Archippus (Philem. 1). This group also includes others who, like Epaphras, independently evangelized their own home cities and founded communities, but then maintained contact with Paul (Col. 1: 7 and 4: 12). For this reason Paul designates him a 'fellow-slave' and 'servant'.

Although the communities did not elect representatives to lead their gatherings, from time to time they did set aside certain people to perform particular tasks on their behalf. But these tasks were extra-mural and not intramural in character, determined by the geographical isolation of the communities. When certain functions had to be fulfilled elsewhere it was impracticable for the community as a whole to carry them out. Instead it deputized one or more members for the task. Such functions could be of several different kinds, e.g. a journey to Paul taking news of the community's progress or monetary aid for the apostle's labours. Epaphroditus, on behalf of the community at Philippi, carried out this task. Paul describes him as his 'fellow-worker' and 'soldier' and as their 'apostle' and 'servant' (Phil. 2: 25). Or again, we have those people 'accredited by letter' from their base communities, who assisted in carrying the collection to Jerusalem — something Paul also refers to as a 'work' (2 Cor. 8: 19). In this instance, there is only a temporary and limited commission to fulfil. All such people, insists Paul, are to be given their due honour by the communities who commissioned them or whom they represent, not because of any superior position that they occupy or official rank that they possess, but on account of the way they carry out their responsibilities and the kinds of helpful services they perform. So with Epaphroditus in mind, Paul encourages his readers to 'honour such men. For he nearly died for the work of Christ, risking his life to complete your service to me'.[14] We find here a further application of the principle of recognition that underlies Paul's whole approach to leadership within the community itself. The worth of leaders, and the acknowledgement they should enjoy, is determined by the quality of their labours, not any inherent status.

(c) Through itinerant colleagues

We now turn to the second group, Paul's more immediate colleagues. Outside the Pastorals (which will be discussed separately later) we do not have a great deal of evidence about the position of Paul's co-workers in the communities where they spend some time. Paul certainly instructs the churches to graciously receive such people when they are in the vicinity. But it is the nature and quality of their work which he commends, not the position they hold in his missionary organization or have by right. Timothy, for example, is sent by Paul to Corinth to remind the community of his message. But Paul has to urge them to 'put him at ease' among them and 'not to despise him' since 'he is doing the work of the Lord as I am' (1 Cor. 16: 10-11a). Timothy's position in the church on his arrival is not automatically guaranteed by his connection with Paul's mission. He should be accepted because he performs the mission God has given him to fulfil. Doubts also existed about the way in which the same community would accept Titus, but Paul's mind was eventually 'set at rest' when he heard that they had received him with the respect due to him on account of his work (2 Cor. 7: 13-15). The sending of Tychicus to Colossae, Timothy to Philippi and Thessalonica, and Titus to Corinth again illustrates the temporary commission such associates of Paul have in the communities to which he sends them. Their worth is endorsed on the grounds of their activities and sense of commitment to the task. He reminds the Corinthians that Titus is his 'partner and fellow-worker in your service' who 'being very earnest', journeys to them 'of his own accord' (8: 17 and 23). Of Timothy Paul says, 'I have no one like him who will be genuinely anxious for your welfare' and goes on to add 'but Timothy's worth you know, how as a son with a father he has served me in the gospel'.[15] Tychicus he describes as 'a beloved brother and faithful minister and fellow servant in the Lord' and says that he has 'sent him for this very purpose' (Col. 4: 7-8). Paul consistently appeals to their faithful performance of the work entrusted to them, not any honorific position they have been

14. Phil. 2: 29-30; compare 1 Cor. 16: 17-18; 2 Cor. 8: 9; Col. 4: 13
15. Phil. 2: 19-23; 1 Thess. 3: 1-8

given. Such authority as these people exercise when they visit the local communities does not differ in principle from that of others in the community with special functions to fulfil.

PAUL'S MISSION COMPARED TO OTHER ITINERANT ACTIVITY WORK

(a) Generally

At this point we can sum up what has been said about the structure and character of Paul's missionary work and compare this with other kinds of itinerant activity in Jewish and Graeco-Roman circles around the same time. Travelling was quite widely undertaken in the first century, if mainly by the well-to-do. We have already noted that philosophic 'missionaries' toured the ancient world disseminating their views. Stoic and Cynic philosophers in particular sometimes operated in this way, their travels and methods being both celebrated in historical romances[16] and derided in satirical essays.[17] We know from Acts that Jewish exorcists travelled around the synagogues of the Dispersion (Acts 19: 13-15), while the Gospels tell us that (individual?) Pharisees journeyed by land and sea to make Gentile converts (Matt. 23: 15). Just how frequently this took place is hard to say: there is little evidence on which one can draw. However there are precedents for the sort of activity in which Paul was involved.

But is there any parallel to the size of his missionary apparatus or to the complex network of relationships built up around it? So far as one can trust the evidence, Cynic philosophers like Diogenes seem to have moved around mainly as individual teachers. Some itinerants, such as the 'prophet' Alexander, travelled with a single partner. Others, who journeyed with a group, like Apollonius, did so with 'disciples', a 'scribe' and 'secretary', not with genuine co-workers.[18] The 'Sophists' also sought payment for their services, a right Paul consistently declined to press.[19] Paul's 'search and destroy' visit to Damascus may suggest that Pharisees travelled with ancillary help to assist them, but this may be affected by his working under the high priest's direction (Acts 9: 7). Apart from the New Testament, we

16. E.g. Philostratus, *Apollonius of Tyana*
17. E.g. Lucian, *The False Prophet*
18. See Dio Chrysostom, *Orationes*, VIII-IX, Lucian, *False Prophet*, 6; Philostratus, *Apollonius*, I, 18, IV, 37-38, VIII, 19, 21 and 24. (Demetrius in IV. 25 and 42. 31 was originally independent.)
19. 1 Cor. 9: 1-18; contrast Lucian, *False Prophet*, 23 and 49

do not really have any evidence for Pharisaic proselytizing in the Diaspora. On Jewish territory outside Judaea Pharisees generally appear, according to the Gospels, in a group.[20] But otherwise Paul's enlistment of full and part-time helpers on his later missionary journeys, at times swelling to a quite substantial company of co-workers, has no parallel in the field of contemporary religious propagation. This could also be said of his mission's continuing close involvement — through messengers, letters and prayers — in the communities founded by it, and their participation — through visits, letters, gifts and prayers — in its ongoing work. The new dynamic in the Christian message and the new quality of life created by it apparently could not be contained within conventional itinerant activities whether religious or philosophic.

(b)   A specific case

The same may be said about one important aspect of Paul's work, the encouragement, collection and transport of financial aid from the Gentile churches for the poor among the saints in Jerusalem.[21] This requires closer inspection because it possesses, externally at least, some parallels with another Jewish institution. The similarities between this and the annual payment of the Temple-tax by Jews (Matt. 17: 24-27) throughout the Dispersion have frequently been noted. Both involved extensive itinerant activity, the creation of groups to oversee the collection and payment, and the acknowledgement of Jerusalem as a distinctive religious centre.

But there are also some significant differences. For example, Paul's collection has a specifically gospel basis for it expresses the gratefulness of the Gentile churches for the foundational preaching in Jerusalem. It also has a cosmopolitan participation for it involves both Jews and non-Jews in giving. As well it possesses a social objection for it aims at the alleviation of the needs of the poor. All this marks it off from the legal basis, national character and essentially cultic purpose of the Temple-tax. At the structural level, there are also variations between them. One is voluntary, the other compulsory. One is gathered in individual homes, the other at central collecting points. One is paid to the Temple authorities, the other presumably to those within the Jerusalem community for charitable disbursement to the poor. So again we

20. Mark 2: 24, 3: 6, 8: 11 and 10: 2; Luke 5: 17, 13: 31, 15: 2, 16: 14 and 17: 20

21. Rom. 15: 24ff.; 1 Cor. 16: 1-4; 2 Cor. chapters 8-9; compare Gal. 2: 8-10; Acts 11: 27-30

have only certain general parallels between these two institutions. Though Paul may have modelled this aspect of his work upon the Temple-tax payment, it differs from the Jewish institution at virtually all levels of its operation.

CONCLUSION

We find then that not only is Paul's conception of the *ekklēsia* distinctive compared to other first century voluntary associations but also his conception of the *ergon* as well. These two, the church and the work, should never be confused, as they generally have in subsequent Christian thinking about the church. Paul nowhere views his missionary operation as an *ekklēsia*, but rather as something existing independently alongside the scattered Christian communities. Nor does it provide the organizational link between the local churches, suggesting the basis for a wider conception of *ekklēsia* of a 'denominational' kind. Paul's mission is a grouping of specialists identified by their gifts, backed up by a set of sponsoring families and communities, with a specific function and structure. Its purpose is first the preaching of the gospel and the founding of churches; then the provision of assistance so that they may reach maturity. While this clearly involves interrelationship with the local communities, Paul's work is essentially a service organization whose members have personal, not structural, links with the communities and who seek to develop rather than dominate or regulate them.

CHAPTER SEVENTEEN

The apostle in the community

From the authority of Paul's wider and narrower circle of 'fellow-workers', we can now turn to the authority of the apostle himself. Before we look at this in connection with the communities, his relationship with three other groups must be considered. Namely, the character of his authority over his *immediate colleagues* in the mission, his position with respect to the *original apostles* in Jerusalem, and his attitude towards *other 'apostles'* who sought to undermine his work. This will prepare the ground for a detailed examination of his involvement in the churches he had founded. All through this discussion the underlying nature of the authority to which even the apostle is subject will gradually come into focus, though fuller explanation of that will take place in the following chapter.

PAUL'S AUTHORITY OVER HIS IMMEDIATE COLLEAGUES

We have already discussed Paul's relationship with such colleagues as Timothy and Titus. He undoubtedly held the pre-eminent place in the work established by him and was chiefly responsible for decisions affecting the movements of his companions. Yet he does not appear to have acted in an authoritarian manner towards them, as if his function was simply to command and theirs only to obey. The presence of a personal rather than formal framework of authority emerges from the familial way in

which he portrays their relationship and the voluntary response
which they make to his requests. So much for what we have seen
to be the case. Can we identify more precisely the nature of the
authority exercised by him here? In an attempt to do this an
appeal could be made to a model of Jewish origin, the institution
of the *shaliach*, i.e. official 'messenger' or 'representative'. Much
of the discussion engendered by this term has centred around the
issue of Paul's commissioning by Christ. But it really has more
relevance to the question of Paul's relationship with his co-
workers. The *shaliach* was, after all, commissioned by men not
God, and required to carry out tasks on their behalf.

The *shaliach* is a messenger of another person with a special,
generally limited, task to perform on his behalf. Outside the
boundaries of that commission he has no authority. He has
importance only so far as he represents the one who sends him
and faithfully carries out his will. He is viewed really as an extension of that person.[1] The *shaliach* institution concerns not the messenger but the one who commissions him. It shows no interest in
the one who is sent, viz as a person in his own right. This provides
some parallel to the relationship between Paul and his immediate
or occasional colleagues. Part of their ministry involved relaying
instructions to the communities from their apostle. We shall look
at the significance attached to their words and the precise character of his authority extended to them as his '*shaliach*' shortly.
But his co-workers have other functions to perform when they are
travelling among the churches. They have a ministry to exercise
in their *own* right, in accordance with the individual gifts they
have been given by God. Paul acknowledges this by mentioning
them alongside himself when referring to his initial work of
apostleship (2 Cor. 5: 11ff.). On other occasions he takes pains to
stress the particular contribution each has made to the advance of
the gospel and the assistance of the churches on their own
initiative rather than at his direction (8: 17). He also eagerly
desires them to be welcomed and received by his communities for
their own sake and given liberty to minister among them.[2] This
does not imply that Paul's colleagues had the kind of heightened
self-conscious authority that characterized the wandering Cynic
philosophers[3], or, in a more muted way, that exhibited by their

1. Ber. 5: 5 and see Gitt. 3: 6 and 4: 1; Kidd. 2: 1; Yom. 1: 15; B. M. 1: 3 and
4. 2: 2
2. 1 Cor. 16: 10-11; 2 Cor. 8: 22 and 24; Phil. 2: 20-22 and 25-28; Col. 4: 7
and 12-13
3. Epictetus, *Dissertationes,* III, 22 and 41ff.

Stoic counterparts. There was a subordination to Paul, though one that was voluntary[4] and 'familial' rather than formal in character.[5] So once again this aspect of his mission cannot simply be understood in terms of parallels that we find in Jewish or Hellenistic circles.

PAUL'S RELATIONSHIP TO THE ORIGINAL APOSTLES

Other apostolic works existed apart from Paul's and had their own missionary commission to fulfil. Peter, for example, had been entrusted with 'the gospel to the circumcised' prior to Paul's call to go to the Gentiles (Gal. 2: 7). Apollos also seems to have concentrated primarily upon the Jews (Acts 18: 24-28). But both Peter and Apollos also contributed occasionally to the life of churches not founded by them. This raises the question of their authority within Paul's communities when they visited them. To begin with, Paul's own practice is illuminating here. He claims no privileged status within communities which he has not himself founded, even when he knows personally many of the people who belong to them. He comes to these as a distinguished visitor seeking an audience, rather than as one who holds a special right of entry into them. Therefore he does not assume any airs of superiority in writing to them, but addresses them as equals. If he regards himself as having certain gifts he can confer on them, they in turn have others from which he will benefit (Rom. 1: 11-12). Though he is 'bold' enough to say certain things to them, it is by way of 'reminder' that he does so (i.e. drawing their attention to matters with which they should have already been familiar) and on the grounds of the general commission as an apostle to the Gentiles that he has received (15: 15-16), of whose limits he shows himself especially conscious (2 Cor. 10: 13-16).

Paul appears to regard the relationship between other apostles and the churches he had founded in the same light. We know, for example, that both Peter and Apollos had visited Corinth and Paul is happy to endorse and encourage their ministry.[6] He is always insistent, however, that the community must *test* the contributions made by such people against the foundation upon which they were built.[7] Elsewhere he lays down the principle that they should not allow visitors to go beyond the 'terms of commis-

4. Compare again 2 Cor. 8: 17
5. 1 Cor. 4: 17; Phil. 2: 22
6. 1 Cor. 3: 5-9 and 21-23, 16: 12
7. Gal. 1: 9; compare 1 Cor. 4: 10-15

sion' they have been given by God (2 Cor. 10: 15). Certainly the foundation apostles in Jerusalem are not accorded any privileged position in relation to his congregations. Though others regard them as 'pillars' of the Christian movement, Paul appears quite unconcerned about their status (Gal. 2: 6 and 9). Indeed he is quite willing to challenge them when fundamental principles are at stake and sets his experience before his churches as an indicator of what their own attitudes should be (vv. 4-20). He also regards the collection for the Jerusalem church as an expression of his communities' gratefulness to it for its fundamental contribution to the spread of the gospel, not as a token of their subordination.[8]

PAUL'S ATTITUDE TO OTHER 'APOSTLES'

Apart from these figures, there are other wandering apostles who also spend time with the communities he has founded. Particularly in Galatia and at Corinth this was taking place with disturbing results. These so-called apostles are not in Paul's view genuine apostles at all, but only spurious counterfeits of whom his church should beware. Paul is therefore extremely scornful of those 'false' (2 Cor. 11: 13) or, as he ironically describes them, 'superior' apostles (12: 11), who go beyond the boundaries of their commission and give themselves a position in local churches to which they have no right. Such men, he says, 'commend themselves' (10: 12 and 18), 'compare themselves with one another' (v. 12) and 'boast beyond the limits in other men's labours' (v. 15). In order that the churches 'may make much of them' (Gal. 4: 17) they 'put on airs', 'take advantage' of others, 'prey' upon them and, in effect, 'make slaves' of those they are to serve.[9] Though Paul on one or two occasions dares to 'boast' (2 Cor. 11: 20) about his authority, he does this only because he has been forced to show how, if he wished, he could outdo their claims (vv. 21ff.). He does not really believe in this procedure (12: 1). And when, on those rare occasions, he 'commends' himself, it is for reasons quite other (6: 4) than those of people who 'pride themselves on man's position and not on his heart' (5: 12). He totally rejects his opponents' approach and insists that it is not the man who commends himself that is accepted, but the man 'whom the Lord commends (2 Cor. 11: 18). Thus if Paul is to boast of anything, he will boast of his 'weaknesses' so that 'the power of

8. 2 Cor. 9: 11-13; Rom. 15: 26-27
9. 2 Cor. 1: 12ff.; 10: 8 and 11: 1ff.

Christ' (12: 6) rather than his own prowess may be seen to be at work in him. Instead of 'taking advantage' (v. 17) of his communities he foregoes the rightful claims of his authority upon them, even when it has the backing of a word of Jesus (1 Cor. 9: 14-15), 'gives himself up to death for them' (2 Cor. 4: 11) and 'suffers' for them (1: 6-7). Since for him life 'is Christ' he 'will not venture to speak of anything except what Christ has wrought' (Rom. 15: 18) through him. All this is summed up in his assertion that 'what we preach is not ourselves but Jesus Christ as Lord, and ourselves as your servants for Christ's sake' (2 Cor. 4: 5). That is the essence and, as we shall now see, the criterion of all his involvement in the life of his communities.

PAUL'S AUTHORITY WITHIN HIS CHURCHES

What kind of authority is it, then, that he possesses vis-à-vis his churches? Significantly, the word *exousia*, 'authority', does not greatly help us here. Paul uses it fewer than a dozen times in his writings, mostly as something he refused to exercise even when it had the support of Jesus' express command.[10] The only two occasions on which he refers to it positively are in contexts where the false apostles in Corinth have left him with no choice but to do so (2 Cor. 10: 8 and 13: 10). Thus to understand his position in the communities founded by him we have to look elsewhere. To begin with, Paul views his relationship with his churches primarily in terms drawn from family life — e.g. as the 'father' who conceived them, as the 'mother' who bore them or as the 'nurse' who cared for them[11] — rather than through analogies from the legal, administrative, political or even religious sphere. A permanent dependence of the communities upon him as of child to parent (or parent-surrogate) does not necessarily follow from this way of speaking. On the contrary, Paul continually encourages his churches to grow up to maturity (or adulthood) in their thinking and behaviour. Although in view of the fundamental role he played in their foundation (1 Cor. 4: 15), and the future role he has in their eschatological presentation[12] — apostle and community are indissolubly tied together from beginning to end — he never suggests this would lead to a severance of their relationship.

10. 1 Cor. 9: 4ff. (3 times), 12 and 18; 2 Thess. 3: 9; 1 Thess. 2: 6 and especially 1 Cor. 9: 14

11. 1 Cor. 4: 14-15; compare 2 Cor. 12: 14; 1 Thess. 2: 11 (father); Gal. 4: 19 (mother); 1 Thess. 2: 7; compare 1 Cor. 3: 2 (nurse)

12. 1 Thess. 2: 19; compare 2 Cor. 1: 14; Phil. 4: 1

Rather Paul's model is the parent-*adult* child rather than parent-*infant* child. (The distinction between these has not been sufficiently noted in discussions of Paul's authority within his churches.)

In the early days of a community's history a heavy burden lies upon the apostle to put his converts on a firm footing with God and one another. But from the very beginning Paul recognizes their self-sufficiency in the Spirit, even though in some areas they may still need his assistance.[13] So in his first letter to the Thessalonians, written fairly shortly after his evangelistic ministry among them, he acknowledges that 'concerning love of the brethren you have no need to have any one write to you, for you yourselves have been taught by God to love one another; and indeed you do love all the brethren throughout Macedonia' (1 Thess. 4: 9-10). When he exhorts them to continue to do so, reminding them of other things that were said to them, Paul is merely expressing his continuing concern for their welfare. But when he goes on to add that 'we would not have you ignorant, brethren, concerning those who are asleep' (1 Thess. 4: 13ff.), he opens up a subject on which *further* tuition is needed by them and which he has a responsibility to give. To a community he has not founded he declares himself 'satisfied about you, my brethren, that you yourselves are full of goodness, filled with all knowledge and able to instruct one another' (Rom. 15: 14). He then adds, 'But on some points I have written to you very boldly by way of reminder, because of the Gentiles in the service of the gospel of God' (Rom. 15: 15). Interestingly the term 'reminder' here covers not only what they well know, but also further *inferences* drawn from it with which they may not have been familiar. But more of that in a moment. they may not have been familiar. But more of that in a moment.

Striking in all this is the way in which Paul seeks to encourage his communities to a deeper point of view, recall them from a false direction or simply remind them of things they already know and practise. The terms he employs are most frequently words of exhortation and appeal, rather than command or decree. By far the most common term used by him in these contexts is *parakalein*, 'appeal', which is used some twenty-three times in his writings.[14] This parallels the use of the term *peithō*, 'persuade' or 'convince',

---

13. 1 Thess. 4: 8; Gal. 2: 3-5; 1 Cor. 2: 12-16; Rom. 8: 9-14

14. E.g. 1 Thess. 2: 11, 4: 1 and 10, 5: 14; 2 Thess. 3: 12; 1 Cor. 1: 10, 4: 16 and 16: 16; 2 Cor. 5: 20, 6: 1, 10: 1 and 13: 11; Rom. 12: 1, 15: 30 and 16: 17; Phil. 4: 2, Eph. 4: 1

in contexts where his preaching to outsiders is in view.[15] Both outside the churches and within them Paul seeks the voluntary decision of those to whom he speaks in favour of the message he brings. Often he attempts this in the most passionate way; 'urging' rather than simply 'asking'[16] or 'saying' to them.[17] We could even conclude that Paul seeks to compel his hearers and readers to transform their way of life without compulsion, so highly does he prize their full consent and commitment to what he has to say.

Significantly Paul never employs the very strong term of command, *epitage̅*, for his own instructions. The three occasions where he does use the noun he has only an opinion to offer and, in the one place where the verb occurs, he refuses to speak in such terms.[18] True, we occasionally find in his letters such terms as *diatassein,* generally translated 'direct', and *paraggelein,* rendered either as 'charge' or 'command' (in the RSV) but the first of these is not used in any strongly legislative way, though the particular passages suggest there was a regularity about many of the guidelines Paul laid down in his churches and that he expected his converts to abide by them.[19] The second term, *paraggelein,* is one used in much the same sense, viz 'instructions' (1 Cor. 11: 17). Apart from his statement 'to the married I give charge . . . ' (7: 10), the remaining five occurrences are in 1 and 2 Thessalonians — four coming from the one passage in the second letter.[20] Indeed all but one example of this, plus a third term, *entole̅* (meaning 'commandment' or 'instruction'), are confined to 1 Corinthians[21] and the two Thessalonian letters.[22]

It is significant that in these three letters, together with Galatians, Paul adopts his most authoritative tone. This must not be ignored, for in these churches serious *departures* from basic teachings on the gospel foundation and spiritual unity of the community are present. Paul therefore employs the strongest possible language in order to bring their members to their senses. The most dramatic example of this occurs in 1 Corinthians when Paul says quite bluntly that 'what I am writing to you is a command of

15. 2 Cor. 5: 11; compare Acts 13: 43, 17: 4, 18: 4, 19: 8 and 26; 26: 28, 28: 23 and 24
16. 1 Thess. 4: 1 and 5: 12; 2 Thess. 2: 1; Eph. 3: 20
17. Gal. 1: 9, 5: 2 and 16; 1 Cor. 7: 8 and 12; Rom. 12: 3 and 15: 8; Phil. 4: 4; Col. 2: 4; Eph. 4: 17
18. 1 Cor. 7; 6 and 25; 2 Cor. 8: 8; Philem. 8
19. 1 Cor. 11; 34 and 16: 1
20. 2 Thess. 3: 4-12 and 1 Thess. 4: 11 (compare 4: 2)
21. 1 Cor. 7: 19 and 14: 37
22. Except Col. 4: 10

the Lord' (1 Cor. 14: 37). However even here he desires that people 'should acknowledge' this and 'recognize' it (1 Cor. 14: 37-38). Failure to do so does not result in forceable exclusion from the community, just non-recognition of the person concerned. Compare too his strong injunction to the Thessalonians that 'whoever disregards this, disregards not men but God' (1 Thess. 4: 8), 'this' being an instruction, given 'through the Lord Jesus'. But his reminder that it is 'God' who 'gives his holy Spirit to you' once again indicates that the truth of his statements should be self-evident to them.

But all this is an exception to the general rule. Paul prefers not to speak in such terms and elsewhere in his letters language of this type is absent. Where he writes to churches who have exhibited a mature stance on most matters and a genuine concern for his welfare, a different spirit is present. Paul's letters to the Philippians is an excellent example of this. Though it contains admonitions of various kinds, these are not conveyed in the kind of strong language that we find in 1 Corinthians and 2 Thessalonians. Mostly he reiterates things they already know and do but, as he says, 'to write the same things is not irksome to me, and it is safe for you' (Phil. 3: 1). His warm letter to Philemon also catches the spirit of Paul's general approach. 'Though I am bold enough in Christ to command *(epitassein)* you to do what is required',he says, 'yet for love's sake I prefer to appeal to you . . . ' (Philem. 8-9). Even his expressed boldness to command stems from his new freedom 'in Christ' rather than some 'legal right'.

THE HEART OF THE MATTER

Two statements both to troublesome communities, reveal the heart of Paul's attitude to his churches. 'We do not lord it *over* your faith', he tells the Corinthians; 'we work *with* you for your joy' (2 Cor. 1: 24). The apostle, for all his divine call, diverse gifts and founding labours, does not set himself in a hierarchical position above his comunities or act in an authoritarian manner towards them. He refuses to do this since Christ, not he, is their master (4: 5). As one subject to Christ himself, he stands *with* them in all that he does. That is why he talks elsewhere of his belonging to the church, not of the church belonging to him.[23] He does not issue his approvals, encouragements, instructions, warnings and censures as one who sits in isolation from the community

23. 1 Cor. 4: 22-23 and 12: 28

but as one who stands within it, surrounded by all the gifts and ministries the Spirit has granted the other members. Even at a distance he can envisage them assembling together with his spirit present in their midst (1 Cor. 5: 3; Col. 2: 5). In order to give expression to this Paul constantly forms new compound words with the prefix *sun*, 'with' or 'co-', to emphasize his fellowship with his communities in all that they experience.[24] He identifies with them in their weaknesses and strengths, their struggles and labours, their sufferings and consolations, their prayers and thanksgiving, their rejoicings and victories. When he speaks to them, he speaks always as one of them, even where he has the severest things to say. So to the Galatians he writes, 'Brethren, I beseech you, become as I am, for I also have become as you are' (Gal. 4: 12).

There are profound reasons for Paul's identifying with his communities in this way and addressing them as he does. Did not Christ identify himself with those he came to aid in the most far-reaching way? God sent 'his own son in the likeness of sinful flesh and for sin, condemned sin in the flesh'. 'For our sake he made him to be sin who knew no sin, so that in him we might become the righteousness of God. *Working together with him*, then, we entreat you not to accept the grace of God in vain.[25] In this respect Paul not only proclaims the gospel message, and all that flows from it, but *embodies* it as well, conveying its life through both his words and his deeds. Christ's identification with mankind also affects the *manner* in which Paul can speak to his converts. For God draws men to himself not through the exercise of his power, but rather the demonstration of his 'weakness' — or so it seems from a human point of view — in the cross (1 Cor. 1: 20-24). But then 'the weakness of God is stronger than men' (v. 25). For this reason Paul cannot imperiously 'command' his readers. When he addresses his communities he does so in 'weakness', 'fear', and 'trembling' (2: 3). But to do this is to speak 'in demonstration of the Spirit and power' (v. 5). Christ 'was crucified', he says, 'in weakness but lives by the power of God. For we are weak in him but in dealing with you we shall live with him by the power of God' (2 Cor. 13: 4). In the death of Jesus lies an understanding of Paul's own authority with the churches he was called to serve.

24. 1 Cor. 12: 26; Rom. 1: 12, 15: 32, 16: 9 and 21; Phil. 1: 7, 2: 2, 17 and 25, 3: 17; Col. 4: 11; Eph. 2: 19, 21 and 22, 3: 6, 4: 16
25. Rom. 8: 3; 2 Cor: 5.21 - 6: 1

CHAPTER EIGHTEEN

The authority of the apostle

This, then, is the framework within which Paul exercises authority among his communities. This does not take place through the coercion of his converts, or the forceful imposition of his will upon them. Rather it is achieved by persuading his communities to accept his point of view. This persuasion is based on his capacity to convince them, by word and by example, that what he desires for them the gospel also requires of them.

THE RELATIONSHIP BETWEEN AUTHORITY AND FREEDOM

Paul's approach to authority did not develop independently of his understanding of freedom but arose in close association with it. He strongly affirms the freedom within which his communities already stand through the gospel he preached (Gal. 5: 1 and 13). He does not place limits upon this, drawing lines around them and only little by little allowing them to extend their freedom into new areas of experience. He recognizes that from the beginning they have freedom in Christ as full and complete as it could be (2 Cor. 3: 3 and 17). Paul's task is to help them discover the real dimensions of that freedom and discern the false versions of it that others might seek to press upon them (1 Cor. 3: 21-23). Their freedom is a reality to be appropriated, not a goal to which they must be gradually introduced. For this reason his instructions to his converts are generally couched in terms of appeal and exhortation, rather than command and decree. Even when he threatens to come to them with a 'rod of iron' and 'punish' or 'not spare' his readers, it is the 'rod', 'punishment' and 'severity' of God's word that he intends to lay upon them to do its work, not some worldly power or weapon by which he can enforce their submission to his will (2 Cor. 10: 3-6). In any case he would prefer to come to them 'with love in a spirit of gentleness'.[1] This explains why, precisely when he fears he may have to take this course of action, he hesitates, holds himself at a distance, allowing the Corinthians time to see for themselves what the real situation is and alter their attitude accordingly. Subsequently accused of vacillating in his plans, Paul replies that 'it was to spare you that I refrained from coming to Corinth . . . For I made up my mind not to make you another painful visit . . . And I wrote as I did that when I came I might not be pained by those who should have made me rejoice, for I felt sure of all of you, that my joy would be the joy of you all' (2 Cor. 1: 23-2: 4). As he says elsewhere, the 'authority which the Lord has given' him is for 'building up and not for tearing down'.[2] Nothing is gained by their conformity to his point of view unless they see the truth for themselves and embrace it fully from their own hearts. A purely nominal obedience does not result in any real growth in their understanding or living.

Paul's approach to authority relates to his view of freedom in another respect as well. We saw earlier that while liberty for him involves *independence* from certain things and for others, only through *dependence* upon Christ does it become possible. The experience of freedom begins through submission to another and only on this basis can it continue and deepen. But we saw also that the life of freedom involves *interdependence* as well, particularly with those who belong to the Christian community, resulting in a mutual service of and subjection to one another. This interrelationship with others is the natural expression of Christian freedom and is the only context within which it can grow to maturity. We have a real paradox here, for precisely through his increasing service to Christ and to others the Christian finds himself becoming progressively more free. This helps us to understand several references to 'obedience' which occur in Paul's letters.

Paul requests the Philippians 'as you have always obeyed, so now, not only as in my presence but much more in my absence' (Phil. 2: 12). On the one hand this may be seen as God's work,

---

1. 1 Cor. 4: 21; compare 2 Cor. 10: 3-6
2. 2 Cor. 10: 8; compare 13: 10

but on the other as their own. Paul is not asking for obedience to himself here so much as to the gospel, for it requires them to 'work out (their) own salvation with fear and trembling'. Paul says this more explicitly to the Thessalonians who, when they received the word of God from him '. . . accepted it not as the word of men but as what it really is, the word of God' (2 Thess. 2: 13). The 'obedience' he has won 'from the Gentiles' (mentioned several times in Romans) also has as its object 'the gospel of Christ'.[3] The 'obedience' of the Corinthians (resulting from Titus' visit among them) has to do with their now standing 'firm in the faith'. This followed the 'repentance that leads to salvation' (occasioned by Paul's earlier letter to them), though Paul also notes how with 'fear and trembling' they received Titus among them. Paul can write to the Corinthians to find whether 'they are obedient' in everything,[4] ask the Thessalonians 'to obey what we say in this letter',[5] and reveal to Philemon that he is 'confident of (his) obedience' (Philem. 21). But here we need to remind ourselves that at the basis of Paul's instructions to his communities lies a call to 'remembrance' and that behind all his appeals is an acknowledgement of their possession of the Spirit.[6] Not only things he has already taught them but even new teaching can be presented to them in this manner. Whatever he says, whether already expressed or yet to be communicated, has its root in the foundation on which their community rests. When a question of conflict arises, he deals with it by drawing their attention to that common starting point and tracing out its consequences for the specific issue at hand.[7]

THE ULTIMATE AUTHORITY OF THE GOSPEL

This leads us to the heart of the matter. What is the ultimate authority to which not only individual Christians and their communities but even the apostle himself are subject? For this 'foundation', or 'common starting point', is the source from which Paul derives his authority. It is nothing less than the *euaggelion*, 'gospel', which he has been called to preach and embody in

3. Rom. 15: 18; compare 1: 5, 16: 17-19 and 26
4. 2 Cor. 2: 9; compare 10: 6
5. Compare here 2 Thess. 3: 14
6. 1 Thess. 4: 8; 1 Cor. 2: 12ff.; Philem. 19-20
7. See chapter 8, footnote 16; also 1 Thess. 4: 13ff.; Gal. 3: 1ff.; Rom. 6: 15ff.; 1 Cor. 1: 17ff.; 2 Cor. 5: 11ff.; Phil. 3: 2ff.; Col. 2: 8ff.; Eph. 5: 1ff.

his life, and hand over to the communities founded by him.[8] Only insofar as he remains faithful to that gospel, in word and life, does he or any other apostle possess its authority and deserve recognition from others. While he endorses the freedom of other apostles to build on the foundation he has laid, Paul also insists that his communities test the contributions made by such people against that foundation itself, as he himself has done (Gal. 1: 9 and 2: 11-21). The foundation apostles themselves, he emphasizes, had nothing to add to his gospel but simply confirmed its legitimacy (2: 6). His churches should also evaluate his own subsequent teaching by that same original message. Paul makes this quite explicit. 'If we ourselves', he says, 'or even an angel from heaven, should preach a gospel at variance with the gospel we preached to you, let him be anathema' (1: 8). The church has the right and power to excommunicate its own apostle if he radically departs from the gospel!

It is interesting to note here how Paul from time to time consciously distinguishes his own inferences from the words of Jesus. In doing so he appeals for consideration on the basis of his having functioned trustworthily in previous situations when his advice had been sought, not on some claim to his apostolic status or infallibility (1 Cor. 7: 25). Although having done this he concludes that he thinks the Spirit has guided him in the reflections (v. 40), he has left the way open for his communities to see how he arrived at them and to judge whether they are legitimate deductions from their gospel premises.

The gospel itself, as key passages in his writings demonstrate, essentially concerns God's saving activity on behalf of mankind.[9] This has been most clearly revealed in Jesus' death and resurrection, presence and return, and in the reconciliation this has effected.[10] At its heart is 'the word of the cross' (1 Cor. 1: 18). But it is also a living and growing reality in the world, transforming individuals and groups and establishing colonies among them. This takes place through the Spirit[11] who comes from God (1 Cor. 2: 12). Two things flow from this. In the first place, the gospel is not just a word or a message, but rather a 'life' and a 'person' (Rom. 10: 14). This remains true whether we think of Christ around whom it centres, the apostle through whom it is transmitted, or even the individual in whose life it takes root. True, the *words* spoken by each are crucial, for without them there might

8. E.g. 1 Cor. 1: 17, 9: 19-23 and 15: 1-3
9. 1 Thess. 1: 5 and 9-10; Col. 1: 26-27
10. 1 Cor. 15: 3-4; 2 Cor. 5: 18-19 et al.
11. 1 Thess. 1: 5; 1 Cor. 2: 4; 2 Cor. 3: 6

not be understanding of what they bring. But no less crucial is what they *do,* particularly the suffering they endure, for in this the very heart of what they bring is revealed (1 Thess. 1: 6). In the second place, Christ himself is both the content of the gospel and the source of its continuing potency. Not only is he defined by the preaching and illustrated by the living of the apostles, but his presence is actualized in it. Not only is he the objective authority to whom they point, but also the subjective authority in whose power they operate. For the Spirit is none other than the power of the living Christ here and now.[12] This two-sided reality explains, by the way, how Paul can speak of the 'tradition' passed on by him to his communities as something received not from men but Christ, even though in fact much of it was handed over to him by earlier apostles.[13] It also means that Paul exhibits *Christ's* authority when he who is only an 'earthly vessel' (2 Cor. 4: 7) in word and deed, in preaching and living, in communicating and suffering, faithfully fulfils the ministry to which he has been commissioned.

This close connection between the apostle and the gospel becomes even more emphatic when Paul talks not about 'the' but about 'my'[14] or 'our'[15] gospel. His speaking in this way betrays not so much the particular interpretation he placed upon the gospel for the Gentiles, as his involvement in it through his preaching and its effects on his communities. The dynamic aspect of the gospel is more in view here than its content. Paul further expresses the connection between the two by his understanding of 'tradition'. In the first place he attached his own initial experience of Christ to the traditions handed on to him by earlier apostles (1 Cor. 15: 8-10). He also regards the 'tradition' as only becoming 'gospel' when someone interprets it through preaching, so that it becomes a living experience for others who receive it and begin to live by it.[16] Again the virtual equivalence of the two in his thinking comes to dramatic clarity when he exhorts, or commends, people to imitate himself. 'You became imitators of us and the Lord', he reminds the Thessalonians (1 Thess. 1: 6). 'I urge you', he says to the Corinthians, 'become imitators of me', even 'as I am of Christ' (1 Cor. 4: 6 and 11: 1). 'Become as I am', he beseeches the Galatians (Gal. 4: 12). 'Join in imitating me', he encourages the Philippians (Phil. 3: 17). So Paul regards himself

12. 2 Cor. 3: 17 and compare Gal. 1: 12 with 1: 16
13. 1 Cor. 11: 23 and 15: 3
14. Rom. 2: 16 and 16: 28; compare Gal. 1: 11 and 2: 2
15. 1 Thess. 1: 5 and 2: 14
16. 1 Cor. 15: 1-3; compare 11: 2 and 23; Rom. 6: 17

as closely identified with the gospel, constructively involved in the tradition and as a clear reflection of Christ as well.

Even so, he does not separate himself off from others. The Philippians are to imitate 'those who so live as you have an example in us' and the Thessalonians have already become 'imitators of the churches of God in Judaea' who suffered from their countrymen as Christ himself had done (1 Thess. 2: 14-15). Paul can move so freely between Christ, himself and certain of his converts precisely because he urges obedience not to himself personally, or primarily to his instructions, but to the gospel in all its ramifications. This gospel has become transparent in him and in some of his readers. All this applies, in some measure or other, to any member of the community who responsibly exercises the *charisma* he has been given and genuinely reflects the fruit of the Spirit in his life. This is why Christians are to submit to one another in the community: each is the bearer to the other, in some degree, of the word and life of Christ. All, as Luther so beautifully expresses it, are 'to be a sort of Christ to one another', and for this reason, as Paul crystallizes this principle, all are to 'be subject to one another out of reverence for Christ' (Eph. 5: 21). But we may go further. Since, according to Paul, the gospel about Christ was prefigured in the earlier Old Testament scriptures (Gal. 3: 8) and elaborated upon in subsequent apostolic traditions including the various Gospel narratives (2 Thess. 2: 15 and 3: 6), it stands as the criterion by which all are to be judged and interpreted, and the power by which we all live.

THE DISTINCTIVENESS OF PAUL'S APPROACH TO AUTHORITY

Drawing together all the threads of Paul's approach to authority, we can conclude that:

(a)   all authority stems from God the Father as revealed in his Son Jesus Christ and is mediated by their Spirit;

(b)   in the prophetic history of Israel, as recorded in the Old Testament scriptures, and in the apostolic development of the church this authority was decisively present; but the person and the work of Jesus Christ, and the message about him enshrined in the apostolic writings, are the *definitive* expression of God's will and normative for all that precedes and follows;

(c)   through the Spirit God continues to speak and work authoritatively, not through coercion of people's personalities but by convincing their minds of the truth and warming their hearts with love so that they freely embrace it;

(d)   authority is exercised through the service of others in word
and deed, not their domination; and Jesus is the example *par excellence* of the way in which this takes place, since 'though he was in
the form of God, (he) did not count equality with God a thing to
be grasped, but emptied himself, taking the form of a servant . . .'
(Phil. 2: 6-7);
(e)   authority is conveyed in this way primarily through the
apostles, who still live in their writings; though in differing
measure all Christians manifest Christ to one another according
to the ministries given them by the Spirit and are therefore instruments of his authority.

This understanding of authority can be distinguished from
other first century approaches. For example, from that based on
the *sacerdotal rights* of the priesthood communicated by succession
of election from one generation of chosen men to another (as
among the Essenes and Qumran community). Or that centred
around a sacred curriculum of *written and oral traditions* preserved
and extended by an educationally accredited series of teachers (as
among the Rabbis and Scribes). Also from that arising from the
individual experience of those who have been mystically enlightened
or who have rationally grasped the truth (as in the mystery
religions and Stoicism) and who, by virtue of that experience
alone, are regarded as qualified transmitters of it. Although some
of Paul's terminology overlaps with what one finds along these
various groups — for example the talk of 'traditions', the making
of 'commands', the expectation of 'obedience' — these words are
not central to his discussions or exercise of authority. The real differences lie in the *content,* for whatever similarity there may be at
some levels, for instance the ultimate grounding of authority in
the divinity worshipped, the means by which authority is conveyed and the type of authority in view markedly differ.

Attempts to find a model for the type of authority Paul
possessed in the Jewish *shaliach* institution have already been
briefly referred to. We suggested that if any parallels were to be
sought, the relationship between Paul and his colleagues provided
a more relevant field for comparison, though even there only
formal similarities came to light. There is an additional problem
here and it accentuates the difficulty of drawing Paul into the
discussion. Jewish missionaries, or prophets, are never described
in *shaliach* terms even by the rabbis. Though the word is used of
those engaged in the collection of the Temple-tax for Jerusalem
this may reflect post-AD 70 practice. Paul oversaw his collection,
but the responsibility for carrying it out largely lay with his
associates. In any case, since the earliest written evidence for the

institution comes from the middle of the second century, the form in which it has been discussed might not have been in existence before the destruction of the Temple in AD 70.

Many more points of contact can be found between Paul's view of apostleship and the self-understanding of the Cynic philosopher, at least as depicted by Epictetus. Both are conscious of a divine call and commission.[17] Both see their task in terms of serving God and teaching men.[18] Both celebrate freedom and wish others to enter into it.[19] Both are willing to suffer in the pursuit of their vocation.[20] Both are engrossed in their calling.[21] Still there are real differences as well. The idea of apostleship is not as clearly articulated among the Cynics; there is no eschatological edge to their proclamation; self-exertion rather than grace is more in the foreground; and suffering is more an exemplary work than something inherent in their vocation. As well, the Cynics in certain respects were individualists, with no real sense of a localized community. Although they propogated the idea of common friendship that potentially exists between all men, they did not see the need for an intensive community life between smaller groups of people.

CONCLUSION

So Paul's understanding of his calling, and the idea of authority inherent in it, cannot be fully paralleled in the activities of the Jewish *shaliach* or the Cynic philosopher. His understanding has more in common with the prophetic vocation of some of his Old Testament forerunners. But the unique character of the Christ whom he preaches and embodies, and the new depth of community life generated by the gospel, have both left their distinctive mark on Paul. Paul's apostolic authority was ultimately a gift, given by Christ supernaturally on the Damascus road, for use in the communities he was called to found through the power of the Spirit. Ultimately Paul owed his idea of community not to any cultural precedent but to the instruction and example of Christ himself.

---

17. Epictetus, *Dissertationes,* III, 22: 23; compare Gal. 1: 1
18. Epictetus, *Diss.,* III, 22: 24f.; compare Rom. 1: 14; 1 Cor. 1: 4 and 15
19. Epictetus, *Diss.,* III, 22: 48, 96f.; compare 1 Cor. 9: 1; Gal. 5: 13; 2 Cor. 13: 12f.
20. Epictetus, *Diss.,* III, 24: 113f.; compare 2 Cor. 4: 10
21. Epictetus, *Diss.,* III, 22: 94f.; compare 2 Cor. 11: 27f.

Conclusion

We have now come to the end of our investigation of Paul's idea of community but, before we conclude, something should be said about the practicability of his view. There can be no doubt this his communities failed to express fully the ideals of common life he held out before them, and that Paul was fully aware of this fact. But it would be a mistake to represent his subtle and distinctive approach to community as therefore idealistic and impracticable. While it certainly differs from alternative views of community present during his time, even other Christian ones, and bypasses the more structured frameworks in which most of them operated, this did not stem from a utopian evaluation of the possibilities of human relationships. Rather it resulted from a sober estimate of their potential 'in the Lord' through the agency of 'his Spirit'.

No one is more realistic than Paul in dealing with the frailties and failures of human relationships and yet he continually sets before his communities a vision of what their common life should, and one day will, be. He sees this as simply the consequence of the life that is in them, and therefore as the reality they must strive to realize. His view of community unfolds necessarily out of his understanding of the gospel and no less than that gospel is it geared to the real contradictions of human existence. Indeed, all the way through this study, we have seen how Paul develops his view of community directly from fundamental gospel realities. For example Christ's radical words, 'Who are my brethren?' and 'When two or three gather together . . .' lie behind Paul's approach to community relations and meeting; Christ's sacrificial service stands as the model and motive for those who have special responsibilities in the community, including Paul himself; Christ's resurrection power acts as the source of the unity between the community's members and as the dynamic and structure of the gifts and ministries exercised within it. So Paul's understanding of community is nothing less than the gospel itself in corporate form!

There is also the fact that his organization of community life contains no detailed confession or code to which people must subscribe, no liturgical order by which their meetings must be governed, no clerical structure of leadership to regulate the control of its affairs and no denominational authority to create between between communities an organizational unity. This does not mean that Paul was unconcerned about right belief and conduct, order and decency in church, and stability and unity within and between his communities, nor that statements of faith and principles of conduct, criteria for assembling, distinctions between members and tangible expressions of fellowship did not exist in them. But none of these were secured by the formal means mentioned above. Yet despite this apparent absence of all institutional means of support, we should not imagine that Paul's work was provisional and incomplete — a series of interim measures later to be superseded by more concrete arrangements. Undoubtedly that is what soon began to happen. Others after Paul did not see things in the same light. In the writings of the following period there occur a series of minor shifts of emphasis through which his understanding of community began to be altered, the unfortunate consequences of which remain with us till this day.

In the Introduction we noted that Paul's idea of community was not only the most detailed, but also the most developed and profound, in the writings of the New Testament. We have now suggested that the superiority of Paul's view is no less apparent if one compares it with the Christian literature of the succeeding centuries. Though no one yet seems to have done it, I would claim more for Paul than just the principal place in early Christian thought about *community*, significant though that might be. Paul may be the first individual, of whom we have record, to formulate and implement an idea of religious community not subservient to those two fundamental institutions of ancient society, the family and the state. Religious communities that possessed a relatively or completely independent status do antedate Paul by several centuries. About some of these we have very little information, though there are others who left a more permanent record. As we have seen, various Stoics were interested in the idea of community, but their discussions tended to remain at the abstract level. They thought more in terms of an international community than of real associations of people in specific places. Such a community was the Qumran sect by the Dead Sea whose self-understanding and practices were carefully committed to writing by the members themselves. But here we have a composite record rather than a personal statement and the outlook of Qumran involved a future political realization of the community's goals.

There is a further side to Paul's understanding of community — the historically significant role it has played, not only in the development of Christian thought and practice but in the formation of more general *social* theory. We do not need to say much about the first. The seminal importance of Paul's ideas for the view of the church held, for example, by Augustine in late antiquity, Calvin and the Anabaptists in the time of the Reformation and, in the last century, movements for the reform of ecclesiastical and missionary structures, is well known. The rediscovery of Paul's approach to community has periodically broken the intellectual systems by which thinking about the church has been constrained, and challenged the institutional frameworks in which its practice has been formalized. Less recognized is Paul's contribution to more general social thought. I give but two examples.

To begin with, many of the basic elements in Augustine's social teaching — and it is one of the truly foundational contributions to Western social thought — have their origin in Paul's writings. Certainly Augustine was a more systematic thinker than Paul and was responsible for creatively elaborating ideas from a number of sources. But commentators too often have credited him with originating certain social ideas and principles which were drawn from Paul's writings. In particular Augustine's highly developed 'organic' view of society has its basis in distinctively Pauline ideas.

A modern example of the influence of Paul generally is provided by Max Weber's adoption of the concept of *charisma*. Its value in the clarification of early Christian ideas of authority had been impressed upon him by a reading of Rudolf Sohm's work on church history and law — Sohm himself having taken the term directly from Paul. Weber gave it a wider sociological relevance and in certain significant respects also altered its meaning. But the roots of his concept and — though Sohm did not see it — the basis for its wider social application, lie in the Pauline writings themselves. But Paul's historical significance does not stop here. For while in view of a changed cultural situation the *practical expression* of his views is not always applicable today, the *principles* underlying them continue to attract the attention of those actively, even desperately, seeking community. His understanding of what constitutes community raises serious questions both for established ecclesiastical structures which claim a historical link with Paul and the counter-culture groups which ardently promise 'community' to those who join them. The former have excluded many of Paul's basic insights into the nature of community and frozen others into a rigid form that prevents their constructive exercise. The latter lack the foundation which alone can give the fullest cohesion and depth to their efforts. Paul's approach to community has stimulated the creation of alternatives alongside these, e.g. house churches and other Christian communities, but these have not always been accompanied by the existence of a contemporary version of Paul's work to complement and enhance their activities. More recently it has spurred the development of cell groups and charismatic fellowships within some traditional structures which have a more interpersonal and less hierarchical character — though these rarely result in a radical reappraisal, along Pauline lines, of the wider institutions. For that reason the principles underlying Paul's idea of community remain as revolutionary and challenging in the twentieth century as they did in the first.

Appendix:
The drift of the Pastorals

When did the drift from Paul's idea of community begin? While some have located the movement away from Paul's view only in the post-apostolic writings of the succeeding period, others have discerned its roots in the New Testament itself, even in writings attributed to or descriptive of Paul himself. In the Introduction we noted the doubts surrounding Ephesians, Acts and the Pastorals.

EPHESIANS

The decision to include Ephesians within the treatment of Paul seems in retrospect to be warranted. Although at a few points different terms are used (e.g. *doma* instead of *charisma*), some new developments occur (e.g. its theology of racial integration) and stronger emphases can be detected (e.g. the church built on the foundation of the apostles and prophets), the extent and character of their usage do not require, though they may still permit, a non-Pauline view of its authorship.

ACTS

We have also freely used Luke's account of Paul throughout our discussion, since it contains much valuable historical information about the background and nature of Paul's activities. While it has

considerable detail on the composition, movements and consequences of his mission, it has very little direct material on Paul's
understanding and practice of community. Where it does throw
light on this, it frequently supports and extends what we find in
Paul's letters, e.g. the household basis of his churches, the
personal links between them, the informality of their gatherings
and so on. In certain matters we find a preservation of pre-
Pauline attitudes, viz concentration on the more extraordinary
works of the Spirit and more prosaic descriptions of the
communities as 'disciples' or 'believers', though in others a
reflection of post-Pauline views begins to appear, i.e. the
occasional use of *ekklēsia* for the community as well as the
gathering, the tendency to standardize Paul's terminology of
leadership through references to elders and the portrayal of Paul
as more accommodating to the Jerusalem authorities than his
letters would suggest. But none of these makes Luke the purveyor
of 'early Catholicism' that many have claimed him to be.

THE PASTORALS

What then of the Pastorals? To compare 1-2 Timothy and Titus
with the other letters of Paul, we will look in turn at their conception of *ekklēsia* and metaphors of community, their view of gifts
and order, their depiction of class and leadership in the community and their understanding of Paul's and his colleagues'
authority. From this discussion, we will evaluate whether the
Pastorals also stem from him.

(a)   Conception of ekklēsia and metaphors of community

The local sense of *ekklēsia* still seems to be preserved in the
Pastorals (1 Tim. 3: 5 and 5: 16), though in one place a more
generic sense is present (3: 15). But the notion of 'gathering' no
longer appears in the foreground; *ekklēsia* is virtually a synonym
for the community. The language of family relationships also
occurs. Indeed the church is expressly described as 'the household
of God' (v. 15). Along with occasional reference to the 'brethren'
(4: 6 and 6: 2) — proportionately less frequent than in any other
Pauline letter except Ephesians — we have the advice to Timothy
not to 'rebuke an older man but exhort him as you would a father;
treat younger men like brothers, older women like mothers,
younger women like sisters . . .' (5: 1-2).
Interestingly enough the community is never described in the

letters as a 'body'. While this idea is also absent from the (late) letter to the Philippians, here we have three letters, not just one, with the operation of the community less prominently in view. The building metaphor occurs in the Pastorals, but in a more static form than elsewhere. Though the church is the property of 'the living God', its function is that of 'the pillar and bulwark of the truth' (3: 15).

So while the terms used in the Pastorals are generally similar to those in the other letters, overall we are presented with a less dynamic view of the Christian community. On the other hand we do not have here, as some have suggested, a sacramental view of the church. Baptism and the Lord's Supper are not so much as mentioned, let alone aggrandized in any way.

(b)   View of gifts and order

The term *charisma* also turns up in these writings, though only in the letters to Timothy with reference to Timothy himself, not members of the community in general (4: 14; 2 Tim. 1: 6). Certainly a wide range of functions is mentioned which in the other letters Paul describes as *charismata* (e.g. prophecy,[1] teaching,[2] exhortation,[3] pastoral care (1 Tim. 3: 8ff.), service (vv. 4, 5), giving aid (5: 26)), but they are not called gifts in the Pastorals. Also all are not said to have their individual role to play — a typical Pauline emphasis. False teaching must be tested, though the responsibility for this devolves on the genuine teachers (2 Tim. 2: 2; Tit. 1: 9-11) and only indirectly on the community at large.

The term *agapē*[4] occurs in these letters, but nowhere provides the ethos within which the members of the community carry out all their responsibilities to another. Only three times in all three writings do we have any reference to the Spirit.[5] There are three allusions to 'prophecies'; two to utterances, probably predictive in character and related to Timothy's commissioning for his task, and one to a pagan prophet from Crete. None refers to any ongoing activity in the life of the community.[6] Teaching now occupies the primary position, along with exhortation. Mention

---

1. 1 Tim. 1: 18 and 4: 14; Tit. 1: 12
2. 1 Tim. 4: 13; 2 Tim. 2: 2; Tit. 1-9, 2: 1 et al.
3. 1 Tim. 4: 13 and 5: 1; Tit. 2: 2ff. and 2: 15
4. 1 Tim. 1: 5; 2: 15, 4: 12 and 6: 11; 2 Tim. 1: 7, 2: 22 and 3: 10; Tit. 2: 2; compare 1 Tim. 1: 14 and 2: 13
5. 1 Tim. 4: 1; 2 Tim. 1: 14; Tit. 3: 5
6. 1 Tim. 1: 18 and 4: 14; Tit. 1: 12

of the more spectacular gifts, such as healings, miracles or glossolalia, is lacking. Since there is a similar lack in Romans as well, perhaps not too much weight should be placed upon this evidence. However, unlike Romans, the Pastorals do not even refer to the apostolic exercise of these gifts.[7] So despite some of the language held in common with the other letters, we appear to be in the presence of a less dynamic approach to gifts and a less participatory view of community. The charismatic dimension seems to have diminished in importance, though it has not altogether disappeared.

(c) Depiction of class and leadership

Yet in these letters, the functions talked about do involve more than just the prominent people in the community. While pastoral and teaching responsibilities are confined to the more mature members of the congregation,[8] widows are also encouraged to engage in a similar ministry within the confines of female relationships (Tit. 2: 3-4). Younger men, and probably their wives, can carry out tasks appropriate to deacons (1 Tim. 3: 8-13). Any two or three members of the church can bring a charge of irresponsibility against an elder (5: 19).

But the role of women suffers more restrictions. The men alone appear to have the privilege of praying in the church (2: 8) — not, as in 1 Corinthians (11: 5), the women as well. Also, women are expressly prohibited from teaching and exercising authority over their husbands (1 Tim. 2: 12), whereas Colossians speaks of the relative freedom for all to teach and admonish one another (Col. 3: 16). The restriction upon women is buttressed in the Pastorals by an appeal to their responsibility for the Fall (1 Tim. 2: 14), though in the other letters Eve's weakness is seen as a warning to all and Adam's responsibility is more firmly in the foreground.[9]

In these writings the *episkopos*, 'the bishop', casts a longer shadow over various aspects of the community's life — organizational arrangements, pastoral care and discipline, its guidance, advancement, protection — than any figure mentioned in the other letters. And the talk about 'aspiring' to be a bishop sits uneasily with comments in other letters about people gaining recognition through devotion to fulfilling other's needs, not con-

7. Compare Rom. 15: 19
8. 1 Tim. 3: 1-7; Tit. 1: 5-12
9. 2 Cor. 11: 3; Rom. 5: 15ff.

centration on acquiring the recognition itself.[10] Yet the language of function rather than office still dominates these letters, for it is a 'task' (1 Tim. 3: 1) which the *episkopos* has (not 'office' as in the RSV). It is those who 'labour' in exhortation and teaching who deserve honour (5: 17). The qualifications laid down for those appointed to such a ministry also indicate that this only took place after they had shown themselves worthy of such work. Yet the description of such work as 'noble' (3: 1), and the emphasis on 'respectability' (v. 7) more than sacrificial service, have a different atmosphere about them.

These two tendencies are also present in the remarks concerning deacons. Although their work is portrayed in functional terms (v. 13) and prior testing is required (v. 10), if they perform well they acquire a 'good' standing or rank for themselves. Again personal moral requirements are stressed at the expense of charismatic endowments. Still, we do not have here anything like an ordination procedure in the later sense[11] and, although a succession of elders is envisaged, it is one of teaching rather than office (2 Tim. 2: 2). In other words, to talk of the institutionalization of the ministry in the Pastorals exaggerates the tendencies towards a more static and exclusive approach to ministry which one finds in their pages.

(d)   Understanding of Paul's and his colleagues' authority

Precisely what role do Timothy and Titus have according to these letters? They are essentially the apostle's representatives, reminding the churches of his teaching and practice and acting towards them as he would if present. It seems too that their association with Paul does not in itself gain them full recognition in these communities. They have to work for that, not by assuming control or asserting their privileged status, but by 'taking heed' of themselves and their teaching, and setting 'the believers an example in speech and conduct' (1 Tim. 5: 13 and 16). Their ministry should also contain a strong note of appeal or exhortation, and they are to develop family relationships with people, not build up formal or sacral power over them.[12] Nowhere is this clearer than in the instruction given to them that 'the Lord's servant must not strive, but be gentle towards all, apt to teach, patient, in meekness instructing his opponents' (2 Tim. 3: 24-25).

10. Compare 1 Cor. 16: 15
11. 1 Tim. 4: 14 (commissioning), 5: 22 (re-acceptance); 2 Tim. 1: 6 (baptism)
12. E.g. 1 Tim. 5: 1-2; 2 Tim. 4: 2

Yet certain tendencies lead in a different direction. The note of command, viz the use of *paraggelein* to command, features more strongly here[13] and terms for rebuke occur more often than in the other letters.[14] For the first time such men also 'preach' to these communities — something that Paul only does elsewhere to outsiders (2 Tim. 4: 2). One cannot escape the impression that Timothy and Titus play a more prominent part in the activities of these communities. While similar kinds of disciplinary action to what we find elsewhere are in view,[15] the apostle's associates are strongly involved in administering it,[16], as with the appointment of *episkopoi* from among the elders (Tit. 1: 5). But they do not exercise the functions of monarchical bishops as some have suggested; the reference to hands being laid upon them has nothing to do with later ordination procedures. We have here a parallel to the setting aside of Barnabas and Paul for their missionary work by the prophets and teachers at Antioch.

The portrait of Paul in these writings also has real similarities with that found in the other materials. The centrality of the gospel in his experience and work,[17] his relationship with his colleagues,[18] the approach to disciple[19] — all have much in common. Yet alongside the gospel an increased importance is given to 'sound doctrine'[20] and the 'sacred writings'.[21] There is a new undertone in the Pastorals, even taking into account the role played by the Old Testament and the apostolic traditions in the other letters. Along with the note of appeal and exhortation, there is an increased tendency for 'commands' and 'rebukes' to be issued on Paul's behalf and a more significant role granted to his associates. In dealing with refractory members, 'Paul' unilaterally excludes two people rather than consults with the community to which the persons concerned belong (1 Tim. 1: 20). Yet despite a lack of emphasis upon the Spirit and the formalization of ways in which 'Paul' speaks about himself, e.g. not only as an apostle but also as a 'herald' and 'teacher',[22] real marks of the apostle do pervade the

13. 1 Tim. 1: 3; 4: 11, 5: 7, 6: 13 and 17; compare 1 Tim. 1: 5 and 18
14. 1 Tim. 5: 20; 2 Tim. 4: 2; Tit. 1: 13 and 2: 15 but contrast 1 Tim. 5: 1
15. 1 Tim. 1: 3-4 and 5: 19-20; 2 Tim. 4: 3; Tit. 1: 9-16 and 3: 9-11
16. 1 Tim. 1: 3 and 5: 20-22; Tit. 3: 10
17. E.g. 1 Tim. 1: 12-17, 2: 3-7, 3: 14-16, 4: 9-10 and 6: 11-16; 2 Tim. 1: 8-12 and 2: 8-13; Tit. 2: 11-14 and 3: 3-8
18. 1 Tim. 1: 2 and 18; 2 Tim. 1: 2 and 2: 1; Tit. 1: 4
19. Compare footnote 15
20. 1 Tim. 1: 3 and 10, 4: 6, 11, 13 and 16, 5: 17, 6: 1 and 3; 2 Tim. 2: 2, 3: 10 and 14, 4: 2-3; Tit. 1: 9, 2: 1, and 10
21. 1 Tim. 4: 13; 2 Tim. 3: 16
22. 1 Tim. 2: 7; 2 Tim. 1: 11

work, nowhere more so in the place that suffering is given in his description of 'his' work.[23]

CONCLUSION

What are we to make of all this? Real similarities exist between the Pastorals and the other letters of Paul and yet also a number of clear differences. All too often these have been exaggerated or overlooked. The content of the Pastorals is neither as far from, nor as close to, what we find in the other letters as discussion of them frequently suggest. Can the differences between them be explained by their later composition and altered historical situation? Possibly. The differences between the earlier letters of Paul and the Captivity letters have been understood in this way.

However the problems here are more severe. Not only are the divergences between the Pastorals and other Pauline correspondence (including Ephesians) *greater in number;* they also move *in another direction.* It seems unlikely that Paul's thought and practice would turn aside into shallower waters, rather than move further in a more profound direction, in the period of time between the latest of the Captivity letters and the first of the Pastorals — especially when only two or three years can have passed. The problem becomes insuperable if the Pastorals are dated back to the fifties. And, quite apart from those already identified, there are other variations. These are the different themes, the contrasts in style and vocabulary and the improbability, in a letter to Timothy, of such statements as 'For this I was appointed a preacher and apostle (*I am telling the truth, I am not lying),* a teacher of the Gentiles in faith and truth' (1 Tim. 2: 7). The reader must judge for himself, but it begins to look as if the first tentative steps away from Paul's idea of community were made, with the best of intentions, in the name of Paul himself!

23. 2 Tim. 1: 11-12, 2: 8-9 and 3: 10-12

Bibliography

Since, as the list of contents shows, the topics treated in adjoining chapters are thematically related, I have arranged this bibliography accordingly. I have restricted the number of entries under each heading to about a dozen articles or books so as not to unduly extend the list, but a number of these contain extensive bibliographical material. No reference is made to standard dictionaries and encyclopaedias, though there are many fine discussions of important terms, e.g. the Theological Dictionary of the New Testament, the Interpreter's Bible Dictionary, the Encyclopaedia Biblica and the Encyclopaedia Judaica. Commentaries are also omitted, but should be consulted on central passages — as should the standard lexicons on New Testament Greek literary, papyrological and epigraphical usage for any serious study of the key terms. Only works written in, or translated into, English are mentioned. I have included among those listed a number of lesser known, particularly Australian, contributions which deserve wider scholarly and general circulation.

Of course many basic texts on this subject remain untranslated, especially from German. Anyone who wishes to investigate these will find ample reference to them in the footnotes of the works cited in the following bibliography, though such works will not necessarily make reference to the more recent discussions of F. Mussner on freedom, J. Hainz on church, G. Theissen on social status, G. Hasenhuttl on charisma, K. Kertelge on ministry and K. Hruby on the synagogue. Various articles in the steadily-appearing *Reallexicon für Antike und Christentum* are also essential reading. These are accompanied by wide-ranging bibliographies: see too the comprehensive list of writings on 'house-communities' in the appendix to P. Stuhlmacher's new commentary on Philemon in the EKK series. Specialists may be interested to hear of unpublished dissertations by C. Hill on 'A Sociology of the New Testament Church' and K. Hemphill on 'Paul's Concept of Charisma', available from Nottingham (U.K.) and Cambridge (U.K.) Universities respectively, and of the enlightening, wide-ranging list of writings dealing with Paul's social and intellectual environment contained in E. A. Judge's article on 'St. Paul and Classical Society', *Jahrbuch für Antike und Christentum*, 15, 1972, 19-36.

Since the manuscript for the book was completed in late 1977, no mention is made of publications after that date.

CHAPTERS ONE AND TWO

ed. S. Benko and J. J. O'Rourke, *Early Church History: The Roman Empire as the Setting of Primitive Christianity*, Oliphants, London, 1971.

F. Cumont, *Oriental Religions in Roman Paganism*, Dover, New York, 1956.

J. G. Gager, *Kingdom and Community: The Social World of Early Christianity*, Prentice-Hall, Englewood Cliffs, 1975.

V. P. Furnish, *Theology and Ethics in Paul*, Abingdon, Nashville and New York, 1968.

W. Halliday, *The Pagan Background to Early Christianity*, Cooper Square, New York, 1925.

E. A. Judge, *The Social Pattern of Christian Groups in the First Century*, Tyndale, London, 1960.

R. N. Longenecker, *Paul: Apostle of Liberty*, Harper & Row, New York, 1964.

G. F. Moore, *Judaism in the First Three Centuries of the Christian Era*, 2 vols, Schocken, New York, 1971.

L. L. Morris, *The Apostolic Preaching of the Cross*, Tyndale, London, 1955.

A. D. Nock, *Conversion: The Old and New in Religion from Alexander the Great to Augustine of Hippo*, Oxford University Press, London, 1933.

S. Sandmel, *The First Christian Century in Judaism and Christianity: Certainties and Uncertainties*, Oxford University Press, New York, 1969.

M. N. Tod, 'Clubs and Societies in the Greek World', *Sidelights on Greek History*, Oxford University Press, London, 1932, 71-96.

CHAPTERS THREE AND FOUR

H. C. Baldry, *The Unity of Mankind in Greek Thought*, Cambridge University Press, London, 1965.

J. Y. Campbell, 'The Origin and Meaning of the Christian use of the word ' ΕΚΚΛΗΣΙΑ ', *Three New Testament Studies*, Leiden, Brill, 1965, 41-54.

L. Cerfaux, *The Church in the Theology of St. Paul*, Herder and Herder, London, 1959.

G. Downey, *A History of the Church of Antioch in Syria*, 1961.

F. V. Filson, 'The Significance of the Early House Churches', *Journal of Biblical Literature*, 58, 1939, 105-112.

B. Gärtner, _Temple and Community in Qumran and the New Testament_, Cambridge University Press, London, 1965.

M. Goguel, _The Primitive Church_, Allen and Unwin, London, 1964.

M. Green, _Evangelism in the Early Church_, Hodder and Stoughton, London, 1970.

E. A. Judge and G. S. R. Thomas, 'The Origin of the Church at Rome: A New Solution?', _Reformed Theological Review_, 25, 1966, 81-94.

E. A. Judge, 'Contemporary Political Models for the Interrelations of New Testament Churches', _Reformed Theological Review_, 22, 1963, 65-76.

A. J. Malherbe, 'House Churches and Their Problems', _Social Aspects of Early Christianity_, Louisiana State University Press, Baton Rouge and London, 1977.

Joan M. Peterson, 'House-Churches in Rome', _Vigiliae Christianae_, 23, 1969, 264-272.

G. La Piana, 'Foreign Groups in Rome during the First Century of the Empire', _Harvard Theological Review_, 20, 1927, 183-354.

CHAPTERS FIVE AND SIX

M. Barth, 'A Chapter on the Church — The Body of Christ', _Interpretation_, 12, 1958, 131-156.

E. Best, _One Body in Christ_, SPCK, London, 1955.

P. A. H. de Boer, _Fatherhood and Motherhood in Israelite and Judaean Piety_, Brill, Leiden, 1974.

D. Bonhoeffer, _Sanctorum Communio_, Collins, London, 1963.

G. Bornkamm, 'The More Excellent Way', _Early Christian Experience_, SCM Press, London, 1969, 180-193.

J. Y. Campbell, 'KOINONIA and its Cognates in the New Testament', _Three New Testament Studies_, Brill, Leiden, 1965, 1-28.

L. Cerfaux, _The Church in the Theology of St. Paul_, Herder and Herder, London, 1959.

V. P. Furnish, _The Love-Command in the New Testament_, Abingdon, Nashville and New York, 1972.

R. H. Gundry, _Sōma in the New Testament_, SNTS, Cambridge University Press, London, 1976.

P. S. Minear, _Images of the Church in the New Testament_, Westminster, Philadelphia, 1960.

J. A. T. Robinson, _The Body_, SCM, London, 1952.

E. Schweizer, _The Church as the Body of Christ_, SPCK, London, 1965.

CHAPTERS SEVEN AND EIGHT

G. Bornkamm, 'Faith and Reason in Paul', _Early Christian Experience_, SCM, London, 1969, 29-46.

E. Ferguson, 'Laying on of hands: its significance in ordination', *Journal of Theological Studies,* 26, 1975, 1-12; and 'Selection and Institution to Office in Roman, Greek, Jewish and Christian Antiquity', *Theologische Zeitschrift,* 30, 1974, 273-284.

A. E. Harvey, 'Elders', *Journal of Theological Studies,* 25, 1974, 315-332.

J. Jeremias, *The Eucharistic Words of Jesus,* SCM, London, 1966.

D. Kemmler, *Faith and Human Reason: A Study of Paul's Preaching as Illustrated by 1-2 Thessalonians and Acts 17, 2-4,* Brill, Leiden, 1975.

H. A. A. Kennedy, *St. Paul and the Mystery Religions,* Hodder and Stoughton, London, 1913.

C. F. D. Moule, *Worship in the New Testament,* Lutterworth, London, 1961.

A. D. Nock, *Early Gentile Christianity and its Hellenistic Background,* Harper and Row, New York, 1964.

D. W. B. Robinson, 'Towards a Definition of Baptism', *Reformed Theological Review,* 24, 1975, 1-15.

R. Schnackenburg, 'Christian Adulthood According to the Apostle Paul', *Catholic Biblical Quarterly,* 25, 1963, 354-370.

(ed.) K. Stendahl, *The Scrolls and the New Testament,* SCM, London, 1953.

G. Wagner, *Pauline Baptism and the Pagan Mysteries,* Oliver and Boyd, Edinburgh and London, 1967.

CHAPTERS NINE AND TEN

G. Bornkamm, 'On the Understanding of Worship', *Early Christian Experience,* SCM, London, 1969, 161-179.

M. M. Bourke, 'Reflections on Church Order in the New Testament', *Catholic Biblical Quarterly,* 30, 1969, 493-511.

H. von Campenhausen, *Ecclesiastical Authority and Spiritual Power in the Church of the First Three Centuries,* A. & C. Black, London, 1969.

H. von Campenhausen, 'The Problem of Order in Early Christianity and the Ancient Church', *Tradition and Life in the Church,* Collins, London, 1968, 123-140.

J. D. G. Dunn, *Jesus and the Spirit,* SCM, London, 1975.

F. Hahn, *Worship in the New Testament,* Fortress, Philadelphia, 1973.

E. Käsemann, 'Worship in Everyday Life: a note on Romans 12', *New Testament Questions of Today,* SCM, London, 1969, 188-195.

E. Käsemann, 'The Cry for Liberty in the Worship of the Church', *Perspectives on Paul,* SCM, London, 1971, 122-137.

T. M. Lindsay, *The Church and the Ministry in the Early Centuries,* Hodder and Stoughton, London, 1902.

W. O. E. Oesterley, *The Jewish Background of the Christian Liturgy,* Peter Smith, Gloucester, 1964.

E. Schweizer, *Church Order in the New Testament,* SCM, London, 1961.

E. Schweizer, 'The Service of Worship', *Neotestamentica,* Zwingli, Zurich, 1964, 333-343.

CHAPTERS ELEVEN AND TWELVE

J. P. V. D. Balsdon, *Roman Women: Their History and Habits*, Greenwood, Westport, 1962.
S. S. Bartchy, ΜΑΛΛΟΝ ΧΡΗΣΑΙ : *First Century Slavery and the Interpretation of 1 Corinthians 7.21*, Society for Biblical Literature, Missoula, 1973.
G. B. Caird, 'Paul and Women's Liberty', Manson Memorial Lecture, University of Manchester, 1971.
G. Dix, *Jew and Greek: A Study in the Primitive Church*, Harper, New York, 1953.
A. Harnack, *The Mission and Expansion of Christianity*, Vol. 2, Williams and Norgate, London, 1908.
S. Heyob, *The Cult of Isis among women in the Graeco-Roman World*, Brill, Leiden, 1975.
M. D. Hooker, 'Authority on her head: 1 Cor. 11.10', *New Testament Studies*, 10, 1963-4, 410-416.
J. Jeremias, *Jerusalem in the Time of Jesus*, SCM, London, 1969.
R. Loewe, *The Social Position of Women in Judaism*, SPCK, London, 1966.
R. MacMullen, *Roman Social Relations, 50 BC to AD 284*, Yale University Press, New Haven, 1974.
A. J. Malherbe, *Social Aspects of Early Christianity*, Louisiana State University, Baton Rouge and London, 1977.
S. B. Pomeroy, *Goddesses, Whores, Wives, Slaves: Women in Classical Antiquity*, Schocken, New York, 1976.

CHAPTERS THIRTEEN AND FOURTEEN

M. Black, *The Scrolls and Christian Origins: Studies in the Jewish Background to the New Testament*, Nelson, London, 1961.
H. von Campenhausen, *Ecclesiastical Authority and Spiritual Power in the Church of the First Three Centuries*, A. & C. Black, London, 1969.
J. D. G. Dunn, *Jesus and the Spirit*, SCM, London, 1975.
G. Forkman, *The Limits of Religious Community*, Gleerup, Lund, 1972.
M. Goguel, *The Primitive Church*, Allen and Unwin, London, 1964.
L. Goppelt, *Apostolic and Post-apostolic Times*, A. & C. Black, London, 1970.
D. R. Hall, 'Pauline Church Discipline', *Tyndale Bulletin*, 22, 1969, 3-26.
E. Käsemann, 'Ministry and Community in the New Testament', *Essays on New Testament Themes*, SCM, London, 1964, 63-94.
D. Powell, 'Ordo Presbyterii', *Journal of Theological Studies*, 26, 1975, 290-328.
L. Sabourin, *Priesthood: A Comparative Study*, Brill, Leiden, 1973.
E. Schweizer, *Church Order in the New Testament*, SCM, London, 1961.
D. M. Stanley, 'Authority in the Church: A New Testament Reality', *Catholic Biblical Quarterly*, 29, 1967, 555-573.

CHAPTERS FIFTEEN AND SIXTEEN

R. Allen, *Missionary Methods: St. Paul's or Ours?* Eerdmans, Grand Rapids, 1962.
W. Beardslee, *Human Achievement and Divine Vocation in the Message of Paul*, SCM, London, 1961.
G. W. Bowersock, *Greek Sophists in the Roman Empire*, Clarendon Press, Oxford, 1969.
A. Deissmann, *Paul: A Study in Social and Religious History*, Harper, New York, 1957.
E. E. Ellis, 'Paul and his Co-Workers', *New Testament Studies*, 17, 1971, 437-452.
M. Green, *Evangelism in the Early Church*, Hodder and Stoughton, London, 1970.
A. T. Hanson, *The Pioneer Ministry*, SCM, London, 1961.
A Harnack, *The Mission and Expansion of Christianity in the First Three Centuries*, Vol. 1, Williams and Norgate, London, 1908.
E. A. Judge, 'The Early Christians as a Scholastic Community II', *Journal of Religious History*, 2, 1961, 125-137.
K. F. Nickle, *The Collection*, SCM, London, 1966.
E. B. Redlich, *St. Paul and his Contemporaries*, Hodder and Stoughton, London, 1913.
D. W. B. Robinson, 'The Doctrine of the Church and its Implications for Evangelism', *Interchange*, 15, 1974, 156-162.

CHAPTERS SEVENTEEN AND EIGHTEEN

C. K. Barrett, *The Signs of an Apostle*, Epworth, London, 1970.
F. F. Bruce, 'Paul and Jerusalem', *Tyndale Bulletin*, 19, 1968, 3-25.
J. D. G. Dunn, *Jesus and the Spirit*, SCM, London, 1975.
D. Hay, 'Paul's Indifference to Authority', *Journal of Biblical Literature*, 88, 1969, 36-44.
E. a. Judge, 'St. Paul and Classical Society', *Jahrbuch für Antike und Christentum*, 15, 1972, 19-36.
A. Kirk, 'Apostleship Since Rengstorf', *New Testament Studies*, 21, 1975, 249-264.
W. Schmithals, *The Office of Apostle in the Early Church*, SPCK, London, 1971.
R. Schnackenburg, 'Apostles Before and during St. Paul's Time', *Apostolic History and the Gospel*, ed. W. W. Gasque and R. P. Martin, Paternoster, Exeter, 1970, 287-303.
J. H. Schütz, *Paul and the Anatomy of Apostolic Authority*, SNTS, Cambridge University Press, London, 1975.
J. Munck, *Paul and the Salvation of Mankind*, John Knox, Virginia, 1959.
R. C. Tannehill, *Dying and Rising with Christ: A Study in Pauline Theology*, Töpelmann, Berlin, 1967.
E. J. Tinsley, *The Imitation of God in Christ*, SCM, London, 1960.

Glossary

Adonis: A fertility and vegetation god, whose cult was brought from Cyprus to Athens in the first century BC and existed only in conjunction with the rites of Aphrodite.

Alexander: The object of a satire entitled *The False Prophet* by the author Lucian, Alexander originated a new form of the cult of Asclepius, the healing god, during the middle of the second century AD in Asia.

Apollonius of Tyana: A contemporary of Paul, an ascetic itinerant teacher and miracle-worker from Cappadocia, whose real and legendary exploits are celebrated in an early third century *Life* by Philostratus.

Apuleius: A Latin poet, philosopher and author, born c. AD 123, whose 'novel' *The Metamorphoses* (more popularly *The Golden Ass*) contains a first-hand account, in fictional form, of rites associated with Isis.

Aristophanes: The great classic poet-dramatist of the fifth and fourth century BC, whose surviving plays include *Lysistrata, The Birds, The Frogs* and others.

Attis: Youthful partner of the Phrygian goddess Cybele, he remained a subordinate part of her cult as it spread to Greece and Rome, but gained official recognition by Claudius and, in AD 150, equal honours.

Cicero: Famous first-century BC Roman philosopher, politician, orator and man of letters, whose views contain both Platonist and Stoic elements.

Clement of Alexandria: One of the most distinguished early Christian 'fathers', head of an unofficial Christian philosophical 'school' at Alexandria in the late second and early third centuries, who united gnostic and Christian tendencies in his thoughts.

Crates: Wandering Greek Cynic philosopher c. 365-285 BC who led a life of voluntary poverty and humanitarian actions after his conversion.

Cybele: The great Phrygian mother-goddess, whose cult became known in Greece in the late third century BC.

Cynics: Individualistic followers of the principles laid down by the fourth-century philosopher Diogenes of Sinope, who practised poverty, rejected conventions and deliberately shocked their contemporaries.

Dio Chrysostom: First-century Greek-orator, philosopher and writer who, like others during his time, combined Stoic and Cynic ideals and, more the exception here, spent much of his later life as an exiled wandering preacher.

Diogenes Laertius:	Author of an early third-century AD survey of the lives and teachings of the ancient Greek philosophers, about whose own circumstances nothing is known.
Dionysiac mysteries:	Dramatic sensual rituals incorporated into the city-state cult in Athens in the classical period, centred around the god of emotional religion who stemmed from Thrace or Phrygia.
Eleusinian mysteries:	An old agrarian cult, integrated into the Athenian state-cult in the sixth century, involving various rites, processions, initiations, etc.
Epictetus:	Stoic philosopher c. AD 55 to 135, originally a slave and student of Musonius Rufus, who before his banishment by Domitian in AD 80 taught successfully in Rome and left behind extensive moral discourses, a briefer manual *Encheiridion* and some fragments containing his views.
Epicureans:	Followers of late fourth and early third-century BC Greek moral and natural philosopher, always a minority group, who favoured the simple, communal life, taught that the gods no longer intervened in human affairs and elaborated a particular cosmology and science.
Essenes:	Monastic urban and rural groups in Judaea and elsewhere, who rejected Greek cultural intrusions and demanded a strict keeping of the Law.
Eusebius of Caesarea:	The first church historian, author of the *Ecclesiastical History* spanning more than three centuries, who was also Bishop of Caesarea and a moderate supporter of Arius.
Gnosticism:	Second-century AD phenomenon, comprising Jewish, Hellenistic, Oriental and especially Christian elements, and stressing the importance of esoteric knowledge and repudiation of the body for attaining salvation.
Helena:	According to tradition, the partner of Simon Magus in his gnostic transformation and miraculous dissemination of early 'Christianity'.
Hipparchia:	Convert of early Cynic philosopher, Crates, who later married him and accompanied him on his travels.
Ignatius:	Influential Syrian Christian bishop, martyred by the Romans in the early second century AD, whose last letters to various churches and fellow-bishop Polycarp insist on a mono-ministerial ecclesiastical structure.
Isis and Osiris:	Egyptian goddess and her husband; from the fourth and particularly second century BC, she became a leading goddess in the Greek and Roman world, eventually gaining official recognition and a wide following.

Josephus:	Jewish general in revolt against Rome, AD 66-70, who went over to the Romans and proceeded to write in Greek an apologetic account of the war, history of the Jews (the *Antiquities*) and account of his life.
Justin Martyr:	Christian apologist in Rome during the second century AD, whose writings, among other things, discuss Jewish scepticism about Christianity, Roman calumnies against Christians and Platonic philosophical views.
Lucian:	Prolific Athenian writer c. AD 120-180, who perfected a special dialogue form and used it, *inter alia,* to great effect against such religious 'imposters' and 'fanatics' as Alexander 'the false prophet' and Peregrinus.
Mishnah:	Collection of rabbinic legal traditions, some pre-dating Christianity, which were set down in writing in the early third century AD.
Mithras:	Ancient Persian god, whose masculine religion spread throughout the Roman world, particularly via the senior orders in the army and business classes, from the late first century AD, but never really gained wide-spread popularity.
Musonius Rufus:	Enlightened Stoic philosopher, born 30 AD, who spent most of his time in Rome: unfortunately only fragments of his works remain.
Origen:	One of the most famous early Christian 'fathers', later judged to be heretical, who continued Clement's fusion of Christianity and philosophy in Alexandria and Caesarea during the third century AD and also defended Christianity against the attacks of such pagan writers as Celsus.
Orphism:	Archaic Greek religious movement, distinguished by having a personal founder, fraternal character and sacred texts; it had an intermittent existence in the classical and later ages.
Pharisees:	Devout, law-centred Jewish group, originating in opposition to Hellenistic cultural intrusions in second century BC, which gained increasing popular respect before and after the Jewish War of AD 66-70 and eventually dominated Jewish religious life.
Philo:	Alexandrian Jew, c. 30 BC — AD 45, who as well as becoming head of the Jewish community in the city, developed a highly sophisticated apologia for Judaism in his many philosophical writings, most of which took the form of allegorical biblical commentaries.
Philostratus:	Member of the philosophical circle patronized by the early third-century Emperor Septimius Severus, and his wife Julia Domna, and author of various philosophical 'lives' including that of Apollonius of Tyana.

Platonism:	Philosophical tradition stemming from Plato which underwent a revival in the first century BC, but did not become widely influential again in its own right till the second century AD.
Plutarch:	Born c. AD 50 and died c. AD 120, Plutarch was an eclectic philosopher-writer, theological interpreter of the Isis mysteries and biographer of famous Greeks and Romans.
Porphyry:	Neo-Platonist philosopher, student of religion and critic of Christianity from the third century AD, a prolific but unoriginal author deeply influenced by Plotinus.
Posidonius:	One of the architects of the first century BC Stoic revival, rejuvenating it through the infusion of Platonist elements, especially imprinting it with a more transcendental emphasis.
Qumran:	Well-known monastic community by the Dead Sea, the finding of whose writings threw light not only on its own 'Essene-like' character but on first century BC and AD Judaism in general.
Seneca:	Important Roman philosopher and statesman of the first century AD, author of ethical treatises, epistles, dialogues, tragedies and prose works, and representative of a more personal, if also more hypocritical, Stoicism.
Simon Magus:	Samaritan pseudo-Christian in Acts, who, according to later traditions, was the originator of a heretical form of Christianity with strong gnostic leanings.
Stoicism:	Philosophical school founded by Zeno in Athens about 300 BC which, by the first century AD, largely dominated intellectual life with its pantheistic world-view, emphasis upon reason, cosmopolitan outlook and disciplined emotional life.
Teacher of Righteousness:	Leader, though not founder, of the Qumran community at some stage during the second century BC, renowned as an interpreter of the Law and the Prophets.
Thucydides:	Famous Greek historian, author of the account of the war between Athens and Sparta, 431-404 BC, which is one of the seminal historical works.
Tibullus:	First century BC Latin poet, of whose life little is known, mainly remembered for the quality of his few surviving elegies.
Xenophon:	Early Greek historian, living mostly in Athens or Sparta, c. AD 428-354, who composed many other works and later achieved considerable popularity among the Romans.